T0298513

New Unions, New Workplaces

In the last two decades new techniques of management, driven by global competitive pressures, have led to a significant restructuring of the workplace. Trade unions have increasingly been on the defensive as organisational downsizing has been accompanied by managerial efforts to encourage company loyalty at the expense of more traditional 'them and us' attitudes. Despite the difficulties they face, there remains much union resilience in the workplace due to new ways of organising and challenging management authority.

New Unions, New Workplaces draws on data from a range of workplaces in the UK, covering manufacturing and aerospace, the NHS and local authorities, the insurance industry and the public and private utilities, as well as data from three unions – the MSF, the AEEU (now merged to form the two sections of AMICUS) and the GMB. The research reveals the topical impact of processes such as team-working and performance pay on union collectivism.

These three unions profess some allegiance to the 'new unionism' and the model of union renewal. The authors probe the real extent of such new initiatives, and produce a model of potential union revival that emphasises the importance of engaging with new management initiatives and mobilising union members around ever-increasing sources of employee discontent.

The authors work in the Employment Studies Research Unit at Bristol Business School, University of the West of England. **Andy Danford** is Senior Lecturer and Researcher in Employment Relations and author of *Japanese Management Techniques and British Workers*. **Mike Richardson** is Researcher and Tutor of Employee Relations and Business Systems, and has taught Economic and Social History at the Faculty of Humanities, University of the West of England. **Martin Upchurch** is Senior Lecturer in International Employment Relations and editor of *The State and Globalisation: Comparative Studies of Labour and Capital in National Economies*.

Routledge Research in Employment Relations

Series editors: Rick Delbridge and Edmund Heery
Cardiff Business School

Aspects of the employment relationship are central to numerous courses at both undergraduate and postgraduate level.

Drawing insights from industrial relations, human resource management and industrial sociology, this series provides an alternative source of research-based materials and texts, reviewing key developments in employment research.

Books published in this series are works of high academic merit, drawn from a wide range of academic studies in the social sciences.

New Unions, New Workplaces

A study of union resilience in the restructured workplace

Andy Danford, Mike Richardson and Martin Upchurch

LONDON AND NEW YORK

First published 2003 by Routledge
2 Park Square, Milton Park, Abingdon, Oxon, OX14 4RN

Simultaneously published in the USA and Canada
by Routledge
270 Madison Ave, New York NY 10016

Routledge is an imprint of the Taylor & Francis Group

Transferred to Digital Printing 2006

Typeset in Baskerville by MHL Typesetting Ltd, Coventry,
Warwickshire

British Library Cataloguing in Publication Data
A catalogue record for this book is available
from the British Library

Library of Congress Cataloging in Publication Data
Danford, Andy.
  New unions, new workplaces: a study of union resilience in the
  restructured workplace/
 Andy Danford, Mike Richardson and Martin Upchurch
    p. cm
  Includes bibliographical references and index.
  ISBN 0–415–26061–2
    1. Labor unions–Great Britain. 2. Collective bargaining–Great
    Britain. 3. Industrial relations–Great Britain. I. Richardson, Mike,
    1947– II. Upchurch, Martin, 1951– III. Title.

  HD6664.D36 2002
  331.88'0941–dc21   2002068148

ISBN 0–415–26061–2

Contents

Figures and tables

Acknowledgements

This research was made possible by a Leverhulme Trust research grant (RF&G/7/9900487).

The authors would also like to thank the full-time officers of the three participating unions, the AEEU, the GMB and MSF for their support and granting of access. Above all, we would like to thank all of the workplace union representatives who took part in the interview and questionnaire stages of the research.

We are indebted to Professor Paul Stewart for his invaluable comments and constructive criticism and special thanks are due to Viv Calway and Stella Warren for their work in transcribing the interview tapes.

Parts of Chapters 3 and 6 are from previously published journal articles. We would like to thank the editors and publishers of *Work, Employment and Society* (Sage Publications) and *Capital and Class* (The Conference of Socialist Economists) for permission to use this material.

Abbreviations

ABI	Association of British Insurers
ACAS	Advisory, Conciliation and Arbitration Service
AXIS	AXA Sun Life Staff
AEEU	Amalgamated Electrical and Engineering Union
AEU	Amalgamated Engineering Union
ASTMS	Association of Scientific, Technical and Managerial Staffs
BAT	British American Tobacco
BIFU	Banking, Insurance and Finance Union
BNFL	British Nuclear Fuels
BSA	Building Societies Association
CBI	Confederation of British Industry
CCT	Compulsory Competitive Tendering
CEGB	Central Electricity Generating Board
CITU	Confederation of Insurance Trades Unions
CPSA	Civil and Public Services Association
CSEU	Confederation of Shipbuilding and Engineering Unions
DTI	Department of Trade and Industry
EBF	Electricity Business Forum
EEF	Engineering Employers' Federation
EETPU	Electrical, Electronic, Telecommunications and Plumbing Union
EMA	Engineering Managers' Association
EU	European Union
EWC	European works council
FDI	Foreign direct investment
FSU	Financial Services Union
GCHQ	Government Communications Headquarters
GIO	Guild of Insurance Officials
GMB	General, Municipal and Boilermakers Union
HCA	Healthcare assistant
HNC	Higher National Certificate
HRM	Human resource management
IDS	Income Data Services
ILO	International Labour Organisation

IPRP	Individual performance related pay
ISTC	Iron and Steel Trades Confederation
JNC	Joint Negotiating Committee
JSSC	Joint Shop Stewards' Committee
JUC	Joint Union Committee
LJC	Local Joint Council
LRD	Labour Research Department
MJC	Magnox Joint Council
MLA	Medical Laboratory Assistant
MLSO	Medical Laboratory Scientific Officer
MNC	Multinational company
MP	Member of Parliament
MEP	Member of the European Parliament
MORI	Market and Opinion Research International
MSF	Manufacturing, Science and Finance Union
NHS	National Health Service
NJC	National Joint Council
NMT	New management technique
NUBE	National Union of Bank Employees
NUIW	National Union of Insurance Workers
NVQ	National Vocational Qualification
OFWAT	Office of Water Services
PC	Personal computer
PCS	Public and Commercial Services Union
PFI	Private Finance Initiative
QC	Quality circle
R&D	Research and development
SBAC	Society of British Aerospace Companies
SIC	Standard Industrial Classification
SWEB	South Western Electricity Board
TASS	Technical, Administrative and Supervisory Union
TGWU	Transport and General Workers Union
TQ	Total quality
TQM	Total quality management
TUC	Trades Union Congress
TUPE	Transfer of Undertakings (Protection of Employment) legislation
UCAD	Universal computer-aided design
UIS	Union of Insurance Staffs
UNiFI	The union for Barclays staff
UNITE	Union of Needletrades, Industrial and Textile Employees
USDAW	Union of Shop, Distributive and Allied Workers
WERS	Workplace Employee Relations Survey
WPD	Western Power Distribution

1 Unions facing up to crisis

Crisis? What crisis?

Trade Unions in Britain have had a difficult time in the last two decades. In terms of the official indicators both membership and density have fallen consistently since the peak years of 1979/80 and this decline has been accompanied with a drop in the numbers of days taken in strike action to the lowest level since records began.[1] Figures for 2000 show a slight improvement in TUC affiliated membership, but it is too soon to say if the downward trend has been reversed. Evidence on declining industrial action in Britain is confirmed by the latest Workplace Employee Relations Survey and presented in *Britain at Work* (Cully *et al.* 1999: 245), which records a drop in those workplaces surveyed taking strike action from 11 per cent to 1 per cent between 1990 and 1998. The decline in trade union membership is not solely confined to Britain and is apparent in many western advanced capitalist countries (Troy 1990; Jeffreys 2000). The reasons for this decline have received much attention. A core reason is structural change in employment and the relative demise of trade union 'heartland' manufacturing industry. The relative growth of service employment, especially in the private sector, together with greenfield manufacturing establishments (some anti- or non-union) means that trade unions experience 'lagged' development due to the time taken to establish unionism in new fields of pasture. There is nothing unique in this phenomenon that should lead mechanistically to forecasts of doom for the trade union movement. For example, trade unionism did not occur spontaneously in the growing car industry of the 1930s and 40s, but took time and effort before employer resistance was overcome (Beynon 1973). Logic would suggest that such basic structural reasons are temporally fixed, rather than permanently embedded. Despite this, decline has sometimes been explained by the emergence of a 'new political culture' which de-emphasises class identity and class solidarity as a result of a concomitant individualisation of the employment relationship (e.g. Phelps-Brown 1990; Beck 1992; Clark and Hoffman-Martinot 1998; Giddens 2000). Such theories have been questioned by others as lacking empiricism and historical perspective (Callinicos 1989: 121–7; Kelly 1998: 108–25), but their grip on policy makers' opinions can be real and lead in turn to the fallacious translation of 'trends' into undeniable 'facts' (Bradley *et al.* 2000). Trade unionism in Britain has been on the defensive for other reasons. Both state and employers have combined to restrict union freedoms by legislative and organisational means. British trade unions, even after the 1997 election and subsequent re-election of a New Labour Government, now face the most pernicious anti-combination laws in the European Union.

The defeats trade unions suffered in the 1980s, steelworkers, civil servants, teachers, seamen, printers and, most importantly the miners, dented the credibility and confidence of the union activists to win their members' case. This allowed space for moderate trade union leaders to develop discourses and policies based on moderation and collaboration at the expense of militancy and combativity. Within this framework of defeat and retreat a re-invigorated employers' ideology based on organisational commitment, entrepreneurial values and the dominant power of the market was also given space to emerge. This new ideology has undoubtedly been designed to create a new atmosphere in the workplace. The 'new' workplace would be based on a de-collectivised and fragmented workforce in which new production and management techniques focus on the business needs of the employer and seek to intensify work under the dubious banner of employee involvement and customer consciousness (Smith and Morton 1993). The combination of these forces, both substantive and ideological, has reduced trade unions' room for manoeuvre and ability to plan strategic responses. As such a 'crisis of representation' has occurred, described by Müller-Jentsch (1988) in terms of a constrained ability of unions to face the challenges of a fragmented workforce, decentralised employment regulation, and the rise of newer and more dynamic sections of the economy.

Individualism and the new worker?

The impact on workers, as mentioned above, has been interpreted by many commentators in ways which suggest that there is a 'newness' in worker attitudes which eschews traditional collectivism and emphasises individual interest at the expense of class solidarity (e.g. Valkenburg 1996). The basis for this thesis is threefold. First is the notion that the international economy is essentially led by new information technology where 'knowledge' work takes precedence over the traditional functions of labour and the individual is liberated in the process from alien pressure. (Bell 1973; Beck 1992). A 'weightless' economy, free of the constraint of national geography, it is argued, has now obviated the need to consider the role of human labour in the productive process (e.g. Coyle 1997; Castells 2000). Second, is the proposition that workers have accepted the need for emotional labour, customer consciousness and entrepreneurial values and have re-invented themselves as new 'model' workers ready and willing to abandon collective solidarity with their work peers in favour of the goals of the employer. This pre-supposes the triumph of customer consciousness and a consumer-led cultural shift, when in fact much of this new emphasis on emotion may be contested terrain (du Gay and Salaman 1992). Hochschild (1983), for example, in raising the concept of 'emotional labour', describes the employer's need for behavioural *compliance* expressed by the employee's ability to display different aspects of 'surface' and 'deep' acting as part of their job. Besides the need for emotional awareness, workers are said to be in need of more 'agility' or even, in the case of some service industries, to possess 'aesthetic' qualities designed to please the customer (Nickson *et al.* 2001). The 'new model worker' is thus a direct product of more sophisticated human resource management (HRM) procedures of recruitment, selection and training which mould 'self-reliant' workers and can sometimes be gender oriented emphasising sexual attraction (Linstead 1995; Noon and Blyton 1997: 121–39; Flecker and Hofbauer 1998; Denzin 1999). Third, are arguments stressing the emergence of a new 'psychological contract' between employer and employee (Herriot and Pemberton 1996). In this scenario the old ideas of collective 'dependency' on the employer for welfare and job security are abandoned in return for the 'employability' of the new worker, a drift to personalised rather than collectivised contracts, and a new sense of individual responsibility for career and skill development.

All three notions are subsumed and adopted within the 'excellence movement' literature (e.g. Peters and Waterman 1982; Peters and Austin 1985), and take as granted the efficacy of the HRM approach (although critics do not). Implicit in the HRM perspective is an acceptance that workers benefit from the liberating effects of knowledge-based work, high commitment regimes or employee involvement. Much literature can now be cited challenging the basis of these arguments and providing concrete examples of why, in the real rather than virtual world, the impact of HRM is either rhetoric or over-stated. Ursula Huws (1999), for example, has criticised the validity of the concept of a 'weightless economy'. In particular, she argues the importance of understanding a variety of types of information workers, ranging from the creative web-site designer through to the most routinised of call-centre operators. Each has its own functional relationship with capital, making it difficult to generalise or categorise as 'knowledge work'. Guest (1990) has argued that HRM must be seen as a 'product of its time' when free market policies pervaded the 1980s years of Reagan. There was much ideological expression of the HRM ideal, in a period when the collective worker was presented as a barrier to a 'free' labour market and the search for a new 'American Dream' emphasised the positive motivational aspects of employer leadership rather than the negativity of down-sizing and industrial restructuring. Legge (1995) has similarly challenged many claims for HRM as rhetoric rather than reality. Warhurst and Thompson (1998), in reviewing the evidence of HRM in practice, conclude that employers' efforts to win the 'hands, hearts and minds' of British workers is in fact an elusive task, where employees for the most 'remain poorly motivated, overworked and under-valued'. There is thus some considerable critique available of the HRM approach to employee relations, based as it is on a decline of collectivism and a rise of new individualism. We know that there is some base for the flowering of non-collectivist attitudes as a result of decline in trade union membership and density, and a rise in non-union workplace establishments. Real changes have also taken place in product and labour markets which in turn have increased worker sense of insecurity and possibly made workers more compliant to employer objectives. What is less easy to determine is the extent to which attitudinal change has developed in practice. The difficulties of unpicking cause and effect arise because there are contradictory tendencies, whereby increased managerial authority and declining collective worker power allow employers room to intensify work through means other than employee commitment to organisational goals (Casey *et al.* 1997; Danford 1999: 101–21; Howell 1999). For example, new ways of organising work or extending working hours will add to senses of injustice and grievance of workers which may in turn act to renew feelings of collective solidarity against the employer.

While some commentators have tried to grasp these contradictory tendencies and make sense of them others have continued to bend the stick towards a postmodern perspective. In some instances this goes so far as to embrace concepts based on Foucauldian interpretations (e.g. Knights 1990), whereby phenomenological approaches are abandoned in favour of *anti*-structural arguments whereby power relationships at work are dispersed rather than concentrated into the employer-employee relationship. Others do not stray quite so far from classic labour process analysis but seek to redefine the dominant forces within the workforce in a *post*-structuralist direction. In this new workplace '. . . the individualising tendencies of capitalist relations of production can accentuate insecurity to a point where privatised efforts to gain a secure identity take precedence over collective efforts to transform the historical conditions that promote such self-defeating tendencies' (Willmott 1989: 371). This refinement does not entirely dismiss the possibilities for the collective worker but, according to O'Doherty and Willmott (2001: 465), seeks to inject 'a self-critical and multi-disciplinary exploration of complex political, economic, psychological and existential processes . . .'. Such doubts over the future of collectivism have in turn led other labour process theorists to decry the seeming take-over of the labour process debate by those either imbued with managerialist perspectives or intent on 'academicising' the role of labour by treating it as an object rather than as a subject active in its own right (Nichols 1991; Martinez Lucio and Stewart 1997). These critiques seek to rescue and restore the centrality of workers' own action in shaping their environment, a process much less likely to preclude the possibility of collective action.

These various strands of thought within the labour process debate do need investigating, and so a key task set by the authors throughout this book in assembling evidence has been to unscramble the dialectic of these relationships. This needs to be done in order to assess the impact of employer-based ideology and practice on union interests and consequently on the potential for union renewal. In tackling this question the authors are aware that there is a danger that the statistics of decline in trade union membership and density, and the contemporaneous decline in strike statistics, may overstate the case that workers are becoming more passive and self-centred. Less is known of the degree of *non-strike* action taking place within workplaces now severely restricted by new legislation. Indeed, as Stirling (2001), indicates, there is a discrepancy in the WERS (1998 Workplace Employee Relations Survey) data between responses from *managers* and responses from *workplace representatives*, of whom almost a quarter report some form of collective dispute over pay and conditions in the previous year. Trade Union Congress (TUC 2000) evidence also suggests a recent increase in legal ballots for strike action, although in most cases this has not been transformed into actual strike action, with disputes being settled without recourse to a strike.[2] Disputes in the Royal Mail, Vauxhall, and the London Underground, early in 2001, have all been significant in the degree to which the workers involved were willing to act illegally or to find other ways of avoiding the law, either by 'show of hands' voting (Royal Mail), mass 'stayaways' and sympathy walkouts (Vauxhall), or defiance of injunctions (London Underground). The patterns of industrial dispute activity may, therefore, be less clear cut than the statistics indicating a fall in union membership and density would suggest. Similarly, whilst official statistics show us the extent of *formal* workplace activity (strikes, ballots, etc.), they tell us little of the *informal* resistance that can continue and which also can be part of collective worker activity. For this reason we argue that the point of production must be a primary focus of research inquiry if we are to fully make sense of the reality of working life in the 'new' workplace, and to understand the wider culture of collectivism.

Work intensification and worker discontent

The argument presented here is that in order to understand what is really happening in today's workplaces the factors likely to generate conflict (and trends within) must be assessed. For example, the employer-generated process of employee involvement and workplace de-collectivisation may restrict the scope for *the effective expression of employee voice.* If conflict is endemic to the world of work then the need for an employee voice cannot be ignored. In Britain, there has been a discernible shift from union to non-union voice representation (Millward, Bryson and Forth 2000: 124–5). What is less clear is the usefulness of the new voice arrangements to the employee. Bryson (2000) argues, for example, that union voice is no better than non-union voice in positively influencing management's behaviour. This contrasts with Freeman and Medoff (1984) who have argued the contrary. However, if it were the case that union voice is more effective for the employee, then the decline of the scope and coverage of unions in Britain will have led to the creation of a distinct 'representation gap' whereby untapped potential for trade union representation is a result. The TUC, recognising this gap, and following a MORI survey, place the potential untapped demand for trade union membership in the UK at five million (a figure which would restore trade union membership to density levels of the late 1970s). Other core reasons for this suppressed demand for trade union representation, besides the general need for an effective voice, are *senses of injustice at work* and gathering *disrespect from employers* (e.g. Kelly 1998: 44–5). Evidence of sensed injustice can be linked to widening income gaps within the workplace, especially the relatively strong growth of directors' and top managers' pay in comparison to employees, as well as perceived or real abuse of managerial prerogative. The gap between rich and poor widened considerably in Britain in the 1980s. Between 1980 and 1990 income of the top ninetieth percentile grew by 47 per cent, while that of the bottom tenth percentile grew by only 6 per cent.[3] By the end of the 1990s incomes of the top ninetieth percentile were approximately five times that of the bottom tenth, as compared to three times in 1970. Some evidence of gathering managerial disrespect of employees is recorded in surveys of bullying and intimidation in the workplace. There is no longitudinal analysis of bullying and victimisation to prove increasing incidence. Nevertheless, it is generally recognised by survey initiators (many of them trade unions) to be an increasing problem worth highlighting in recent years because of its intensity (LRD 1997). A recent survey published in 2000 by the University of Manchester Institute of Science and Technology, for example, supported by both the TUC and CBI (Confederation of British Industry), reported 47 per cent of employees witnessing bullying at work in the last five years, with one in four saying they had been bullied themselves in that period.[4] Outside of workplace surveys, Kelly (1998: 46) in his discussion of mobilisation theory, refers to data collected in the *British Social Attitudes* survey indicating that 'levels of mistrust in management among the general population have been rising' (between 1984 and 1995) whereas the percentage of employees 'who have a say in decisions affecting their work' has been falling. Abbot (1998) suggests that the Citizens Advice Bureaux, where the number of work-related problem inquiries has been ever increasing, may now be acting as an alternative source of worker help in the absence of trade union presence. Furthermore, *the intensification of work* is likely to be a key factor generating employee discontent. A review of evidence on work intensification by Green (2001) indicates a rise in work intensification in the UK during the last decade based on both extensive and intensive forms of exploitation. Longer working hours are concentrated in an increasing proportion of the workforce, while measures of work intensification suggest an increase in work effort in the private manufacturing sector during the 1980s and in the public sector in the 1990s. The *Trade Unions Into the 1990s Project* conducted from Warwick University by Waddington and Whitson (reported in 1995, 1996) surveyed just less than 6,000 trade union activists on membership grievances and found staffing levels and workload as two of the three most reported causes of grievance. Increasing levels of felt-job insecurity have also been linked to work intensification and cost cutting in a survey conducted by Burchell *et al.* (2002) for the Joseph Rowntree Foundation. Job insecurity has particularly affected professional workers, who, according to the survey, went from the most secure group of workers in 1986 to the least secure in the 1990s. Burchell *et al.* (2002) argue that the rise of job insecurity is now associated with workplaces permeated by a lack of trust, a sense of loss of control over the pace of work, and a sense that workers were being made to work too hard. The range of potential workplace grievances, and the sense of unfairness, seem therefore to be combined with a general worry of future security in today's workplace. However, before presenting evidence on these concerns it is important to examine in more detail the contextual changes in the economy that may help shape and determine the constraints, limitations and opportunities for organised labour.

The new political economy

Changes in world political economy have arguably been driven in the last two decades by capital's desire in the Group 3 countries of North America, the European Union and Japan to recoup declining domestic profit rates by creating and exploiting new markets abroad (Harrison 1994; Bryan 1995; Harman 1995; Brenner 1998).[5] Advanced industrial capital, acting though world trade organisations and agreements, as well as by the strategic investment of Group 3-based multinational companies (MNCs), has encouraged the deregulation (or re-regulation) of international financial markets and the liberalisation of tariff barriers in the poorer two-thirds of the world. The consequences of this 'globalisation' process have been numerous. A whole intellectual industry has developed around the 'globalisation thesis', painting the above processes as an inevitable and immovable natural force from which there is no escape (e.g. Ohmae 1990, 1996; Horsman and Marshall 1994). The process has engendered an ideological offensive on behalf of capital seeking to subject labour as an object of these global forces leaving no room for dissent against the 'logic' of capital. In practical terms this has meant a drive towards labour flexibility as well as market flexibility and a withdrawal of the state from many of its former commitments to protect the individual worker from excessive employer power. For labour this has often meant an employers' offensive to intensify work though new organisational practices and industrial restructuring. Such themes have already been addressed in our discussion on the individual worker. The outcomes of this global processes being an increase in job insecurity (as workers' flexibility is translated as greater disposability), and internal cost-cutting as enterprises off-load all but their core activities (Standing 1997: 11; Cappelli *et al.* 1997). Combined with job precari-ousness has been deterioration in working conditions aimed at both intensifying and extensifying worker exploitation (Rubery 1996; Danford 1999: 159–87). In the UK, for example, average weekly working hours have lengthened for a significant proportion of the workforce and stress levels have increased. A recent report from the International Labour Organisation on mental health in the workplace found that in any year three out of ten UK workers experience mental health problems, largely as a result of the introduction of 'an array of new technologies and methods of work organisation stemming from inexorably rising productivity requirements' (ILO 2000).

   The justification for these processes has fed back into the globalisation myth as states have sought to justify the creation of favourable conditions for inward foreign direct investment whilst attributing blame for job loss in the trading sectors to the immovable forces of globalisation. From the mid-1970s onwards neo-liberal ideologists began in the UK to develop a case attributing the blame for low competitiveness in Britain to excessive trade union power (Pratten 1976; Caves 1980). Thacherism in the 1980s sought both through legislation and encouragement of employers to marginalise unions as a response. Rather than roll back the frontiers of neo-liberalism, New Labour has become a keen proponent of 'new growth theory', seeking to solve the problem of declining international competitiveness by raising the stock of human capital through incentives and exhortations on employees to engage in higher-level skills training (Coates 2000: 48–9). This approach concentrates on the supply side of the labour market and assumes that unemployment is a result of skill gaps in the economy. But, as Panitch (1994: 83) argues, such an approach ignores the fact that recurrent crises of overproduction have led capital to try to drive down wage costs and increase exploitation in *both* 'high skill, high wage' regimes *and* 'low skill, low wage' regimes alike. Concomitantly, New Labour has not fundamentally reversed or altered the orientation on market internationalisation and the need for flexible labour markets but has instead pursued its Third Way strategy of accommodation to market internationalisation. Prime Minister Blair, in his introduction to the 1998 Fairness at Work White Paper, outlined that the new UK employment legislation 'seeks to draw a line under the issue of industrial relations law. . . . Even after the changes we propose, Britain will have the most lightly regulated labour market of any leading economy in the world ' (Department of Trade and Industry, 1998). Whilst labour market deregulation reached its peak in the Anglo-Saxon economies in the 1980s and 1990s it has now infected public policy in the exemplary social market economies. In the neo-corporatist case of Germany, evidence suggests a deliberate fragmentation and erosion of the co-determination model (Carling and Soskice 1997; Streeck 1997; Hassel 1999) and in Austria, the once all-embracing ethos of macro-corporatism is now challenged (Gerlich 1992). One of the chief casualties in these cases has been a decline in the authority of national or sectoral collective agreements, and their replacement with enterprise-based bargaining (Milward *et al.* 2000). In the UK case this is reflected in an absolute decline in the scope and coverage of collective agreements. In the German case by a withdrawal by some employers from the peak employer organisation discipline either partially (in the old West Germany), or generally (in the old East Germany), leading to downward or negative wage drift from previously all-embracing agreements (Upchurch 2000).

If the globalisation thesis were to be believed then the plight of organised labour would indeed be very difficult. However, as many critics have argued, the reality is somewhat different and many of the core aspects of the thesis are overstated. First, as Hirst and Thompson (1996: 67) have shown, much of the increase in world trade takes place within the Group 3 bloc rather than between the Group 3 and developing nations. Similarly the pattern of foreign direct investment (FDI) is fairly closely confined to the Group 3 plus the newly industrialised countries of east and south-east Asia (Dicken 1998). The threat to western workers of capital flight comes not so much from third-world countries but rather from within competitor nations in the advanced industrial world. Only in highly labour-intensive, low-cost production industries, such as textiles and clothing, is there likely to be a shift of production from north to south. As such there are strict limits to capital's alleged 'footlooseness' (Allen 1995; Dicken 1998). Competition between capital based in western nations is nothing new, and is likely to be a continuation of previous patterns of competition, albeit more intensified. Second, globalisation, to the extent that it can be determined, is not a mystical arrangement of natural forces that cements the structure of society leaving no space for human action but is partly a social process determined by individual choice and the actions of élites. As such their actions can be challenged from below and new agendas can be fashioned. The revisiting of World Trade Organisation agendas under pressure from the Seattle, Prague, Genoa and other demonstrations bears witness to this fact. The *processes* of globalisation have, for example, undoubtedly led to a greater disparity of income throughout the world between rich and poor. However, this is a result not of invisible market forces but instead is a consequence of the decline of collectively bargained wage solidarity (Mahnkopf 1992), government taxation policy and the deliberate withdrawal by the state from welfare support for the unemployed and sick (Atkinson 2001). Both are functions of employer or state policy and as such can be reversed. Third, the claim that organised labour is totally emasculated in the face of capital's ability to up and leave needs to be challenged. New production techniques associated with just-in-time have arguably created more scope for the exercise of worker power as the threat of strike action has speedy ramifications beyond the factory gates in an inter-related but dissaggregated production system (Auerbach 1989; Bradley *et al.* 2000: 149–68). Evidence of international union solidarity in response to internationalised capital, as well as resistance to the impacts of globalisation at the national level, are amply assembled by Moody (1997) in *Workers in a Lean World*. At the level of the corporation, evidence from the US at least, would suggest that new forms of union organising are capable of harnessing corporate research data and aggressive anti-corporate campaigns to give renewed energy and meaning to trade union activity. The splendid tale of *Ravenswood*, for example, as told by Juravich and Bron-fenbrenner (1999) gives insights into the variety of ways in which trade unions at the workplace can act beyond the confines of the factory gate to challenge the power of multi-national corporations.[6] The reality of the new political economy is thus more difficult to decipher than first thoughts might suggest. It is argued here that there is a tenuous link between the interests of employers and the prevailing ideology used to justify renewed forms of worker exploitation. Trade unions are then faced with a strategic dilemma in the face of this ideological offensive, its HRM content, and its translation into new forms of working. On the one hand the processes of individualisation have some social and material basis in the new workplace (and the reformed old workplace). This poses difficulties for collectivised approaches and has been met in many instances by a shift towards more collaborationist union practice. On the other hand work is getting harder for the majority of workers while income inequality is increasing. The resulting rising sense of injustice suggests a more militant and aggressive union stance is necessary. Union renewal is dependent on success in its ability to solve these contradictions, and it is to these prospects that we now turn.

The new unionism

For trade unions the decline associated with the new political economy could not be allowed to continue. The survival of unions as a social entity is clearly threatened, irrespective of agreement on the causes of decline. This has a knock-on effect on the social position of the trade union full-time official, whose job comes under fire as trade union subscription income falls.

Analyses of official trade union responses to decline in the UK have covered the initial 1980s retreat into business and single unionism, consumer unionism, the 'servicing approach' as well as more recent attempts to emulate more participative and inclusive approaches based on the organising model (see Heery 1996). The withdrawal into business unionism and the re-enforcement of the servicing approach was a reflection of unions' limited room for strategic manoeuvre but also indicated an ideological retreat on behalf of union leaders away from the efficacy of union combativity against the employer. The New Realism of the 1980s reinforced passivity within unions that allowed even more space for the gathering employer offensive to develop. The TUC's adoption of the 'organising model' and New Unionism in 1996 can be interpreted not only as an attempt to redefine the constituency of union membership, but also as an opportunity to expand the space for strategic union choice and recruit more 'distant' workers previously outside core membership areas (Kelly and Heery 1989: 189). The foundation of the TUC's Organising Academy in 1998 followed a general refocusing of the internal workings of unions developed earlier with the 're-launch' of the TUC in 1994. The process of internal restructuring was designed to generate a 'new ethos and sense of mission', while the TUC encouraged unions to examine their own internal democratic procedures and to develop more open campaigning approaches to attract non-traditional groups of workers to the trade union cause (Heery 1998). In an attempt to get closer to the hearts and minds of members and potential members a shift in trade union marketing techniques was also apparent at this time. Instead of recruitment being almost an adjunct to the trade union activists' and officials' roles and duties signing up new members was now taken as an important aspect of trade union work entailing a shift in resources and time. In addition the TUC encouraged the use of member surveys to help identify potential needs of members and potential members. Various telephone hotlines to identify and give advice on 'bad bosses', bullying and discrimination, or debt counselling are now offered by the TUC or affiliated unions. Discounts on energy supply through *Union Energy* or stakeholder pension schemes are available, and many affiliated unions now offer extended discount schemes, insurances and credit union facilities (TUC 2001). Such schemes are not, however, perceived as the sole recruitment strategy (as was the implication under the period of consumer unionism), but are an adjunct to a more member-focused TUC approach.

The process of membership expansion is a progressive one whereby deeper consolidation of existing membership areas (often in already unionised establishments) is supplemented by expansion into previously non-union territory, and also by movement into areas beyond the workplace into the wider community. Figure 1.1 illustrates the processes involved whereby more distant expansion requires more advanced recruitment and organising activity. This will move recruitment further away from traditional core workplace memberships, and will involve a greater risk of failure and be more costly in terms of

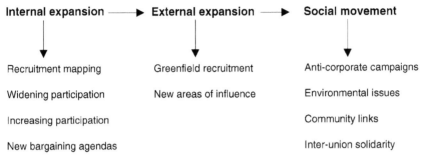

Figure 1.1   Methods of trade union expansion.

organisational resources. The organising model, if applied to maximum effect, would involve a parallel process of engagement in all three aspects of membership expansion. A more timid approach would entail a 'staged' movement. In reality we can argue that the process of moving from 'internal expansion' through 'external expansion' and then on to 'social movement' is a difficult act for trade union leaderships to pursue given their general inertia and hostility to internal politically based upheaval. Nevertheless, as a survival strategy there are few alternative options (other than defensive merger) for unions to embark upon. Pressures to move from one stage to another will continue, albeit in the more conservative British case, on a slow and fragmented basis with much internal resistance from within the union bureaucracy.

The encompassing appeal to 'non-traditional' union members (translated as women, non-whites and youth) as well as the deepening of bargaining agendas to include such issues as training, bullying and discrimination might allow unions to rebuild their social legitimacy in the workplace. In defining its new turn the TUC and many affiliated unions looked abroad to the experience of unions in the USA, Australia, New Zealand and the Netherlands (Oxenbridge 1997; Bronfenbrenner *et al*. 1998; Heery *et al*. 2000). The organising approach, led by the US example, champions community unionism and a 'social movement' approach which seeks to encourage legitimacy of unions in wider civil society. Trade union membership in the USA had shrunk to a far greater extent than in the UK during the 1980s and 1990s, and hence union leaders were faced with a much more severe crisis important enough to threaten the very survival of unions. In addition Voss and Sherman (2000) argue that a new leadership had emerged less tainted with the bureaucratic corruption of the previous generation of leaders and within whose ranks some, at least, were active campaigners from the events of 1968. At grass roots level new, younger activists from single-issue campaigns and student movements against sweatshops had joined unions, seeking to transfer and continue their activism into the labour movement. The extent of change in the US may be in danger of being overstated in the rush to find a panacea for organised labour's *travails* (Eisenscher 1999). Despite this the US model does appear to represent a *change* in union activity and as such it is important in itself.

Table 1.1   The US 'model' of union organising.

Political implications (after Brecher and Costello 1999)	Organisational implications (after Heery et al. 1999)
• Organise at a pace and scale that is unprecedented	• Planned organising campaigns, with targets subject to review and revision
• Build a new and progressive political movement of working people	• Reliance on 'lead organisers' to oversee campaigns and foster union activism
• Construct a labour movement that can change workers' lives	• Participation of activists through organising committees
• Create a strong new progressive voice in American life	• The use of workplace 'mapping techniques' to systematically target and recruit non-members
• Renew and refocus commitment to Labour around the world	• Identification of current concerns and grievances, often through surveys or focus groups, to develop campaigns
• Lead a democratic movement that speaks for all American workers	• Use of 'actions' such as badge wearing, street theatre, petitions, demonstrations and protest strikes to raise union profile
• Institutionalise the process of change	• One-to-one recruitment, if necessary through house calls
	• 'Like-for-like' recruitment (e.g. young-young, women-women, black-black)
	• Press and publicity awareness of successes
	• Identification of pressure points and levers against anti-union employers (e.g. corporate exposés)
	• Community support via alliances with community organisations and pressure groups

The US model can be described both in terms of political change and in terms of organisational change, as Table 1.1 illustrates.

Such new forms of organising, and the emphasis on recruitment and self-reliance at the expense of servicing, are likely to encourage activism rather than passivism and as such, can prepare unions to re-engage with employers on a more adversarial basis. Activism and participation have been argued to be central to the concept of *union renewal* as opposed to the broader notion of *membership revival*. Fairbrother (2000a: 18), for example, refers to union renewal as:

> ... the way unions organise and compose themselves in the circumstances of restructuring and reorganisation at the workplace level and beyond so as to lay the foundation of active, engaged, and participative forms of unionism in the context of the flux and flow of labour-capital relations.

However, there remain doubts as to the penetration of such an organising culture into the heart of the British union machinery. While many unions claim to adopt the organising approach the new activity and focus in most cases remains at the level of deepening member penetration in already organised workplaces. Recruitment at greenfield establishments has so far been rarer, and often confined to the activities of the academy trainees or union's own equivalents. It may be that the initial concentration on workplaces where unions already exist is sensible in terms of union resources and time, while the new Employment Relations legislation on union recognition is an obvious focus for increasing the work of specialist recruitment officers.[7] Even here, recent survey work by Heery and Simms (2001) report that a third of unions report no use of the new Employment Relations Act to recruit or secure recognition, and fewer than 20 per cent of ten unions surveyed report frequent use of the new legislation to gain access to plants to recruit. Progress towards 'community' or social movement unionism remains restricted, with the ISTC (Iron and Steel Trades Confederation) appearing to be the only union showing substantial commitment to the community unionism approach, moving to organise and recruit in areas outside their traditional sphere of influence. A number of reasons can be identified to explain this more minimal penetration. First, are differences of opinion as to the efficacy of parts of the US approach in the UK context, where unions have proved more resilient and employers less conflictual. This view reflects the fact that the crisis of unionism and membership decline has not been so severe in Britain as it has in the US. Not all UK unions have thus embraced new unionism and some have adopted only variations on the theme. Three key unions, the TGWU (Transport and General Workers Union), the AEEU (Amalgamated Electrical and Engineering Union) and the GMB (General, Municipal and Boilermakers Union), have so far remained outside the TUC Organising Academy umbrella, preferring instead to develop their own approaches. The GMB, for example, appears to have eschewed the 'like-for-like' approach to organising officers and preferred instead to recruit regionally based recruitment officers with some lay activist experience within the GMB (interview notes). Second, increased activism from below is likely to threaten union leaders' power and authority, thus restricting the degree to which power and authority is likely to be devolved. British trade unions have a long history of turf battles between political factions fighting for leadership and control. In particular there is an organic political connection between the union leadership and mainstream Labour parliamentary politics which has often conflicted with the more radical left-wing politics of the rank and file (Flanders 1975; Coates 1984; Darlington 1994a). Releasing power from above through the avenue of 'participation' thus has threatening overtones for union leaderships. Third, hard-pressed local and regional officials may simply not have the time or energy to spend more time on recruitment at the expense of attending to an ever-increasing workload of grievance and tribunal claims (Snape 1995). Managerial insistence on organisational priorities at the expense of trade union work, the general level of work intensification, and the reining in by some employers of union 'facility' time (particularly in the public sector), would all have taken their toll on union activists already operating in a 'cold climate'. Diffusion downward of the new 'organising culture' will be delayed as a consequence (Carter 2000). As a result of these challenges the TUC public version of the organising model also appears more cautious and less ambitious than the US variety in its scope and content (Carter and Fairbrother 1998). It places much more emphasis on 'putting organising first' by shifting union resources towards recruitment and training existing full-time officers in recruitment and organising than the more aggressive anti-employer or social movement aspects of the US 'model'. New Unionism, according to the TUC, is about:

- promoting organising as the top priority and shifting the union movement towards an organising culture
- increasing union investment in recruiting and organising, strengthening lay organisation, and using dedicated and trained organisers
- helping unions break into new areas and win recognition
- sharpening unions' appeals to new workers and those at the rough end of the labour market.[8]

This more cautious approach reflects some of the aforementioned caveats as well as the delicate balance of power relationships between the TUC and leading affiliates. The TUC's Organising Academy does bend towards more open and participative approaches, with most of the recruits being young and recruited on the basis of having 'talent, energy and sheer determination' with a 'flexible and imaginative approach to the resolution of issues' (cited in person specification for TUC Academy recruits, TUC 1997). However, there remain limitations to the initiative. As Heery *et al.* (2000) indicate, the trainees have so far brought in 7,500 new recruits to the participating unions and a further 18,000 through associated campaigns. Whilst no doubt an achievement it is still small beer to the half million recruits the TUC affiliated unions need each year just to stand still. Second, the appointment of Academy Organisers and the secondment to affiliated unions means that the trainees are invariably operating one step removed from the union official machine. As such they sit uncomfortably with the union bureaucracy and are likely to lack power or authority within the union to have much influence in shifting the union towards an organising culture. They are also dependent on the union leadership for their career prospects after 'training' and are likely as a result to remain cautious and neutral in challenging those union leaderships obstructive to genuine participative change in the union 'from below'. If new unionism is to work in the UK it will need to become deeply embedded in the culture of trade union operations and will also need to resolve questions of power and authority in unions to the advantage of participative and inclusive approaches.

Finally, a decade or so of union retreat in the workplace may have sapped the energy and spirit of all but the most committed union activist. In the organisational context trade union representatives are subject to continuing employer goodwill in order to fulfil an unimpeded role of interest representation. Employer attempts to marginalise unions and restrict collective activity in recent years will have strained relationships. The continuing resilience of the workplace representative is testament to the commitment of ordinary workers to collectivist values and possibly also to the strategic intent of many employers to a continued policy of 'negotiated control' of the labour management problem (Hyman 1989: 190). There is no doubt that this voluntary union activity has become more rather than less difficult in the average workplace. The temptations of employers to subvert negotiated control by the construction of alternative forms of direct participation have increased. The tasks of maintaining trade union presence and, perhaps more importantly, influence over managerial prerogative have become more difficult as a result. Within the discourse over new unionism and new methods of recruiting there is, therefore, a need to address the proposition that new recruitment gains must be consolidated into participative workplace bargaining if they are not to be left high and dry and dependent on extra 'servicing' from local activists or full-time officials. The word 'participative' is also potentially problematic in itself when addressed to trade union workplace activity. In particular, some commentators have referred to a 'democracy deficit' in the unions whereby decision-making structures are unrepresentative of membership (and potential membership) diversity (Cockburn 1995; Labour Research 1998; Healy and Kirton 2000). Fairbrother (2000a), in attempting to formulate more precisely what is meant by trade union participation, places considerable emphasis on a particular definition of participation:

> A union organised on the principle of membership participation is one where the leadership and members place emphasis on the active involvement of members in the genesis and development of union policy, in the execution and administration of bargaining and negotiation, in the development of organisation and the control of officials . . . The purpose of communication and the provision of information and resourcing in the union aims to supplement and stimulate membership participation . . . relations between leaders and members are two way . . . (Fairbrother 2000a: 29).

There are other ways of assessing the degree of participation. For example, Fosh (1993) rehearses the distinction between *formal* and *informal* participation whereby formal participation will include attending meetings and voting in elections, and informal participation would entail activities such as reading union material and interacting with shop stewards. The distinction between participation, involvement and the additional concept of 'inclusiveness' in union affairs at workplace level is thus far from straightforward. *Inclusiveness* is also a function of the degree to which union workplace representatives at workplace level *involve* members in decision-making (through frequency of meetings, regularity of newsletters and surveys, etc.), as well as the extent to which union agendas are *widened* to include issues of importance for women, youth and ethnic minorities as integral to workers' interests. This suggests a more active relationship between leading workplace union activists and the rank-and-file membership, complementing the activist-leadership relationship emphasised in Fairbrother's definition. Given its recency, the onset of *e-collectivism* propelled by the increasing use of email and web-based technology provides an interesting test of unions' ability and willingness to release this information and power. Research by Greene *et al.* (2001) suggests that only a few unions (e.g. UNISON) have utilised the new technology to open up limited opportunities for self-organising. A more likely union response appears to be a continuing 'domination of union web sites and other electronic communication means by the same cliques as in more traditional modes'. Discussion-based and unmoderated sites are generally absent from the official union domains, leaving the creation of more adventurous and democratic options to rank-and-file initiative. Such reactions by the union leaderships to the new opportunities represented by e-technology suggest a continuation of the servicing approach rather than a shift towards participative organising.

While some degree of servicing will be inevitable there is an argument for claiming that the organising approach will not be sustainable unless any new areas of membership growth are integrated into the union through active involvement in the negotiating machinery. The question goes beyond 'organising for recruitment' to one of 'organising against the employer'. As such, if union renewal is to occur, it must take place within the context of appropriate and effective union responses to changing managerial tactics concerning labour control and productivity in the new workplace. Figure 1.2 illustrates the argument, whereby 'new management initiatives', such as work restructuring, the introduction of teamworking or continuous improvement programmes, may trigger (or not) a union response which requires successful organising if the union is to maintain and sustain its position of power and influence within the workplace. The organisational response *vis-à-vis* the employer must engage the employer in workplace change or, as Stewart and Martinez Lucio (1998) argue, in the 'new politics of production' to maximise the chances of success, and must mobilise members and recruit non-members in the process. Our evidence on these points, presented in Chapter 2, would indicate that there is a positive relationship firstly between the introduction of new management practices and the depth of employee discontent, and secondly between the ensuing grievances and the scope of union bargaining activity. These unfolding relationships uncover a re-collectivisation of employment relationships in the 'new workplace', based primarily on an employer-provoked collectivisation of employee discontent.

The process by which unions engage management-driven workplace change is therefore of interest. Kelly (1998) has attempted to address this dynamism by drawing upon earlier work on mobilisation emanating primarily from the US by

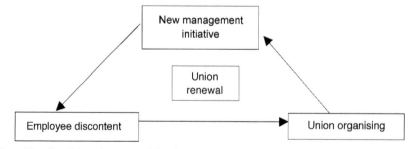

Figure 1.2   Conditions for successful union renewal.

Tilly (1978) and McAdam (1988). The argument is that propensity to organise collectively is a function of perception of interests (collective or individual), organisational capacity, and opportunity within the employer-employee balance of power. Whether or not mobilisation occurs is in turn a function of local leadership and the ability or willingness of that leadership to direct workers' sense of injustice towards management (rather than some external agent). As such, mobilisation is a dynamic process subject to contradictory battles within worker consciousness and often turning on 'critical incidents' within the workplace which provide opportunity for insurgent (anti-management) leadership. The dynamic nature of the process also means that the same or similar incident in two similar workplaces might produce different union responses according to the different union leadership or state of worker consciousness. Research thus lends itself to case study approaches, even down to the extreme micro level of 'who said what, when and to whom' variety of Fantasia (1988) in his fascinating study of the 'culture' of solidarity. Such an approach, however, can be overly voluntaristic and dependent on rank-and-file spontaneity. Internal union dynamics also need to be assessed. Darlington (1994a: 283–4), in his case studies from Merseyside for example, offers the prospect of different political types of leadership inducing a spectrum of variable membership responses from passivity and 'reformism' through to militancy and 'revolutionary socialism'. The passivity induced by 'reformist' leadership, in this exposition, Darlington argues, can lead to the union local leadership exercising 'control from above' and dissipating potential mobilisation opportunity. Similarly Bain and Taylor (2001) in their work on call centres, refer to 'counter mobilisation' whereby opportunities to exploit critical incidents over employee discontent are missed as employers 'counter mobilise' (sometimes by dismissing leading activists) or 'dissipated mobilisation' when key union bodies fail to support local activists during decisive episodes. These some- times contestatory relationships between rank-and-file and union leaderships over questions of power and influence also need consideration (c.f. Darlington 1994a: 31–3; see also Danford 1999: 160–8).

The new discourse of partnership

Against this background of complications and doubts there has emerged a new discourse on partnership at work which now overlays debates on trade union renewal. The TUC now seeks to span both the partnership *and* organising model agendas, having launched in January 2001 its 'Partnership Institute' to accompany the already existing 'Organising Academy'. The motive for partnership has three key sources driven by employers, unions or Government in varying combinations. First, is the mutual gains approach emanating primarily from the US which seeks to reinforce business unionism by encouraging a 'win-win' perspective on union-employer collaboration (Kochan and Osterman 1994; Kochan 1999). This is arguably a continuation by other means of the single unionism ethos in the UK that appeared as a key strategy in some sectors in the 1980s. Second, is the reference to the 'European Model of Social Partnership' which has gathered some ground as European Social policy agendas 'deepen' and as left reformist and liberal political thinkers raise eyebrows at the debilitating effects of neo-liberal free market agendas (Albert 1993; Hutton 1995; Kapstein 1999). Such an approach argues for institutional support for stakeholder power, including more legitimacy for workers' representation. Third, is the preferred model of the current UK Government which de-emphasises the 'social' aspects of partnership and re-emphasises a perceived need for 'partnership' at work as a lever to build productivity coalitions between employees and their employers in a joint productivity effort (Knell 1999). The word 'social' is conspicuously absent from official Government publications implying a distancing from both trade union influence (as one of the social partners) and the implications that creating thick institutional support would have for the necessary upward re-regulation of labour markets and bargaining frameworks (Tailby and Winchester 2000: 374). The various strands of partnership thinking and practice have in common a consensual-based approach to employee relations, implying an emphasis on information giving and consultation rather than negotiation. Such an approach would seem to have some empathy with employers' attempts to introduce the practice (rhetoric or otherwise) of employee commitment and gel with trade union strategies aimed at restoring trade union influence in an era of reduced scope and content of traditional collective bargaining. For the TUC, for example, social partnership 'means employers and trade unions work together to achieve common goals such as fairness and competitiveness. . . . it is a recognition that although they have different constituencies, and at times different interests, they can serve these best by *making common cause wherever possible* (authors' emphasis)' (TUC 1997: 1). How then, does the new discourse of partnership in the British workplace measure as a response to the 'crisis of representation' we have already identified?

For the TUC partnership is seen as 'the most effective approach to improve the working lives of trade union members and an essential element in any strategy to improve organisational performance' (TUC Partnership Institute 2001: 3). The appeal to organisational performance is linked in this strategy to a recognition of the need 'to convince employers that collective bargaining is a collective good – and that the decline of collective bargaining has deprived the UK of a powerful force for delivering positive change in the workplace.' (TUC Partnership Institute 2001: 7) Partnership is thus approached as a potential lever to organisational recognition and legitimacy where an employer strategy of recognising union bargaining rights and using trade unions to facilitate change is preferred to one of imposing change unilaterally. What is not clear here is the distinction between employer strategies of recognising unions through a process of consultation as an alternative to negotiation. By referring to 'collective bargaining' rather than 'negotiation' the TUC fudge the difference. In practice this difference is crucial to an understanding of how interest representation may develop in a workplace. On the one hand partnership, in granting union representation a new legitimacy, may act to encourage union *membership* within the organisation. Haynes and Allen (2001) argue this case and cite the examples of MSF (Manufacturing, Science and Finance Union) in Legal and General and USDAW (Union of Shop, Distributive and Allied Workers) in Tesco as examples. What is less clear are the precise 'terms of engagement' that arise between union and employer within partnership deals and the level of *member participation* that arises as a result. For example, in their sample survey of 240 organisations with current or past membership of the Industrial Participation Association, Guest and Peccei (2001) find a 'generally low level of direct participation in work decisions and of representative participation in organisational decisions' with an inference that 'greater emphasis is placed on employee contribution than on employee welfare and rights and independent representation. In many cases, management would appear to be gaining more from the practice of partnership'. If Guest and Peccei's evidence is confirmed as the dominant trend in the reality of partnership then a strong argument can be made that partnership as a strategy for union renewal is likely to be deficient.

The reliance on consensus as a paradigm has also not surprisingly been criticised for creating a *collaborative* framework at the expense of traditional adversarialism (Kelly 1996), and for pacifying the rank-and-file membership in the interests of consensus (Ackers and Payne 1998). For McIlroy (1998: 543) the apparent merging of government, employer and union objectives has also meant a certain 're-legitimisation' of collectivism, but on the condition 'that it be imbricated with management objectives'. As such the partnership approach creates a potential contra-pole of attraction to the more aggressive implications of the organising model of union renewal. Tested against the possibilities of 'internal expansion' (Figure 1.1), on the evidence presented, the partnership approach may fail to widen participation within union workplace membership but may succeed in opening up new bargaining areas, albeit with an emphasis on the employers' agendas. If there are doubts about partnership as a renewal strategy within the terms of internal expansion what, however, are the prospects for external expansion into new and greenfield sites ?

In probing this question it is useful to examine evidence of new recognition deals that have emerged immediately before and after the 1999 Employment Relations Act and which post date the WERS data. An Incomes Data Services Report in July 2001 reviews the pattern of new recognition deals one year after the enforcement of the statutory right to recognition and finds that the number of new recognition deals has risen sharply over the previous three years, with some unions (and employers) clearly anticipating the legislative change (IDS 2001). Ninety four per cent of deals surveyed were for full recognition, which is a higher percentage than that recorded in previous years. The style of deals agreed is not generally recorded, and so it is not possible to determine the impact of a partnership approach. Gall and McKay (2001), however, in collecting evidence from both unpublished Labour Research Department-TUC records and Employers' Federations, also report an upturn in the rate of union recognition and a decline in de-recognition in the latter part of the 1990s when compared to the earlier part of the decade. In presenting their evidence they review the pattern of union recognition and de-recognition, constrained recognition (where full bargaining rights on all issues are limited), as well as a small but significant continuation of employer attempts to suppress recognition or substitute for union voice, and an equally small but significant number of cases where single union or 'beauty contest' deals have re-emerged onto the scene since the 'fall away' of such deals from their heyday in the mid-1980s. According to Gall and McKay some of these single union deals involve employers' attempts to select an 'appropriate' union which 'may be a union prepared to eschew a traditional bargaining relationship in favour of "business unionism" or "partnership"'. They cite the AEEU as the most successful union in winning contests for such sole recognition which, they claim, is largely as a result of its declared commitment to 'partnership contracts' as opposed to the more 'traditionalist' approach of GMB and TGWU. Some evidence of the different approaches of unions is confirmed in the IDS survey, which again cites some recent AEEU single union deals signed in greenfield manufacturing sites and contrasts these with the more aggressive factory gate recruiting (often on a competitive basis) of the GMB and ISTC. Despite these examples there is clearly not enough quantitative or qualitative evidence available to vigorously assess the impact of the partnership approach as a strategy for external union expansion. More research on this question is clearly important.

Scope and content

The task of this book, in facing up to the union crisis, is to confront these contradictions and problems and to try to assess what is 'new' about workplaces and unions in contemporary Britain and to comment on the limits of this 'newness'. As with all social research the task of researchers is to unpick the rhetoric from the reality and to place what might appear to be trends in the overall context of real and consistent change. Assessing the balance between change and continuity is no easy task, and is itself subject to the perspective of the researchers. The example of Ross and Hartman's 1960 predictions of the 'withering away of the strike', which quickly fell on stony ground in the changed mood of the combative late 1960s and 1970s, is a case in point (Ross and Hartman, 1960). The focus of the research is unions at the workplace rather than unions as a national entity (although the national union is by no means ignored in the analyses). The reason for this is twofold. First, there has been a general absence (with some notable exceptions) of workplace-based studies since the 1970s when such 'classic' studies as Lane and Roberts (1971) *Strike at Pilkingtons* appeared. The period tempted academic inquiry because of the evident workplace turbulence of those times and included *inter alia* studies such as Batstone *et al*'s (1977) account of leadership style among shop stewards, and other sociological studies by Beynon (1973), Nichols and Armstrong (1976), Nichols and Beynon (1977) and Pollert (1981). The increasing relative quiescence in the workplace in the following decades does not mean, in the authors' view, that workplace studies are consequently of limited value. Indeed it is only through an understanding of changes in the labour process, and of the political economy that engenders those changes, that we can fully understand the prospects for union renewal. We also have too little knowledge of the kinds of grievances and disputes that are being addressed by unions in the workplace and which can form a catalyst, in the right conditions, for a resurgence of collective combativity. Secondly, there is a dynamic to unions that cannot be explained solely by examining the internal structure or official policies of unions but which can be better understood by relating to the internal tensions and contradictions within the unions themselves. Micro-study of unions at the workplace is a vital tool in developing this understanding.

This book attempts to address prospects for union renewal by returning to the workplace and placing union responses in their wider context of changes in political economy, changes in labour markets, changes in the organisation of work, and shifts in union organisational strategy. In doing so the trade union response to change is examined and alternative strategies for renewal are hopefully assessed. Rather than deny the continued salience of employee need for collective voice it is apparent that such voice is becoming increasingly suppressed in today's workplace. What then, are the prospects for unions at the workplace tapping the sources of discontent and engendering union renewal in the process? This question is also tackled in Chapter 2 by presenting evidence from the new workplace. The revision of management–union relations in the context of organisational change is recorded. The types and frequency of complaints and grievances processed by union workplace representatives in the survey are analysed, and patterns of leadership and the participative approaches (or otherwise) adopted by representatives with their members are assessed. It is in this chapter that the mass of quantitative data is presented. Chapters 3–6 examine different sectors covering manufacturing, aerospace and insurance in the private sector and local authorities and NHS (National Health Service) Trusts in the public sector. Some additional evidence from privatised utilities is also presented. In each of these sectoral chapters a contextual description covering changes in the relevant industries and organisations surveyed is given, together with more qualitative data obtained from interviewing the union workplace representatives as well as full-time union officials at regional, district and national level.

The research design is described in the Appendix. The data were collected primarily from workplace union representatives in three unions (the MSF, AEEU and GMB) across a variety of workplaces in different industries in the South West of England. The authors' are acutely conscious that workers are subjects who can influence and shape events and not just objects of greater structural influences. Because of this some attention is placed on leadership profiles and degree of participation within the workplace union, as well as more general data on types of grievances and concerns that dominate today's workplace bargaining agendas. Data for the MSF have come from five sectors in aerospace, general manufacturing, insurance, NHS trusts and universities. The occupations reflect MSF's spheres of influence and include technical and specialist engineering workers, medical technicians, health visitors and clinical psychologists in the NHS trusts, and a range of occupations in the (largely) single-union insurance offices where MSF has a presence. For the GMB, data were collected from

privatised utilities (for example, electricity and gas), nuclear power, manufacturing and local authorities. The occupations covered are mostly manual with
a mix of craft and non-craft. For the AEEU, data came from aerospace,
manufacturing private utilities and nuclear power generation. Stewards
represented mostly manual craft workers but also some semi-skilled and unskilled
employees.

The three unions are, of course, different in terms of their tradition and
representative structures. The MSF (Manufacturing, Science and Finance) was
formed in 1988 following a merger with ASTMS (Association of Scientific,
Technical and Managerial Staffs) and TASS (Technical, Administrative and
Supervisory Union). In certain respects the two marriage partners were very
different. ASTMS had a membership of workers in professional, technical and
supervisory jobs which included both the engineering industry and finance.
Whilst the membership was fairly conservative, reflecting its occupational base,
the leadership was generally left Labour and held together by the idiosyncracies of
its leader Clive Jenkins. TASS, on the other hand, had its base among technicians
in the heavy engineering industry, had at one time been amalgamated with the
engineers' union AUEW, and had a leadership of officials strongly attached to, or
influenced by, the Communist Party. The merger brought obvious political
tensions, and whilst many full-time officials were from TASS the activists of
ASTMS appeared to be well placed in the new merged branches. Branches in fact
now retain a relatively high degree of autonomy when compared to other unions,
reflecting the dominant tradition of the old ASTMS within the new union, rather
than the officer-led tradition of TASS (Carter, 1991). The union adopts a system of
senior and junior representatives as workplace activists and was one of the first
UK unions to officially adopt the organising model, despite apparent tensions in
the relationship between national and regional officials in its interpretation and
implementation (Carter, 1997). One of the reasons for moving early to the
organising approach was a financial crisis in the union as a result of declining
membership associated with the general fall in manufacturing employment. This
has created additional tensions in the union as full-time officer numbers have been
gradually trimmed back, whilst at the same time a requirement to shift towards
organising and recruiting new members (and with it increased servicing
demands) has been made.

For many years after the last war the GMB was characterised by a power
structure dominated by the regional full-time secretaries working in close
harmony with the General Secretary. Local workplace representatives had little
autonomy and it was only in later years, as union competition increased and key
unofficial disputes occurred, that this regime was relaxed and more attention was
given to workplace representation (Beynon 1984). The union consequently
adopted a steward system relatively late, partly as a move to a more open style
and partly as an alternative to the previous overconcentration of power with
regional officials. (Maksymiw, 1990; Fairbrother 2000b: 38–40). The GMB has
also traditionally adopted a managerial servicing relationship with its
membership based on systematic research of member needs and aspirations and

the provision of resources and support via regional full-time officers. In 1990 the 'New Agenda' was adopted which sought to extend the subject matter of bargaining in the light of membership needs. Subscription levels have also been tailored to reflect different work contracts, with lower rates for part-time and low-paid workers (Willman *et al*. 1993: 52). This managerial approach filters down to workplace level, where a 'constitutional' relationship between stewards and members is typical, with the steward 'representing' the members on a formal basis to management, and with less emphasis on mass members' decision-making structures. Following the release of its 'Into 2000' policy document and 'Partnerships for Success' campaign full-time officers are now actively encouraged to seek partnership agreements with employers.[9]

The AEEU (Amalgamated Engineering and Electrical Union) is the result of a 1992 merger between the engineers' union AEU (Amalgamated Engineering Union) and the electricians' and plumbers' union EETPU (Electrical, Electronic, Telecommunications and Plumbing Union). Both unions had craft origins and have been closely associated at different times in their past with troubled political in-fighting between left and right. However, by the time of the merger both unions' leaderships were right-wing dominated, and the merger process was thus made easier as a result. The AEU had long had a system of shop steward representation at the workplace, a democratic power structure whereby district full-time officials were directly elected by the membership, and a decision process characterised by formal accountability throughout the union structure. Such a devolved structure led to considerable factionalising but also a strong steward representative structure (Undy *et al*. 1981). The merger with the EETPU led to the consolidation of a large right-wing dominated union that was willing, after the years of retreat in the 1980s, to continue a policy of 'business unionism' and the pursuit of single-union deals. It also meant a weakening of the AEU's democratic tradition and a dismantling of the district-based power structure in favour of centralised control. Despite these changes strong workplace representation has remained, with a relatively high degree of membership participation.

In January 2002, the AEEU and MSF merged to form a new union AMICUS. Although a rationalisation of branches and duplication of resources is inevitable in the longer term, at the time of writing the two constituent unions had retained their own distinctive sections (AMICUS-AEEU and AMICUS-MSF).

2 Union organising in the new workplace

Introduction

Contemporary business writers often proclaim a recent paradigmatic shift in the nature of work organisation. The 'new workplace' inhabited by the majority of British employees is held to be 'post-Taylorist', 'post-Fordist', 'post-bureaucratic', 'de-regulated', 'de-collectivised' and 'individualised'. Subject to a plethora of cultural change programmes and new management initiatives, employees in both private- and public-sector employment are assumed to enjoy ever-increasing flexibility, autonomy and participation at work.

In fact, many writers in the labour process tradition continue to highlight the limitations of these 'new paradigm' assumptions and point to the resilience of essentially Taylorist forms of work design and management control conceptualised by Braverman's (1974) seminal thesis. Nevertheless, as Warhurst and Thompson (1998: 19) argue, some things have changed. Intensified global competition, ever-evolving computer technologies, new management practices and the diffusion of market relations into large public- and private-sector workplaces have catalysed organisational innovations which directly implicate labour utilisation strategies and work reforms.

These 'new workplaces' (in fact, the vast majority are restructured 'old workplaces') have been variously conceptualised as 'World Class Manufacturers' (Schonberger 1996), as Mutual Gains Enterprises (Kochan and Osterman 1994), as High-Performance Organisations (Wood 1999) and as sites of High-Performance Work Systems (Ramsay *et al.* 2000). To the extent that one can generalise from a complexity of organisational practice, in the private sector the new workplaces can be characterised as those which incorporate a variety of participatory and commitment techniques such as teamworking, quality circles or their equivalents, flexible work organisation and two-way communications. When these techniques are used together as coherent 'bundles' of practice (Wood 1999) then a positive association with hard organisational performance measures may be expected (Kochan and Osterman 1994; Ramsay *et al.* 2000).

There is another dimension to work restructuring in the state sector. Managements have followed strategies aimed at individualising workers and redrawing the employment relationship through greater use of numerical and temporal flexible work contracts (Fairbrother 2000b). Moreover, the introduction of privatisation, market testing, compulsory competitive tendering and best value policies by both Conservative and Labour Governments has increasingly acted to commodify labour and weaken the public-sector traditions of trust and commitment to service (Webb 1999). In the new public-sector workplaces, the latter 'normative' aspects of control are being replaced by what Webb refers to as 'performative' control. Performance management systems geared to maximising 'efficiency' and minimising service cost have created a new dominant mode of direct control over employees.

What are the industrial relations implications of these changes, and in particular, how should trade unions respond? Those writers who espouse a neo-pluralism, based on the ethics of trust between stakeholders, assume that co-operation with management agendas might enable unions to regain a central place in the regulation of the employment relationship. For example, Kochan and Osterman (1994) have argued that to maintain their influence in the 'mutual gains enterprise', trade unions must construct new consensus-based relationships with management and should take a lead in ensuring that high-performance work reforms operate efficiently and are sustained. In a similar vein, management attempts to deregulate the employment relationship and 'reorganise collective workforces on an individualistic basis' (Fairbrother 1996) have led some writers to defend the development of workplace partnership relations. Ackers and Payne (1998) and Bacon and Storey (1996) have argued that the direction of management policy towards both individualisation (in terms of employment contracts, wages systems and communications) and a new collectivism (the organisation of workers into teams and group-based employee involvement schemes) threatens to undermine the traditional collective basis of trade unionism. In response to this 'fracturing of collectivism' we are advised to eschew the sterile debate between militancy and moderation; and trade unions are urged to develop shared objectives with employers and to campaign for ever more complete and meaningful forms of partnership to secure a more participative workplace (Ackers and Payne 1998: 546).

This assumption of one best road to union renewal requires closer inspection. Meaningful partnerships require equal partners. And if one party in the employment relationship has enjoyed dominance in terms of the balance of power between capital and labour over the past two decades then the development of partnership at work would expect that party (the employer) to surrender a portion of its accumulated power. In fact, we have little evidence to suggest that employers are prepared to act in this way. Ironically, many neo-pluralist writers concede as much. Ackers and Payne (1998) highlighted how the CBI and the Institute of Directors have been hostile to any legislative reform that might potentially strengthen trade unions. And at the workplace level, case study research of partnership organisations has found little evidence that underlying management attitudes towards joint governance has changed, indeed, many managers would be happier with a continuation of union exclusion agendas (Bacon and Storey 2000: 425; Guest and Peccei 2001).

However, there is a more fundamental flaw in the theoretical underpinnings of neo-pluralism. If trade unions are to defend the legitimate interests of their members, then in the context of contemporary capital accumulation strategies in the private sector and the deepening of bureaucratic rationality in the public sector, there may be a dwindling number of issues upon which they can co-operate with management and an expanding number about which they differ. Moreover, as Martinez Lucio and Stewart (1997) have argued, reconceptualisations of the labour process around new forms of collectivism, the individualisation of work, and ultimately the individualisation of the subject, all tend to deny independent, employee-originated collectivism. The same writers (Stewart and Martinez Lucio 1998: 76–8) have argued that in dwelling upon socio-technical or institutional change analysts of the implementation of lean production or high-performance workplace techniques tend to draw attention away from the active and complex role of labour organisation in challenging managerial agendas. In fact, we have seen the development of a new politics of production based on independent trade union agendas governing such matters as teamworking, health and safety and employee representation, and geared towards realigning management objectives with respect to labour control of the effort-reward process. There are now a good number of case studies of this politics of production. They emphasise that trade unions are not always marginalised or forced into co-operative subordinate relations with management regimes in the 'new workplace' (for example, Danford 1999; Martinez Lucio *et al.* 2000; Rinehart *et al.* 1997; Stewart and Wass 1998).

In the context of these different debates over the complexity of trade union behaviour at work, this chapter explores the patterns of labour management practices, management–union relations and trade union responses to change in the restructured 'new workplaces' of the South West of England. We present survey-based quantitative data investigating processes of union renewal at work. National surveys have tended to paint a pessimistic picture of the condition of British trade unions. The different Workplace Employee Relations Surveys (WERS) – drawing primarily on data provided by managers – have traced a long decline in union power and influence at well established, union recognised workplaces (Millward *et al.* 2000). Similarly, Gallie *et al.*'s (1996) 'trade unionism in recession' project painted a picture at the beginning of the 1990s of British unions clinging onto recognition, posing few challenges to managerial prerogatives at work, and dependent upon either employers' goodwill or their preference for stable collective bargaining over the more messy, individualised management practices. In the current environment of politico-economic change and greater trade union optimism, the key questions explored in this chapter are: (i) to what extent do workplace union representatives feel that the long trend of declining union organisation and influence has gone into reverse? (ii) How are union representatives responding to current work reforms? (iii) Is there any evidence of a recollectivisation of workplace relations in the unionised sectors?

Workplace union characteristics

The questionnaire component of the research design (described in the Appendix) comprised two surveys of workplace representatives. The first was of 356 departmental union representatives and the second was of 70 senior union representatives (or convenors). This chapter draws on quantitative data from both surveys.

The representatives who participated in the survey were predominantly employed at large workplaces. Fifty-seven per cent of respondents worked at establishments with more than 500 employees; 27 per cent worked at establishments of between 201 and 500 employees; and 16 per cent at establishments with less than 200 employees. Only 19 per cent of the representatives were women and this reflected the under-employment of women in the aerospace and manufacturing sectors in particular. Most of the women representatives were concentrated in MSF's NHS and insurance work areas (56 per cent and 46 per cent of respondents respectively), and in the GMB's local government areas (39 per cent).

Union membership densities for each workplace were calculated from membership and potential membership data provided by the survey of senior representatives. Where possible, these membership data were cross-checked with statistical records maintained by regional union offices. The overall membership density was 65 per cent but this varied between unions. In the AEEU areas average membership density was 86 per cent; in the GMB areas membership density was 66 per cent; and in MSF areas the density was 50 per cent. In addition, membership density was much higher in the aerospace and manufacturing workplaces (72 per cent) compared to the private- and public-services workplaces (55 per cent).

The small size of our public-sector sample prevents valid comparisons with the much larger 1998 WERS sample. However, the same cannot be said for our private-sector sample which included many of the larger firms in the South West economy. Millward *et al.* (2000: 92) argue, on the basis of the WERS management responses, that the decline in private-sector union density is primarily due to a withering of employees' support for membership in workplaces with recognised unions plus a lack of recruitment processes. By contrast, our data suggest that in particular key segments of the private sector (aerospace, manufacturing, insurance and privatised utilities) support for trade unions is not withering; membership densities in *large firms* with recognised unions remain relatively high.

The number of members per workplace representative is a further indicator of the strength of workplace union organisation. The means of union members per union representative were significantly lower (meaning greater organisational strength) in our survey establishments compared to the national patterns identified by the 1998 WERS survey. For example, the mean of members per representative in establishments of 500 or more employees was thirty-five to one in our survey compared to the corresponding WERS figure of fifty-three to one. The surveys also asked representatives how much time they spent on union activity both at the workplace and outside working hours. The WERS survey found that 72 per cent of *senior* workplace representatives spent less than five hours per week representing union members. By contrast, the representatives participating in our survey, of whom only a *minority* were senior representatives, spent significantly more than this; an average of nearly seven and a half hours per week.

The high-performance workplace

The questionnaire surveys explored the labour management dimensions of high-performance human resource policies in the local work areas represented by each union representative. The data provide overall patterns of management practice and patterns of difference between industrial sectors.

The significant increase in the levels of Japanese and US foreign direct investment in the UK during the 1980s catalysed considerable interest in the new management techniques of foreign manufacturing transplants and their impact upon UK workplace relations. Despite this, a national survey of union activists completed in the early 1990s found no evidence of widespread emulation in British firms and a relatively low incidence of teamworking, job flexibility and quality circles (Waddington and Whitston 1996). However, the current WERS data suggest that during the last decade a more pervasive process of work restructuring has taken hold. For example, in 1998, 65 per cent of workplaces deployed most employees in teams and 68 per cent of large workplaces utilised problem-solving groups involving employees (Cully *et al.* 1999). Our questionnaire survey of union representatives in the South West's key employment sectors confirms this general trend although the presence of these functional flexibility practices varied between sectors.

Following initial exploratory interviews with senior union representatives three management practices associated with work organisation and functional flexibility were covered in the survey: teamworking; job or task flexibility; problem-solving quality circles/continuous improvement groups (hereafter described as quality circles). Five practices associated with numerical flexibility were covered: working time flexibility; outsourcing; use of sub-contract staff; temporary staff; part-time staff. Four human resource management practices associated with employee commitment strategies were used: team briefings; single-status conditions; job evaluation processes; performance related pay or merit pay schemes. Table 2.1 shows the pattern of use of these different practices in the local areas represented by the different union workplace representatives.

The more intensive capital accumulation strategies of British firms in recent years and the parallel process of new managerialist control and marketising reforms in the public sector have increased labour utilisation rates and secured a more efficient and flexible consumption of labour power. This is reflected in the adoption of particular practices such as teamworking, task flexibility, continuous improvement and the use of more flexible employment policies. As a result, many workplaces in the private and public sectors have been subject to labour rationalisation and labour intensification. Our survey of union representatives

Table 2.1.   The percentage of union representatives reporting the use of selected management practices in their area, by sector, $n = 356$.

	All union reps (%)	Aerospace & m'fact (%)	Services (%)	Private sector (%)	Public sector (%)
More workload – staff reductions	67	71	62	70	58
Teamworking	60	70	64	70	33
Job flexibility	57	67	41	65	32
Quality circles/*kaizen*	46	67	14	59	8
Working time flexibility	31	30	34	35	21
Outsourcing	35	43	19	41	16
Sub-contract labour	42	53	27	51	17
Temporary contracts	48	44	54	46	54
Part-time contracts	33	28	42	30	45
Team briefings	77	83	68	84	55
Single status	10	13	6	11	9
Job evaluation	49	48	50	52	39
PRP/Merit pay	39	43	32	50	7

tended to confirm these trends. For example, Table 2.1 shows that a good majority of all union representatives across all sectors confirmed that their local work areas had been subject to 'workforce reductions resulting in remaining staff taking on greater workloads'. This was reinforced by an additional set of questions which asked the union representatives to indicate whether or not various changes to their role had taken hold. For example, 81 per cent of respondents indicated that 'the representative's role had become more difficult due to increased work pressure'.

As Table 2.1 shows, 60 per cent of all union representatives reported the use of teamworking in their own work areas, 57 per cent reported the presence of job or task flexibility and 46 per cent reported the use of quality circles. All three management practices were more common in the aerospace-manufacturing sector compared to services and significantly so in the private sector compared to the smaller public-sector sample of predominantly GMB manual workers and MSF technicians and health professionals. Teamworking was most often reported in utilities (80 per cent), aerospace (70 per cent), manufacturing (69 per cent) and insurance (62 per cent). Quality circles were surprisingly common in manufacturing (75 per cent) and aerospace (63 per cent). It could be the case that in these centres of production the durability of quality circles, or their equivalents, is greater than some analysts of TQM (total quality management) assume (for example, Hill 1991; Proctor and Mueller 2000).

In the private sector generally and in aerospace-manufacturing in particular, the data also suggested evidence of the use of 'bundles' of these practices characteristic of the high-performance workplace (Wood 1999). For example, 39 per cent of representatives in the private-sector workplaces reported that teamworking, job flexibility, quality circles and team briefings were all used in their local work areas; 64 per cent of representatives reported that at least three of these practices were used. In the aerospace-manufacturing sectors, 45 per cent of representatives reported that all four practices operated in their areas; 67 per cent of representatives reported that at least three of these practices were used.

There was a significantly different pattern of use of numerical flexibility practices in the form of flexible hours, outsourcing and non-standard employment contracts. Working time flexibility measures, such as flexitime and job-sharing, tended to be much higher in the non-manual areas of work represented by GMB and MSF activists. They were also more common in the insurance sector workplaces and in the local government work areas. The outsourcing of work and use of sub-contract labour were more prevalent in both the AEEU's and MSF's aerospace and manufacturing work areas. A significant proportion of GMB representatives in the local government case studies also reported the use of outsourcing as a result of compulsory competitive tendering. The utilisation of both temporary and part-time contracts was more common in the GMB's and MSF's spheres of influence in insurance, the NHS trusts and local government.

National surveys of union representatives and industrial relations managers have identified an increasing use of human resource management practices such as management communications through team briefings, job evaluation schemes and more individualised forms of pay determination (Cully *et al*. 1999; Waddington and Whitston 1996). Our survey identified the same patterns in the major employment sectors of South West England. For example, the use of team briefings was reported by 77 per cent of union representatives and by 93 per cent of AEEU and GMB representatives in the privatised utilities, 89 per cent of MSF representatives in insurance and 83 per cent of AEEU and MSF representatives in the aerospace-manufacturing sector. However, only 7 per cent of the GMB representatives in local government reported their use. In the latter case, more indirect, representative forms of communication and consultation predominate.

Job evaluation schemes and individualised pay determination were also in widespread use in some sectors, particularly in MSF spheres of influence in insurance and aerospace-manufacturing and amongst sizeable minorities of craft areas in aerospace, manufacturing and the utilities. This suggests an increase of monitoring of individual effort in these skilled manual and technical-administrative staff areas. By contrast, the use of individualised pay schemes such as performance-related pay and merit pay were virtually absent from the GMB's and MSF's spheres of influence in the public sector, a reflection of the strength of public-sector union opposition to different government attempts to dismantle or weaken national pay bargaining.

Finally, despite the widespread rhetoric of equality of status and employment conditions heard in many contemporary work organisations, few of the union representatives in our survey reported the use of single-status conditions. The only sector to report any significant adoption of single-status arrangements was local government where harmonisation agreements involving the integration of manual workers into white-collar staff grading structures were being introduced following a 1997 national agreement on pay and conditions. Overall, only 10 per cent of union representatives across sectors reported the existence of single status, a figure that is only marginally higher than the 1991 survey results reported by Waddington and Whitston (1996). By contrast, although the 1998 WERS survey identified 41 per cent of workplaces as single-status organisations, these data were based on management reports. Our survey merely highlights the possibility of a different perspective from those who represent workers who may still feel that the principles of single status and equality at work remain ideological constructs.

Management–union relations at work: getting worse or getting better?

In the context of the general pattern of decline in union power and influence over the past two decades we attempted to measure the union representatives' subjective assessments of both local management–union relationships and their employers' attitudes to unions, and the extent to which these had changed in the two to three years following the election of the Labour Government in 1997.

Three questions were used to explore management–union relations. First, the workplace union representatives were asked to express the relationship between the union's representatives and management at their workplace along a scale of one to five, with one representing 'a close and harmonious relationship' and five representing 'a them and us relationship'. Second, the representatives were asked to express their employer's general attitude to trade unions along a similar scale with one representing 'supportive' and five representing 'hostile'. Third, the representatives were asked to express their own line manager's general attitude to trade unions with one representing 'supportive' and five representing 'hostile'. The mean scores for these responses are presented in Table 2.2.

Separate results for the three trade unions are not presented because there were no significant differences from the total workplace representative scores. The scores for all union workplaces representatives indicate a tendency towards a 'them and us' management–union relationship rather than a more unitarist 'close and harmonious' relationship. Despite this, the union representatives tended to perceive their employer's general attitude to trade unions as more supportive than hostile and this was more clearly the case for their own line manager's attitude. These differences suggest that management–union relations at the workplace level are both complex and multi-layered and that pessimistic accounts of the negative impact on unions of the devolvement of certain industrial relations responsibilities to line managers may be misplaced.

There were also some significant differences between the different employment sectors covered in the survey. For example, in the aerospace, insurance and university (technicians) sectors general management, employer and line management attitudes were perceived as being more antagonistic to trade unions (apart from university technicians' line managers). Similarly, employer and management attitudes were perceived as significantly more antagonistic in the aerospace-manufacturing sector and in the private sector.

Table 2.2   Union representatives' views on their relationship with management, by sector, n = 356.

	Relationship between mgmt & representatives (mean scores)	Employers' attitude to TUs (mean scores)	Line managers' attitude to TUs (mean scores)
All	3.11	2.88	2.60
Aerospace[a]	3.31	3.11	2.69
Manufacturing	3.20	2.86	2.73
NHS	2.65	2.49	2.26
Insurance	3.23	2.96	3.08
Universities	3.40	3.07	2.07
Utilities	2.90	2.60	2.40
Local government	2.59	2.47	2.47
Aerospace-manufacturing[b]	3.28	3.04	2.69
Services	2.88	2.66	2.44
Private sector[b]	3.23	3.00	2.71
Public sector	2.78	2.57	2.27

[a] Kruskal-Wallis tests found significant differences on these scores between the seven employment sectors for all three questions ($p = 0.001$).

[b] Mann-Whitney 2-tailed tests found significant differences on these scores between manufacturing and services and between the private and public sector for all three questions ($p = 0.001$ in each case).

The union representatives were asked whether their employer's attitude to trade unions had changed compared to three years ago. As the three unions were surveyed sequentially, this represented the period of 1996–9 for the MSF representatives and 1997–2000 for the AEEU and GMB representatives. The question captured the period of change from a Conservative to a Labour Government in 1997 with a view to investigating any softening of employer attitudes in the new macro-political environment. The results are presented in Table 2.3. These show that, contrary to expectations, significantly more union representatives felt that their employer's attitudes had hardened rather than softened. There were no differences in results between the three unions but there were some significant differences across sectors. In particular, union representatives in the aerospace-manufacturing sector were more likely to report a hardening of employers' attitudes than their counterparts in the service sector although it should be noted that 40 per cent of MSF representatives in the insurance sector reported a hardening of attitudes as did 30 per cent of AEEU and GMB representatives in the utilities sector.

It should also be noted that over 20 per cent of union representatives in aerospace and insurance reported a softening of employers' attitudes. There was a greater difference between the private and public sectors in that union representatives in the public sector were less likely to report a hardening of attitudes. This might reflect the re-emergence of the public sector as a 'model employer' and a prime site for the adoption of the Labour Government's workplace partnership agenda (Stuart and Martinez Lucio 2000).

Table 2.3   Change in employers' attitude to trade unions (1997–2000), $n = 356$.

	Union representatives reporting that employers' attitude to TUs had hardened (%)	Union representatives reporting that employers' attitude to TUs had softened (%)
All	27	15
Aerospace	31	22
Manufacturing	32	5
NHS	10	12
Insurance	40	20
Universities	14	0
Utilities	30	7
Local government	18	18
Aerospace-manufacturing	31	16
Services	21	12
Private sector	32	15
Public sector	13	12

Overall, however, the data suggest that the employers' attitudes to trade unions had mainly hardened or remained unchanged since 1997. This may well be a logical reaction on behalf of some employers to Prime Minister Tony Blair's attempts to distance the Labour Party from its traditional trade union base. The New Labour project has involved an ideological shift from a 'labourist' social democracy to a support of globalisation, neo-liberal economics and deregulated labour markets. In this context, New Labour has adopted a unitarist position on industrial relations involving unquestioning support for free enterprise, especially big international business (Marquand 2000), opposition to any trade union that impedes modernisation and only limited legislation on trade union rights (McIlroy 1998; 2000; Undy 1999).

Employee discontents: on the increase

Organisational restructuring and work reforms in the high-performance workplace might be expected to enhance employees' sense of job satisfaction through responsible autonomy (Friedman 1977) and job participation (Cully *et al.* 1999; Gallie *et al.* 1998). Such changes should also be reflected in the grievances pursued by individual workers (Waddington and Whitston 1996) and it would be logical to assume that levels of employee discontent might decrease in the high-performance workplace. National survey evidence paints an ambiguous picture here. Whilst the 1998 WERS survey of employees showed relatively high levels of job satisfaction, operationalised by job influence, pay, sense of achievement and respect from management, the same survey also provided evidence of growing employee discontent in the form of increasing individual grievances, the doubling of workplaces seeking advice on such grievances from ACAS (Advisory,

Conciliation and Arbitration Service) and a growth in the number of workplaces subject to claims at an industrial tribunal (Millward *et al.* 2000: 226). Kelly's (1998) analysis of British Social Attitude surveys and the large increases in workplace grievances indicated by Citizen's Advice Bureaux data highlights a similar trend of widespread employee discontent even though this is rarely expressed in collective forms.

Waddington and Whitston's (1996) earlier national survey of trade union activists highlighted a pattern of membership grievances that arose from the contradiction between employee job participation in environments of increasing work intensification. Similarly, Gallie *et al.'s* survey of employee satisfaction in the context of the restructured employment relationship found that employees were generally experiencing upskilling and greater personal involvement in their work but at the expense of substantial work strain resulting from an intensification of work effort (1998: 232). Our survey of workplace union representatives and qualitative data showed similar patterns of employee discontent, and indeed, increasing discontent, linked to private-sector employers' more intensive capital accumulation strategies and new managerialist strategies in the public sector. The union representatives were asked to identify the different types of membership grievance they had pursued over the past three years and whether the incidence of such grievances had changed. The results are presented in Table 2.4.

The incidence of different grievances is considerably greater than that identified in Waddington and Whitston's (1996) national survey. The salience and rising incidence of discipline, management attitudes, staffing levels, workloads, working hours and flexibility as grievance issues derives from the adoption of lean staffing regimes and tight management control in many of the work establishments surveyed. These more common grievances lend support to the argument that in Britain, the concept of labour intensification may involve not

Table 2.4   Membership grievances pursued by union representatives, $n = 356$.

	Union representatives pursuing grievance (%)	Union representatives reporting increase in incidence* (%)
Staffing levels	48	60
Workloads	47	71
Discipline	53	43
Working hours	46	52
Flexibility	35	51
Health and safety	64	50
Management attitudes	52	57
Pay	61	47
Grading	57	61
Redundancy issue	43	60
Training	35	43

*   These are proportions of those union representatives who had pursued these grievances.

only workers being pushed harder by management in certain circumstances but also that the porosity of the working day is being closed up by a variety of changes in working practices (Nichols 1997: 110). Thus, as Gallie *et al.* (1998) and Waddington and Whitston (1996) argue, the centrality of work intensification in workplace relations has major implications for the health and safety of workers, a relation that has been researched more rigorously by Nichols (1997). It is also no surprise, therefore, that of the eleven grievance types listed, health and safety-related grievances were the most widely reported.

Pay and grading issues were also common sources of grievance. Our statistical analysis established a significant correlation between the incidence of pay and grading grievances. This may be partly a function of employee discontent over job evaluation outcomes. However, we found no general correlation between the incidence of pay grievances and the use of performance-related or merit pay (although there was a strong correlation between such grievances and performance-related pay in the insurance sector). This suggests that even in economic environments of low inflation, collective pay grievances remain significant.

The survey data also identified some significant sectoral differences. For example, grievance issues associated with tighter management control were reported in all sectors. Grievances linked to discipline were common in the GMB's local government occupations (63 per cent), in aerospace and manufacturing (58 per cent) and in MSF's NHS trust membership (39 per cent). Grievances over workloads were most frequently reported in the utilities sector (61 per cent), aerospace and manufacturing (52 per cent) and local government (44 per cent). Grievances over management attitudes featured in aerospace and manufacturing (59 per cent), in the utilities (54 per cent) and in local government and the NHS (38 per cent). Grievances connected to health and safety issues were most common in local government (78 per cent), utilities (71 per cent), aerospace and manufacturing (70 per cent) and insurance (50 per cent).

Pay grievances were prevalent in aerospace and manufacturing (73 per cent) but were also common to the individualised pay regimes of the insurance sector workplaces (60 per cent). Finally, the AEEU's spheres of influence in the skilled occupations in aerospace, manufacturing and the utilities were the prime locale of training-related grievances (60 per cent). This suggests that the availability of concrete 'upskilling/multi-skilling' training programmes is a particular source of tension and discontent amongst these occupations.

Trade unions and job participation

National surveys of patterns of work reorganisation and job participation have focused on the extent to which employees' gain a sense of influence and involvement through working in teams and small problem-solving groups. For example, the 1998 WERS survey has identified teamworking as a central element of the new forms of work organisation and it found that around 35 per cent of UK workplaces operate a semi-autonomous form of teamworking (Cully *et al.* 1999: 42). Another employees' survey by Gallie *et al.* (1998) found that large proportions of quality circle members felt that they exerted significant influence over work organisation and quality issues. One implication of such findings is that direct employee participation in teams and quality circles may either marginalise trade union influence or catalyse a shift in workplace union strategy towards co-operation and partnership (Bacon and Storey 1996). In fact, numerous case studies of union response have shown how trade unions are more prone to adopting oppositional positions based on a strategic reaction to transparent management control imperatives (see for example, Danford 1999; Martinez Lucio *et al.* 2000; Rinehart *et al.* 1997; Stewart and Wass 1998).

To investigate the impact of job participation techniques on union influence we created a variable differentiating between those activists who *do not represent teamworkers or quality circle (QC) members*, activists who *do represent either team workers or QC members* and activists who *represent workers who are both team and QC members*. To control for a potential public-sector effect we used only the private-sector data (aerospace, manufacturing, finance and private utilities) where such job participation techniques were more widely used.

The union representatives were asked whether they exerted 'a lot', 'some', 'a little' or 'no' influence over decision-making on pay, on jobs and working conditions in their local departments and on the management of the whole workplace. Table 2.5 presents these data as two collapsed categories denoting either 'some or a lot of influence' or, 'little or no influence' thus providing rudimentary patterns of difference. An additional picture of union influence is provided by an assessment of whether different employment issues are subject to negotiation with union representatives or 'weaker' consultation. These types of data provide information on the extent to which there is joint regulation of the

Table 2.5   Influence of union representatives over decision-making, by representation of teamworkers and QC members, $n = 259$.

	Some or a lot of influence (%)	A little or no influence (%)
Decisions about pay*		
Not teamworkers or QC members ($n = 56$)	26	74
Teamworkers or QC members ($n = 76$)	53	47
Teamworkers and QC members ($n = 127$)	58	42
Decisions about jobs and working conditions in the department*		
Not teamworkers or QC members	38	62
Teamworkers or QC members	67	33
Teamworkers and QC members	73	27
Decisions concerning the management of the whole workplace*		
Not teamworkers or QC members	15	85
Teamworkers or QC members	33	67
Teamworkers and QC members	29	71

*   Chi-square test significant at the 0.001 level.

Table 2.6   The extent of joint regulation, by representation of teamworkers and QC members, $n = 259$.

	Negotiation (%)	Consultation (%)
How is pay decided?[a]		
Not teamworkers or QC members ($n = 56$)	66	34
Teamworkers or QC members ($n = 76$)	80	20
Teamworkers and QC members ($n = 127$)	85	15
How are hours of work decided?		
Not teamworkers or QC members	68	32
Teamworkers or QC members	65	35
Teamworkers and QC members	71	29
How are new working practices decided?[a]		
Not teamworkers or QC members	46	54
Teamworkers or QC members	60	40
Teamworkers and QC members	67	33
How are redundancies decided?		
Not teamworkers or QC members	33	67
Teamworkers or QC members	52	48
Teamworkers and QC members	48	52
How is the use of non-permanent staff decided?[b]		
Not teamworkers or QC members	17	83
Teamworkers or QC members	35	65
Teamworkers and QC members	50	50
How are grievance cases decided?[a]		
Not teamworkers or QC members	63	37
Teamworkers or QC members	72	28
Teamworkers and QC members	83	17

[a] Chi-square test significant at the 0.05 level. [b] Chi-square test significant at the 0.001 level.

employment relationship between managers and union representatives (Cully *et al*. 1999). The data are presented in Tables 2.5 and 2.6.

The data presented in these tables show that the activists who do represent teamworkers or QC members, and particularly those who represent teamworkers *and* QC members, felt they exerted significantly greater influence over management decision-making and the regulation of the employment relationship compared to their counterparts who do not represent such workers. Both influence over decisions about pay, jobs and working conditions, and joint regulation over pay, hours of work, new working practices, redundancies, use of non-permanent staff and grievance cases were significantly higher for union activists who represent teamworkers and QC members.

These data contradict pessimistic assumptions that new job-participation techniques inevitably marginalise local union influence. We also considered the

Table 2.7   Membership grievances pursued by union representatives, by representation of teamworkers and QC members.

	Workplace reps pursuing grievance (teams and QCs) (%)	Workplace reps pursuing grievance (no teams or QCs) (%)
Staffing levels	62	28
Workloads	58	36
Discipline	66	49
Working hours	55	38
Flexibility	50	26
Health and safety	72	64
Management attitudes	63	43
Training	50	22

counter-argument that these data might merely reflect a process of union incorporation through involvement in job-participation techniques. To put this another way, could teamworking and quality circles generate a more co-operative, 'partnership' approach to management–union relations that might then generate feelings of greater union influence? To check this we compared results for differences in management–union relations between the three groups of activists using the scaled questions presented in Table 2.2. If the incorporation argument were to hold true then we would expect to see evidence of more harmonious management–union relations reported by activists who represented teamworkers and quality circle members compared to those who did not. In fact, although there were slight differences in the mean scores, none of these was significant.

Table 2.7 provides further evidence of union independence – and employee discontent – in the context of high-performance work systems. The data show some significant differences in the incidence of job participation-related grievances reported by union activists who represent both teamworkers and quality circle members compared to those who represent neither of these groups of workers. These patterns highlight a contradiction between job participation and labour intensification and management control in the 'empowering' institutions of teamwork and problem-solving groups. One might logically expect the union representatives for teamworkers and QC members to report a lower incidence of these grievances as job participation and influence engender higher job satisfaction (Gallie *et al.* 1998). Instead, for every grievance issue listed, the union activists who represented workers in teams and quality circles reported significantly higher levels of incidence than those activists who represented neither group of worker. The clear implications for union strategy are that rather than follow a 'social relationship for co-operation' with employers (Bacon and Storey 1996: 72), the material outcomes for many workers whose labour processes are subject to job reform and a 'fracturing of collectivism' requires that unions adopt a more strategic, oppositional and militant response.

Overall, these different data do not support the proposition that workers have become 'enriched' by the use of job-participation techniques. Neither do they suggest that their union representatives have become either incorporated or marginalised by their application. Instead, as our case study data show (for example, see Chapter 3), it is not the nature of the work reforms themselves but the propensity of union activists to adapt the form of their workplace union to the work reforms that can result in enhanced trade union influence at work and organisational renewal.

Recollectivisation at work?

The scope of collective bargaining between unions and employers provides a further index of union influence and strength. This is because the range of issues subject to negotiations constitutes a constraint on management's unilateral control at work and thus reflects prevailing power relations between employers and trade unions (Brown *et al*. 1998; Millward *et al*. 2000). By measuring underlying shifts in the scope of collective bargaining (operationalised by focusing on six employment issues) the WERS surveys have detected little change during the 1990s. However, this has not prevented some commentators from endorsing the 'hollow shell' thesis by arguing that the scope of bargaining has indeed narrowed or that the depth of union involvement has diminished (Brown 1993; Brown *et al*. 1998).

Our survey of trade union representatives in the South West did not measure change in bargaining agendas but it did ask union representatives to indicate the current scope of their negotiations. The representatives were asked which issues, from a list of twenty-two, had formed part of their negotiations with management during the previous three years. These included basic terms and conditions such as pay, hours, and holidays; issues associated with organisational change and the labour process, such as restructuring and labour flexibility; issues associated with equal opportunities, such as family-friendly policies and gender and race discrimination; and issues encompassing numerical flexibility, such as the use of non-standard employment contracts. The most common bargaining issues reported were health and safety (69 per cent of all union representatives), collective pay awards (61 per cent), organisational restructuring (47 per cent), workplace stress (42 per cent) and redundancies (41 per cent). Negotiations on holidays, labour flexibility, hours flexibility, skills training and the employment of non-permanent staff were also reported by large minorities of representatives. Negotiations on equal-opportunity issues were less common. For example, only 10 per cent of representatives reported covering racial discrimination, 15 per cent covered sexual harassment, 17 per cent covered sexual discrimination though 26 per cent covered maternity and paternity leave. Surprisingly, these equal-opportunity issues tended to be raised more often in the male-dominated aerospace and manufacturing sectors.

Utilising the scope of collective bargaining as a proxy for union strength we investigated a number of factors related to union activity that might influence this.

Table 2.8   Factors influencing the scope of collective bargaining.

	Bargaining scope	
	Standardised B coefficients	Significance
Manual or non-manual union	0.050	not significant (n.s.)
Total number of grievances handled	0.316	$p = 0.001$
Total number of new management practices	0.266	$p = 0.001$
Total time spent on UB	0.227	$p = 0.001$
Industrial action, past 3 yrs	0.121	$p = 0.01$
Percent of employees in area who are non-members	0.161	$p = 0.01$
Active due to strong belief in TU principles	0.003	n.s
Active to help others	0.088	n.s
Active to become involved in decision-making	0.070	n.s
Influence 1: over pay, working conditions, site mgmt	0.148	$p = 0.01$
Influence 2: negotiation or consultation	0.044	n.s.

$n = 356, r2 = 0.555.$

OLS regression analysis was used to measure the impact of different independent variables on bargaining scope, a summative scale, dependent variable comprising an aggregate of up to twenty-two bargaining issues covered in management-union negotiations. The industrial sector was controlled for and this had no significant impact upon bargaining scope. The results are presented in Table 2.8.

The first point to note is that the individual orientations and motivations of the union representatives had no significant effect on the scope of their workplace bargaining agendas. Neither did the sectoral or manual/non-manual occupational base of their work areas. The variables that did have a significant effect tended to be those that reflected processes of recollectivisation in the context of work restructuring. The total time spent on union business (both at work and away from work) is a more reliable indicator of union commitment than individual orientation or belief and this measure did have a significant, positive effect on bargaining scope. Union militancy is also associated with broader bargaining scope; union representatives who had been involved in some form of industrial action over the previous three years were more likely to include a larger number of issues on their bargaining agendas. Union representatives who felt they exerted more influence over decisions concerning pay, local working conditions and the management of the workplace (Influence 1) were more likely to display the confidence to broaden their bargaining agendas although whether or not they felt that employment issues were subject to negotiation or consultation (Influence 2) had no significant effect. The proportion of non-members in the representatives' work areas was also positively associated with bargaining scope. Although this seems a surprising result the relationship was particularly strong in work areas where membership density was between 50 and 70 per cent; in areas where membership density was weaker than this the association with bargaining scope was negative. This suggests that in those work areas where trade union membership was substantial but not 100 per cent, representatives were attempting to increase recruitment from a position of relative strength by strategically broadening bargaining agendas to engage the interest of non-members and new employees.

Finally, perhaps the most significant result of this regression analysis is that the two factors which were most strongly associated with union strength were the total number of grievances dealt with by the union representatives and the total number of new management practices that were employed in the representatives' own work areas. The latter was a summative variable aggregating the use of the different job participation techniques, temporal and numerical flexibility techniques, and human resource management techniques listed in Table 2.1. In a similar vein to this analysis, Gallie *et al.* (1998) found that HRM-style bureaucratic control techniques were likely to become more intensive in workplaces where trade unions were influential. Following Edwards (1979), Gallie *et al.* suggest that these management techniques have been used to counteract the spread of trade unionism, particularly into white-collar areas. However, they also suggest an alternative line of causation, albeit more tentatively, that where the management techniques have been introduced, workers might become more disposed to support unions (1998: 77). By introducing the extent of employee discontent (incidence of grievances) into the equation, our analysis shows that the latter line of causation is the more likely. Where a greater mass of work restructuring management practices are introduced, employee grievances increase (additional bivariate analysis showed a strong relationship between the two variables) and both variables are strongly associated with the scope of union bargaining, and hence union strength. This key positive association, and the additional significance of union militancy and the time activists devote to union business, suggest that the union representatives in many larger workplaces in South West England have been engaged in a collectivisation of employee discontent. Or to put this another way, a recollectivisation of employment relations in the 'new workplace'.

Conclusion

In the context of the more intensive capital accumulation strategies of private-sector firms, and the deepening of bureaucratic rationality in the public sector, the survey provides preliminary evidence of widespread workplace restructuring. In our private-sector sample, this has involved the introduction of 'bundles' of labour flexibility and participatory practices, such as teamworking and quality improvement programmes; in the smaller public-sector sample the use of numerical flexibility was more apparent. However, in both cases the union representatives reported patterns of staff reductions, greater work pressures and increased workloads. These patterns were confirmed by our data on the character and increasing incidence of employee grievances which highlighted patterns of discontent in the context of tighter management control and widespread work intensification.

In a post-Thatcherite politico-economic environment in the UK which has not been as favourable to trade unions as some activists and union officers had hoped, it comes as no surprise that many union representatives felt that their employers' attitudes to trade unions had either remained unchanged or had hardened since the first New Labour Government's election victory in 1997. If employers seek 'continuous improvements' in cost reductions and operational efficiency then they are still more likely to regard trade unions as a hindrance to change than as partners in change. Many writers in the managerialist tradition have likewise responded to this by assuming that the adoption of high-performance workplace innovations must inevitably, and indeed, necessarily exclude alternative trade union agendas and union renewal along traditional lines (see Stewart and Wass 1998 for a summary and critique of these positions). Such assumptions seem strengthened by the implications of the results of the national WERS surveys which highlight a decline in union strength, a decline in employee support for union membership and a lack of new recruitment in long-established workplaces where unions are already recognised (Millward *et al.* 2000). But these results are derived from managers' accounts of change in industrial relations. By contrast, our survey draws primarily on data provided by departmental and senior workplace union representatives and it comes as no surprise that a different pattern of union influence and strength emerges. In particular, we have found that a good number of workplace unions in the South West of England have not been inactive in the face of significant work reorganisation and a rising incidence of employee discontent. For example, many unions at workplaces where job participation techniques have been introduced have maintained their influence by consciously adapting their union organisation to the new conditions of 'fractured collectivism'. More generally, a good number of unions have succeeded in collectivising the rising incidence of employee discontent rather than merely provide support and a 'service' to the individual instances of this collective worker experience.

Perhaps the most distinctive result of the survey is this. In an area of the UK not noted for a strong trade union consciousness or militancy, many, though by no means all, of the recognised unions in larger workplaces have been more resilient in terms of organisational strength, more proactive as agents of change at work, and more adept at recollectivising the workplace than the pessimistic national surveys suggest. Despite the predominance of partnership discourse in contemporary British industrial relations, our research provides evidence of the durability of an independent workplace unionism still able to defend the separate interests of its members.

3 Job reform and recollectivisation in the aerospace industry

Despite the general decline in manufacturing and concomitant rise of services and telecommunications, the UK's aerospace industry remains a powerful, though discrete, sector within the national economy. A large proportion of graduate engineers and highly skilled technicians and production staff are concentrated in the small number of aerospace firms located mainly in the South West, South East and North West of England. And unlike much of the rest of British manufacturing, these firms have been sites of relatively high levels of investment in research and development, innovative technologies and skills training.

Since the end of the Second World War, the industry has been characterised by a high degree of concentration of ownership. A small core of civil and defence aerospace companies has benefited from different forms of state intervention and support aimed at securing defence industrial capacity (Lovering 1990). During the Cold War period, high levels of demand for defence products and generous 'cost-plus' supply contracts with successive UK governments created the environment for skilled job expansion, union recognition and superior employment conditions (Lovering 1990, 1986; Webb 1998). These favourable conditions for organisational stability went into reverse from the mid-1980s onwards when the Thatcher Government's adoption of a neo-liberal approach to manufacturing was followed by a thaw in East-West Cold War relations. A combination of cyclical recession in civil aerospace markets, company privatisation, the implementation of defence contract competitive tendering processes and successive rounds of defence spending cuts catalysed significant organisational restructuring.

Lovering (1998: 156) has argued that it would be difficult to find any other industrial sector in Britain which has undergone such a radical, rapid and wide-ranging transformation. Five key components of this restructuring are highlighted.

1. *Massive labour rationalisation.* This has been particularly acute in the shop-floor, technician and middle management occupations. It has involved widespread compulsory redundancies, job insecurity and low staff morale (see Lloyd 1999); and many redundant staff have been forced into lower paid, lower skilled, less permanent employment (Webb 1998).

2. *Strategic change.* The previously bureaucratic and inflexible aerospace companies have become more reflexive, market-responsive organisations seeking expansion into international markets.
3. *Cultural change processes.* These have involved a transformation from a militaristic and bureaucratic management culture into a modernised HRM approach incorporating the full range of current new management discourse.[1]
4. *A rationalisation and consolidation of production technologies and capacity.* This has involved the introduction of new technologies, the use of new production control techniques and the reorganisation of employment into new business units. Moreover, economies of scale brought about by joint venture arrangements, full merger policies and the increasingly international collaborative nature of defence and civil projects have induced a shift towards lean, mass-production techniques (Bradley and Pirie 1997).
5. *Reform of industrial relations.* The process of labour rationalisation and an accompanying purge of union militants undermined the strength of the industry's workplace unions and resulted in a shift towards the individualisation of pay and a reduction in the scope of collective bargaining. The aerospace companies have also introduced new forms of labour deployment, such as teamworking, and have adopted various employee involvement techniques in a quest to enhance market competitiveness.

Despite recurrent crises in its civil and defence markets and consequent extensive rationalisation of plant and labour, it would be wrong to treat the UK's aerospace industry as a typical site of manufacturing decline. The industry remains a prime contributor to British manufacturing performance and output. In 1998, aerospace had an annual turnover of £17 billion, it employed 155,000 workers and made a positive contribution of £2.6 billion to the UK's balance of payments (SBAC 2000). Therefore, the aerospace industry constitutes a significant – and under-researched – site of radical and rapid organisational restructuring. As we shall see, much of this restructuring has involved a greater use of contingent workers and sub-contracting, a proliferation of business units and increasing use of such work innovations as teamworking. To put this another way, work organisation in Britain's aerospace industry has been subject to a 'fracturing of collectivism' (Bacon and Storey 1996), a process, these authors argue, which can potentially erode the collective mass upon which trade union organisation is built.

This chapter provides an analysis of this restructuring and investigates its impact on the industry's two largest trade unions, the AEEU and MSF. We investigate three key processes of organisational change: labour rationalisation; managerial decentralisation and plant unitisation; teamworking. In this context of change, we then compare the extent to which the different AEEU and MSF workplace unions have been able to 'recollectivise' the workplace through organisational renewal based on membership mobilisation and participation.

The research base

The South West of England is home to one of the largest concentrations of aerospace design and manufacturing activity in the UK (Webb 1998; Western Development Partnership 1994). Most of the largest aerospace firms are located in the region and all of their larger plants were included in our fieldwork. The AEEU interviewees represented primarily skilled mechanical and electrical production workers whilst MSF interviewees represented primarily technical and engineering staff. Additional interviews were carried out with plant personnel managers and full-time union officers (see Appendix). The analysis also draws upon the aerospace sector sub-set of the questionnaire data presented in Chapter 2. Table 3.1 provides a profile of the aerospace plants and the AEEU/MSF union organisation.

Table 3.1   Company-union profiles.

Company	Product	Total workforce (1999–2000)	Peak workforce (year in brackets)	AEEU and MSF membership (density in brackets)
Honeywell	Electronic & hydraulic control systems	1000	3000 (1990)	AEEU 600 (100%) MSF 168 (74%)
BAe Systems	Airbus wing assemblies	4000	5800 (1990)	AEEU 850 (100%) MSF 710 (33%)
GKN-Westland, Helicopters & Aerospace	Military and civil helicopters	5000	8500 (1987)	AEEU 700 (100%) (Aerospace) MSF 1350 (74%)
Messier-Dowty	Aircraft landing gear	950	2000 (1994)	AEEU 400 (98%) MSF 120 (40%)
Matra-BAe Dynamics/ BAe BASE	GW systems Engineering	420 (Bristol) 650 (Plymouth)	4700 (1986) 1000 (1997)	Bristol: MSF 35 (12% de-recognised) Plymouth: AEEU 190 (85%)
Matra Marconi Space	Civil space hardware	350 (site to be closed)	500 (1993)	MSF 180 (80%)
Rolls-Royce Military Engines	Military aero engines	5249	13,000 (1978)	AEEU 1800 (100%) MSF 1700 (86%)
Smiths Industries, Civil & Defence	Avionic instruments & computers	1500	3200 (1990)	AEEU 300 (100%) MSF 200 (33%)

Labour rationalisation

Concerns for employment security and 'factory survival' constitute a recurrent constraint on workplace union organisation in the aerospace industry. In the South West plants, many workforces have been reduced by 50 per cent or more since the late 1980s. In every plant visited, significant labour reductions have been implemented in both shop-floor and technical staff areas. For example, during the last decade, the skilled manual workforce at BAe Systems was reduced from 2,500 to 1,200, at Rolls-Royce from 4,000 to 2,104, and at Smiths Industries from 990 to 450. White-collar staff in technical areas have also suffered waves of redundancies. The most severe examples are Matra-BAe Dynamics, where over 3,000 engineering, technical and clerical staff have been made redundant since the late 1980s, and Matra Marconi Space which implemented a phased closure of its Bristol site during the period of the research. The site employed over 200 graduate engineers and scientists.

This labour rationalisation has inevitably damaged the AEEU and MSF workplace union organisations. For example, the AEEU lost every one of its workplace representatives at BAe Systems during a redundancy in 1995; 75 per cent of its representatives at Rolls-Royce were made redundant in 1991/92; and between 1990 and 1995, the number of its recognised representatives at Smiths Industries had been reduced from 38 to just three. The MSF workplace unions were affected by a similar pattern of activist loss and victimisation. During the same period, many leading MSF Unity Left activists[2] were selected for redundancy at BAe Dynamics (now Matra-BAe), GKN-Westland, Messier-Dowty and Smiths Industries; in 1991, the complete MSF representatives' committee was dismissed at BAe Dynamics and the union was subsequently derecognised.

Although both unions succeeded in winning industrial tribunal and Court of appeal victimisation claims for some of these activists it was the survivors in the factories who faced the critical challenge of rebuilding their workplace unions. As the AEEU convenor at Rolls-Royce put it:

> We were in a desperate situation in 1992 when Number One shop closed, they bloody destroyed us . . . We used to have 72 shop stewards and they destroyed them. We finished up where there was 8 of us round the table. We had to totally rebuild in every shop.

By the end of the decade, these survivors had largely succeeded. In many plants, the remaining workplace representatives were able to tap into a latent trade union consciousness – which was particularly resilient on the shop-floor – and construct new networks of activists and local representatives. In some cases, individuals who were perceived as having potential leadership skills were tapped on the shoulder and persuaded to stand, in other cases volunteers would come forward. Gradually, shop steward and office representative positions were filled as groups of members realised that without activists the union organisation would atrophy.

Table 3.2   Union membership density and member-representative ratios.

	Membership density (mean %)	Mean of member- representative ratios
AEEU (aerospace plants)	98	35:1
MSF (aerospace plants)	60	45:1
1998 WERS data (all establishments > 500 employees)	42	53:1

Table 3.2 provides means of union density and mean ratios of union members to representatives in the aerospace plants where the AEEU and MSF were recognised. It compares these with national WERS data for all establishments of 500 or more employees. The data indicate a strength in representative organisation in the aerospace plants well in excess of the national average. This is partly a function of the strength of trade unionism in the aerospace sector generally but is also a result of a systematic rebuilding of union organisation in the aftermath of mass redundancy. The AEEU workplace unions have consistently maintained very high membership densities and low member-representative ratios; the pattern for MSF is more uneven with membership densities ranging from 33 to 85 per cent (for recognised unions) and member-representative ratios ranging from nine to one at Honeywell to 100 to one at BAe Systems and 120 to one at Messier-Dowty.

The job insecurity caused by successive redundancy programmes has been compounded by the employers' increasing use of sub-contract labour and the transfer of component and sub-assembly work abroad. The use of sub-contractors for significant components of the design and manufacturing processes has a long tradition in the aerospace industry and, to some extent, has been used to cheapen production costs and weaken trade union numbers (Smith 1987). In the past, many of the major sub-contractors to the South West's aerospace plants have tended to be located in the UK, though some distance from the plants themselves (Boddy *et al.* 1986). However, the new emphasis on internationalising inputs and, for political reasons, locating some production in main export markets, has led to a greater share of aerospace work being performed outside the UK. This has led in turn to such companies as BAe reconstructing themselves as global specialists in system integration drawing on component production and assembly skills on an international level (Lovering 1998: 162, 163).

In the questionnaire survey of union workplace representatives, 53 per cent of AEEU stewards reported the use of outsourcing of work packages compared to 23 per cent of MSF representatives whilst 45 per cent of AEEU stewards reported the use of sub-contract labour compared to 43 per cent of MSF representatives. The greater use of outsourcing and sub-contracting in AEEU spheres of influence reflects the internationalisation of production inputs in the industry.

However, many of the AEEU stewards interviewed felt powerless to halt this process of globalisation. For example, during the period of the research, the stewards at BAe Systems and Rolls-Royce threatened industrial disputes over management plans to outsource part manufacture to sub-contractors in Japan and the US respectively. But on both occasions, in an environment of 'factory survival', the stewards did not feel sufficiently confident that their members would support industrial action even though, in the case of Rolls-Royce, the transfer of work resulted in the loss of 135 jobs. A similar pattern of union impotence has been reported in the North American aircraft industry, where unions have been unable to prevent the problem of 'runaway jobs' through internationalisation (Bluestone *et al.* 1981; Seidl and Kleiner 1999).

The AEEU stewards took a more militant stance against increasing employer attempts to manage work fluctuations by utilising sub-contract labour and temporary agency labour on site. This was partly because the visible use of sub-contract workers can be a more emotive issue for the rank and file in an environment of labour reductions and job insecurity. At most plants, the AEEU stewards had succeeded in blocking all attempts to use non-permanent labour on site. The use of fixed-term contract staff was sanctioned in two plants. At BAe BASE, a limited use of fixed-term staff was approved provided attempts were made to convert these to permanent status. At the GKN-Westland plant, over 200 sub-contract manual workers had been employed to meet peaks in production demand. However, this practice was tightly regulated by a short-term contract labour agreement with the AEEU which incorporated such protections as skill qualifications, equal pay and employment conditions with permanent employees, guarantees of permanent employment or discharge after 12 months and no compulsory redundancies whilst contract workers are employed.

Therefore, although the AEEU workplace unions could exert little influence over the internationalisation of sub-contract work they were still able to maintain either a regulation or exclusion of sub-contract and agency labour on site in order to protect their members' work. In the questionnaire survey, 68 per cent of AEEU stewards indicated that the use of non-permanent labour was subject to negotiation with management rather than consultation. By contrast, only 29 per cent of MSF representatives indicated the issue was subject to negotiation. This is surprising given the MSF traditions of closely regulating the use of sub-contract design staff by way of procedural agreements, the use of MSF-approved contractors (involving the imposition of closed shop arrangements) and the use of sub-contract bans as the first stage of any industrial dispute. However, the data reflect a decline in MSF's willingness to influence sub-contract and agency labour utilisation. This is due, in part, to the impact of Conservative Government legislation banning closed shops and secondary action. But MSF has also become more supportive of labour flexibility. Before the MSF merger, TASS was opposed to the use and extension of sub-contracting because it removed work from its membership base in engineering plants and it could be used to undermine wages and conditions (Smith 1987). The leading MSF officer for aerospace in the South West explained how this opposition had weakened:

What we've recognised is that if you want to maintain core workforce stability then greater flexibility is required to allow management to manage workload peaks effectively. Really, to stop work going out the door these days can be fatal, you must have more flexibility.

This change in attitude was reflected in the regularity of employment of sub-contract staff in MSF areas. For example, at the time of the research, nearly 500 sub-contract technical staff were employed at GKN-Westland and a personnel manager at BAe Systems revealed plans to recruit up to 600 sub-contract staff.

To sum up, in the face of severe labour rationalisation and loss of union activists over the past decade and more, all AEEU and some MSF workplace unions in the eight aerospace plants have succeeded in maintaining high membership densities and robust representatives' organisation. Although both groups of workplace unions have been powerless to respond to the internationalisation of sub-contract work, the AEEU has maintained significant levels of influence over the use of sub-contract labour on site. By contrast, MSF has abandoned some of its traditional controls over sub-contract labour and has signalled a willingness to countenance greater numerical flexibility in the hope that core workforce security may be enhanced.

Decentralisation and plant unitisation

Although collective bargaining in the UK's aerospace industry has always been characterised by single-plant bargaining over pay, the process of decentralisation expanded after 1989 when the Engineering Employers' Federation (EEF) withdrew from national bargaining over other employment conditions with the Confederation of Shipbuilding and Engineering Unions (CSEU) (Pickard 1990). During the 1990s, decentralisation intensified as Britain's aerospace companies attempted to rationalise capacity and create more flexible, market-responsive organisations by converting single factories into multiple profit centres. Aerospace engineers argued that a 'chaotic environment' of market variances required factory restructuring involving the introduction of lean business units, centres of manufacturing excellence and cellular working each having the agility to meet changing customer requirements (Bradley and Pirie 1997; Blundell and Pirie 1997).

Human resource managers and union representatives at each plant reported greater devolvement of industrial relations duties to line management. Team managers and supervisors were taking on more responsibility for such issues as disciplinary and grievance problems, establishing new employment contracts for new staff and establishing new shift patterns. Furthermore, a process of intra-plant business 'unitisation' had taken hold in four out of the eight aerospace firms visited. At the Rolls-Royce factory in Bristol, the previously single Military Engines Division plant had been fragmented into twelve separate business units each based on either a customer group or key product sub-assemblies and engineering processes. Different union representatives described these units as 'mini-factories' operating within the main factory; each had its own managing director, management hierarchy and team of human resource managers. At BAe Systems in Bristol, five business units were responsible for wing design and manufacture for five different aircraft groups. In addition, fourteen operating centres responsible for different design, assembly and engineering processes reported to the business units and each were accountable for profitability and costs. At BAe BASE in Plymouth, the factory of just 650 staff was divided into five separate and autonomous 'value chains' each responsible for a product group or key manufacturing process and each employing its own staff. And at GKN-Westland, a single helicopter design and production plant had been divided into a large helicopter division and a smaller aerospace division which in turn was subsequently divided into two autonomous business units responsible for helicopter transmissions and structures. These different divisions and units were then further sub-divided by a matrix structure which disbanded traditional functional organisation in favour of product-based operating units.

Such organisational changes have clear ramifications for the organisation of industrial relations, the regulation of employment conditions and union organising at the plant level. The AEEU and MSF workplace unions responded in contrasting ways to the changes. The AEEU stewards tended to take a more oppositional stance to decentralisation and consciously organised to maintain site-wide regulation of employment conditions, whereas the MSF representatives tended to adopt a more reactive and acquiescent position.

The AEEU response

In every plant, the AEEU stewards refused to countenance a weakening or fragmentation of site-wide regulation of employment conditions through unitisation and decentralisation. Equal employment rights and conditions for all members, irrespective of business unit, constituted an essential guiding principle of their trade union collectivism. The countervailing problems posed by business unitisation were well summed up by an AEEU steward at Rolls-Royce:

> Previously all things came under one boss and all was dealt with by ourselves. Now each one of those business units has its own team of management. Therefore, when we've got collective agreements on site, then if there's nine of these different business groups, there's nine different answers you get . . . It's been an absolute nightmare for us in these last three years, and I've got to say, it's getting worse.

The AEEU unions responded to these problems by adapting their traditional work group-based model of steward representation so that steward accountability to a site union executive took precedence over steward representation of local members. In every aerospace factory visited, the AEEU workplace unions had succeeded in maintaining single, site-wide bargaining arrangements that covered all business units and departments. In most cases, this had been achieved by restricting the freedom of movement of local stewards – and line managers – by imposing much stricter lines of accountability between the local stewards and a central site executive comprising senior stewards. A senior steward at Smiths Industries summarised this approach:

> We insist that the manager consults with the shop steward first and then the steward comes to see us to see if it's okay . . . So yes, we've maintained accountability between the manager, the shop steward and the site executive of the union. We still control it 100 per cent. Management can't do anything, they can't move labour without our permission, they can't work extra overtime without our permission. We're in charge. It's a good job here.

If enterprising managers attempted to bypass these structures and deal directly with individual stewards then the strength of the union organisation in these workplaces tended to frustrate such initiatives. For example, one HR manager at Rolls-Royce described occasions when business unit managers had requested meetings with local stewards and each time had found themselves confronted with '19 or 20 different shop stewards from across the site marching into the room and sitting on the opposite side of the table'. And at GKN-Westland, a management attempt to devolve collecting bargaining to business units during 1996 was met by sustained AEEU opposition and militancy. In this case, the management had divided the GKN-Westland aerospace division into two business units, helicopter transmissions and structures, and had insisted on separate bargaining arrangements and withdrawing recognition from the AEEU's single-plant convenor. The AEEU stewards responded by securing a 93 per cent ballot vote in favour of strike action and, over a ten-week period, organising a series of one-day and half-day strikes, sectional strikes and an overtime ban. The dispute was settled when management was forced to concede the principle of a single convenor covering both business units and a single co-ordinating shop stewards' committee to overlook committees in the two units. Sustained industrial action had preserved site-wide regulation of employment conditions.

The MSF response

The response of the MSF workplace unions to these changes was more uneven and generally weaker compared to their AEEU counterparts. The process of business restructuring and unitisation was generally perceived by the MSF representatives as capricious and confusing which had an unsettling impact on the workplace union organisation. One MSF representative at BAe Systems complained of cycles of pro-and anti-union managerial behaviour in tandem with the management changes caused by incessant business restructuring. Similar sentiments were expressed by MSF representatives at other plants but unlike the AEEU, the MSF representatives did not display the inclination or the power to prevent a fragmentation of bargaining and regulation where managers requested it. For example, at Rolls-Royce, which was one of the better organised MSF plants, the senior MSF representative complained during an interview in 1998 that:

> Last week they announced another major re-organisation which is not actually clear to us yet. The managers themselves don't seem to understand what the full impact of it is. But it appears to be going down this business group route even more . . . We find it difficult to keep pace with the organisation, the way the company changes.

By the end of 1999 the same senior representative had indicated to management his acceptance of the decentralisation of bargaining to local business units. Similarly, in contrast to the AEEU strike described above, the MSF union organisation at GKN-Westland had been unable to mobilise resistance to the decentralisation of collective bargaining to business units in 1996. The result was not just a dismantling of site-wide regulation of MSF employment conditions but a weakening of the MSF bargaining group as one representative explained:

> The shop floor voted round about 90 per cent in favour of taking industrial action in defending their bargaining group and our members voted totally the opposite way, it was about 86 per cent against taking any action whatsoever. So our bargaining group got split up whereas the shop floor bargaining group maintained their existing structure which shows how ludicrous the situation was. There was no real need to split other than to weaken the overall strength of the bargaining group. So we [MSF] have now got a bargaining group that feels browbeaten. We don't see that taking any action is going to help our cause or make anything different and we've got very demoralised.

This weaker response to organisational restructuring is in some respects predictable considering the traditions of lower incidence of industrial action by technical workers, a more instrumental approach to trade unionism and an inability or unwillingness to resist the restructuring activities of employers (Carter 1988; Smith 1987; Smith and Whalley 1996). These weaknesses have been compounded in recent years by the general decline in trade union power, the partial individualisation of technical workers' wages and an accentuation of career concerns. Consequently, different MSF representatives in five out of the eight plants reported difficulties in recruiting activists because of 'work pressures, apathy and a fear factor', 'a perception that becoming a union representative is damaging to your career', and 'the merit system victimises you . . . you can go for years without getting any merit reward at all'. Moreover, these constraints have prevented the MSF unions from reorganising their representatives so as to ensure the same surveillance of decentralised management actions secured by the AEEU stewards. Tables 3.3 and 3.4 provide quantitative indicators of these differences.

In various ways, the data in Tables 3.3 and 3.4 indicate much greater organising activity by the AEEU workplace unions. Table 3.3 provides evidence that the

Table 3.3 Frequency of representatives' meetings and their meetings with management (reported by senior workplace reps, $n = 19$).

	One per week (%)	More than monthly (%)	Monthly (%)	Few times per year
Frequency of union representatives' meetings				
AEEU representatives	57	43	0	0
MSF representatives	17	33	33	17
Frequency of meetings with site management				
AEEU representatives	71	14	0	14
MSF representatives	17	25	17	42

AEEU representatives hold shop stewards' meetings and meetings with site management considerably more frequently than their MSF counterparts. This may be partly a function of a tradition of more intense bargaining activity by manual workers' unions. However, it also reflects the AEEU's determination, in the context of decentralisation and unitisation, to maintain union regulation over employment conditions on a site-wide basis. Firstly, by way of regular meetings with management and secondly, by securing local steward accountability and

Table 3.4 Change in representative's role in recent years (all aerospace workplace representatives, $n = 136$).

	Agree (%)	Disagree (%)	Undecided (%)
More difficult due to increased work pressure			
AEEU representatives	79	9	12
MSF representatives	86	4	10
More negotiations with line management[a]			
AEEU representatives	50	17	33
MSF representatives	27	41	33
More negotiations with senior management			
AEEU representatives	61	18	21
MSF representatives	51	29	20
More communications with members[b]			
AEEU representatives	77	7	16
MSF representatives	54	18	28
Time spent on union business			
AEEU representatives	9.5 hours per week		
MSF representatives	5.9 hours per week		

[a] Chi-square test significant at the 0.001 level.
[b] Significant at the 0.05 level.

co-ordination through more regular stewards' meetings. Further evidence of this is shown in Table 3.4 which provides various indicators of the changes in the representative's role during the recent years of workplace restructuring. There are significant differences between the AEEU and MSF representatives. Both sets of representatives have found that their union work has become more difficult due to increasing work pressures. However, despite this constraint, the AEEU stewards are spending a relatively greater amount of time on union business, they are communicating more with their members, they are experiencing more negotiations with senior management and significantly more negotiations with line management.

To sum up, managerial decentralisation and business unitisation has generated a number of organisational problems for workplace unions in the aerospace industry. These qualitative and quantitative data suggest that of the two largest unions in the industry, the AEEU has responded more effectively to these challenges by a process of organisational adaptation and stricter monitoring of managerial action at the departmental and workplace level.

Teamworking

The third key dimension of workplace restructuring to be considered is team-working. Cellular working or teamworking, labour flexibility, *kaizen*/quality circles and team briefs had been introduced in some work areas in each of the eight aerospace factories visited. Eighty-two per cent of the AEEU stewards surveyed and 64 per cent of MSF representatives worked in team areas; 78 per cent and 52 per cent respectively reported the use of labour flexibility measures; 77 per cent and 55 per cent respectively reported the use of *kaizen*/quality circles; and 89 per cent and 86 per cent respectively reported the use of team briefings.

There is much literature on the impact of teamworking on the labour process and labour regulation but much less on its impact on local union organisation itself. In fact, the recasting of the division of labour and labour deployment under teamworking has significant implications for the organisation of workplace unions in the aerospace industry, an organisation which has been conventionally constructed around functional and craft demarcations in both shop-floor and technical staff areas.

The AEEU response

Cellular working was the predominant form of team-based work introduced in the AEEU's shop-floor areas. The fragmentation of single plants into business units and operating centres was compounded by the conversion of function-based factory organisation (assembly shops, fitting shops, lathe shops, milling, and so on) into multi-functional cells responsible for particular product families, particular groups of sub-assemblies or key multi-functional processes, such as toolroom cells. In most of the factories, these changes were introduced in the mid-1990s. The cell size varied from four to twenty production employees, each graded according to competence, and each cell was subject to multi-layered supervision comprising a team supervisor or leader, a cell manager responsible for a cluster of cells, and an operating centre/departmental manager. Most of the AEEU stewards interviewed felt that the key change to their labour processes was one of task enlargement through a combination of multi-tasking, self-inspection and assuming responsibility for quality and quantity of output. In some cases, it was felt that the introduction of cellular working into craft-based areas also resulted in deskilling by functionally and spatially focusing work organisation (Martinez Lucio *et al.* 2000). For example, a steward at Rolls-Royce commented:

> We've now got a structure which is based on NVQ levels and competencies and very often the company does not want to train our people totally and wants to train for task rather than for a craft . . . Multi-skilling is an illusion because if you have a cellular system making bevel gears then all you ever do is make bevel gears whereas under our old structure you could be making gears, cases, blades, whatever. Your job was more diversified and the skill level was higher, the interest was higher. You would truly be a craftsman.

This recomposition of the labour process caused a significant modification of the old craft and function-based division of labour around which the traditional AEEU work group system of steward representation was built. Without steward vigilance, and a reorganisation of steward representation, the new cellular working created the conditions for undermining shop steward influence over work changes and local managerial prerogatives, as the following steward at Messier-Dowty made clear:

> It's made a hell of a difference to how we can influence working practices. Whereas before, the management always used to come to the works committee to discuss issues, changes in hours, changes in practices, labour deployment and those types of issues, now they don't. Now they try to get it through the back door by enticing one or two teams into accepting certain changes without involving the union at all.

In every factory, AEEU stewards have responded to this threat by reorganising their work group representation. In most cases this has involved amending procedural agreements to ensure that each steward has the right to represent and enter groups of cells, so that as one steward explained, 'we don't fall into the trap of calling them section stewards or cell stewards, they're shop stewards . . . they've got the right to go from cell to cell and we insist upon that'.

The introduction of teamleaders on the shop-floor posed a further threat to AEEU shop steward influence at these factories. The teamleader role has been variously described as implementing management policy (Kenney and Florida 1993), managing 'disturbance' in production routines and flow (Delbridge *et al.* 2000), and facilitating and coaching staff (Hales 2000). However, from a shop steward's viewpoint, teamleaders can also be perceived as taking on a more ambiguous role as both co-worker and manager (Danford 1999: 146; Durand 1999). At BAe BASE and GKN-Westland, the traditional foreman's role was retained although there were elements of self-management at BAe BASE. However, at the other plants the AEEU stewards had to contend with the new dimensions of the teamleader's role. For example, at Smiths Industries and BAe Systems, it was feared that the introduction of a part worker, part manager role would create resentment and animosity in the teams and might eventually marginalise the representational role of the shop steward. The stewards at Smiths Industries responded to this threat by successfully barring the introduction of teamleaders:

> We would never have gone down that path. There is no way we would accept a manual worker telling other manual workers what to do . . . The foremen are there to manage, not us, and I don't think we should ever be telling each other what to do or disciplining each other because it would break the ranks up and they would fight each other and it would be an unholy war.

At BAe Systems, the AEEU succeeded in curtailing and controlling the managerial facets of the teamleader's role in three ways. First, by securing an agreement that removed teamleaders' disciplinary powers and ensuring they devoted most of their working time to production work. Second, by gaining recognition rights for teamleaders which thus placed them under the control of shop stewards (previously, foremen had been separately represented by MSF). And third, by securing a new communications agreement that allowed shop steward representation at all briefings between management and teamleaders and at all teambriefings. Shop stewards were also allowed to check the content of communications cascades.

However, at Messier-Dowty and Rolls-Royce, the introduction of more autonomous cell leaders with management functions posed a more serious threat to shop steward influence. For example, during 1997, the management at Messier-Dowty decided to 'professionalise' the cell leader's role by recruiting young graduates externally rather than appoint from the shop-floor. The AEEU senior steward commented on this:

> These graduates haven't got a clue about industrial relations! I tried to get the company to make sure that whenever a cell leader from outside is brought in, that they get a crash course on industrial relations and the procedures and agreements we've got. They've never done it. As a result I get more conflicts now that we've been split up into cells. Things like discipline, absenteeism, how they work labour deployment.

The AEEU responded to these new supervisory conditions by displaying a readiness to mobilise unofficial forms of industrial action. This placed limits on the process of managerial decentralisation and the particular arbitrary decisions of teamleaders, foremen and line managers. In six out of the seven plants with

AEEU union organisation, the stewards described the use of unofficial actions to counter management initiatives. The most common form was the unofficial overtime ban, variously referred to as 'morris dancing' (BAe Systems), 'going shopping' (GKN-Westland) and 'going fishing' (Messier-Dowty and Smiths Industries). At Smiths Industries, the practice of 'going fishing' had become so well established that the AEEU convenor would bring a fishing rod to mass meetings as a sign of intent:

> Some years ago, I came in Friday morning and inside my union office, someone had bought me a fishing rod. I couldn't go fishing if I tried! Whenever we have a factory meeting now, I take my fishing rod and I don't have to say anything them to them all. Someone says, 'are we going fishing then?' I say, 'that's up to you brother!'. . . We did so recently, the company was trying to implement practices without discussing them with us. We would just have a factory meeting and say we're sorry, we're just not going anywhere with this and somebody said, 'well we'll just have to go fishing then'. But as soon as you go fishing, oh boy oh boy, they [management] are knocking on your door and saying how much they want to talk to you. It's the only time they listen.

The stewards also organised other actions, such as a refusal to attend teambriefings or a refusal to comply with new working practices. For example, when the Messier-Dowty management introduced a new electronic clocking procedure to book operatives' working time to different jobs it was discovered that disruption of this procedure could jeopardise the company's production control system. One shop steward explained:

> We had a new cell leader who was telling blokes they weren't pulling their weight. The leaders were using the electronic system to gauge how fast the members were working. We've had an agreement for years saying when this electronic system came in, that we would never be chastised over times on the job. The cell leader looked at the computer print out, said this man's two hours down on that job and started giving him a bollocking. The blokes came up to me and said what do we do? I said it's in your own hands, my suggestion is you don't use the system. So they didn't. It took management three days to realise that nobody was booking on. This cell leader, he got transferred to engineering.

The MSF response

Some of MSF's technical staff were affected by cellular working on the shop-floor, however, the introduction of integrated project-based teamworking (IPTs) into design and planning areas constituted the more significant change for most MSF members. Project teams were introduced at different stages during the 1990s.

These teams had two main objectives. First, to create a multi-functional environment which supports the process of designing quality and manufacturability into the product at an early stage. Second to compress the development cycle of a project from conception to initial production.

Project teams come in different forms. The more durable teams borrow from the Japanese practice of assembling a group of engineers from different functions who are then assigned to a development project for its full duration. Other project teams may have specific objectives of a limited duration and could be used on an *ad-hoc* basis to resolve one-off challenges. A typical aerospace project team would comprise development engineers; design engineers; stress engineers; draughts-persons; planning engineers; production engineers; project management staff; and procurement staff.

Most of the MSF representatives felt that teamwork had not significantly altered the skill and task composition of the technical worker's labour process although, in the context of labour rationalisation, the new teamworkers were expected to complete a greater mass of work packages more rapidly. However, this new form of technical labour utilisation created two significant organisational problems for the different MSF workplace unions. First, the traditional organisation of workplace representatives by a department-based office committee system (defined by the MSF rule book) was made redundant. The introduction of project teams fragmented, and in some cases dismantled, the traditional large, function-based technical offices. As one MSF representative at Rolls-Royce observed:

> We had a Design Office with hundreds of blokes stuck behind drawing boards. We had a Stress Office with 80 blokes stuck behind PCs. And a Detail Office with 120 people on drawing boards. And what management did was to break that down into integrated project teams so that if you were designing a component then rather than do things sequentially, that's design, detail, stress and back again, the idea is you'd get everyone around the same table and do all the elements of the design simultaneously. So whereas previously, we had a very well organised Design Office, now that's been broken up into project groups and we have actually found it quite difficult to think our way through that and adapt our organization to match what the company is doing.

Second, this organisational fragmentation was compounded by the emergence of a significant degree of transience in staff deployment. Engineers and other technical staff were expected to move from team to team, office to office, in accordance with the dynamics of project team management. These changes had serious ramifications for workplace union organisation and the requisite amount of activists needed to represent and mobilise members. As an MSF representative at BAe Systems explained:

> Since they implemented integrated teams we've had a migration of people, a workforce that is constantly moving around, which makes my life difficult

keeping contact with people ... It means that the designers, and we had predominant union membership within the design office, are now scattered all over the site. We really need a mountain of union reps if we are going to cover the whole workforce properly.

Our research found that, unlike their AEEU counterparts, the MSF workplace unions had failed to reorganise their systems of workplace representation in response to the organisational restructuring and fragmentation caused by teamworking. This was partly due to the increasing work pressures faced by union activists and partly due, in some plants, to a failure to recruit sufficient activists. But it was also attributable to a reluctance by many to break out of a 'design office mentality', as one representative put it. These processes have enabled the aerospace employers to weaken MSF's influence over the regulation of employment relations. For example, at BAe Systems, management was able repeatedly to bypass an unusual MSF sub-contract labour agreement that required team consultation and approval prior to sub-contract utilisation. This was attributed to insufficient numbers of representatives available to police the agreement and to influence MSF members.

The research did uncover examples of participative workplace unionism and mobilisation of MSF members in some plants, focusing on such traditional bargaining issues as pay determination and redundancy consultation. However, unlike their AEEU counterparts, no evidence emerged of any attempts by MSF representatives to establish a role in the organisation of technical work, or to reorganise in response to workplace restructuring. Neither were the MSF representatives likely to organise industrial action to counter local management initiatives. Despite the radical organisational restructuring experienced in the aerospace industry, MSF activists have still displayed a tendency to be unconcerned with reforming the labour process (Smith and Whalley 1996). These interview observations are supported by quantitative survey indicators presented in Table 3.5.

The data provide indications of the extent of the workplace representatives' influence over certain dimensions of the employment relationship. The determination of pay, changes to working practices and the use of non-permanent staff were more likely to be subject to negotiation with management, rather than weaker consultation, in AEEU bargaining areas compared to MSF areas. This was particularly the case for changes to working practices and the use of non-permanent staff. Moreover, the data show that the AEEU stewards felt they exerted significantly more influence over jobs and working conditions in their own work areas compared to MSF representatives.

Recollectivisation and its organisation

Earlier in this chapter we described the severe impact of labour rationalisation on the different unions and the extent to which they were able to rebuild an effective workplace organisation. In this section, we explore the systematic activity that lies

Table 3.5   Workplace representatives' influence over key work issues (all aerospace workplace representatives, $n = 136$).

	By negotiation (%)	By consultation (%)
How is pay decided?[a]		
AEEU representatives	99	1
MSF representatives	74	26
How are working practices decided?[b]		
AEEU representatives	82	18
MSF representatives	58	42
How is the use of non-permanent staff decided?[a]		
AEEU representatives	68	32
MSF representatives	29	71

	Some or a lot of influence (%)	Little or no influence (%)
How much influence over the pay of your members?		
AEEU representatives	58	42
MSF representatives	45	55
How much influence over jobs and working conditions in your area?[b]		
AEEU representatives	81	19
MSF representatives	58	42

[a]   Significant at the 0.001 level.
[b]   Chi-square test significant at the 0.05 level.

behind recollectivisation at work and how organisational renewal was either sustained or constrained. Three key facets of this are considered: communications, membership recruitment and leadership.

The AEEU

Although the AEEU workplace unions regularly produced site newsletters and distributed minutes of JSSC (Joint Shop Stewards' Committee) meetings, far more emphasis was placed upon regular stewards' meetings followed by informal but systematic verbal communications with members. The stewards at every plant stressed the centrality of communications for effective member participation. A typical 'cascade' system comprised a weekly meeting of senior steward negotiators immediately followed by a full meeting of shop stewards. The stewards would then report outcomes to members and discuss these in small sectional meetings or on a 'one-to-one' basis. Different stewards felt that this constituted a more open and inclusive system compared to the traditional shop steward approach when activists often expected the rank and file to obey their instructions without comment. One senior steward said:

We encourage criticism. Sometimes people come back about certain questions and I think we've acted on those. And the members have several ways of communicating back to the activists. First of all, we do run an open-house operation. The trade union office isn't something remote, the convenors are not remote. We like to feel that we do operate an open-door policy.

The creation of full-time, senior union roles with permanent offices and the use of centralised 'check-off' subscription collection systems can potentially cause a distancing of leading activists from the membership. The AEEU convenors responded to this by undertaking regular, and in some plants, daily membership patrols. A senior steward described this:

Every day I patrol the site. In all, we've got four site executive members who will go on daily patrols around the site, talking to members all the time, dealing with problems. And the members expect to see you! . . . You might have some isolated areas and they do like to see you and they want to talk to you.

Despite the abolition of the pre- and post-entry closed shops contained in the employment legislation of successive Conservative Governments in the 1980s and 1990s, the different AEEU workplace unions had succeeded in maintaining close to 100 per cent union membership. The reasons for this included most employers' implicit or explicit support for recognition, diligent shop steward recruitment activity amongst new starts, a resilient trade union 'craft culture' and more broadly, a strong trade union consciousness on the shop-floor. The larger plants provided union recruitment sessions during the formal induction of new employees, and all but one of the plants supplied the names of new starts to the AEEU convenors. Only at Smiths Industries had this employer co-operation been withdrawn. In this case, the shop stewards responded by involving the membership as a whole in the recruitment process. In particular, peer pressure was applied to new starters and non-unionists; any individual who refused to join would receive no help or training from his or her colleagues.

The ability of activists to maintain an effective, participatory workplace union organisation is partly contingent upon the nature of the members' attitudes towards the union and in turn, the influence of leadership style on membership commitment (Greene *et al.* 2000). Classic typologies of leadership approaches have outlined dichotomies between the 'delegate' type who acts solely in accordance with membership mandate and the more independent 'representative' type who may take additional actions based on personal convictions (Batstone *et al.* 1977); or dichotomies between adversarial/militant and co-operative/partnership approaches (Kelly 1996). Useful as such models are heuristically, they fail to capture the complexity and psychology of leadership behaviour and the ways in which union activists have been forced to adapt to the unfavourable political environment of work of the past decade.

When asked to reflect upon their role and leadership style, many of the AEEU stewards interviewed described the new challenges arising from these conditions and particularly, the difficulties faced in meeting the shifting aspirations and demands of the membership. In years gone by, engineering shop stewards were more likely to receive the support of the rank and file without having to go out and fight for it. Their role was then to go out and fight management along the shifting frontiers of control at the point of production, provided they had sufficient self-confidence. But in the 'new workplace' shop stewards do not have the same room for manoeuvre in challenging managerial prerogatives and increasingly membership aspirations cannot be fully realised. For example, one convenor who had experienced four decades of industrial relations in the aerospace industry described the changing leadership role in this way:

> I believe the role of the shop steward is more difficult today than it ever was. If I think back to the 1960s, whilst in one sense it was harder in that you had a real gaffer – they were hard-nosed bastards – but it was also easier because everybody saw them as that. Today, with the industrial relations laws, successive Governments including the present one, are not akin to trade unionism. Always we're misunderstood, always the tabloid press say we strike over cups of tea, etc., there's still a lot of Colonel Blimps about in the *Daily Telegraph* and I believe that trade unionism is maligned generally. It's very difficult for a shop steward today, with all that in mind, to be able to act in the way that we did then. And there's more and more responsibility of course. The aspirations of the members today are different from those in the 1960s and 1970s. The level of support isn't the same. You automatically had the membership then, you don't get that today, it's hard. The aspirations of the membership are so high that when we don't get what we want, then the stewards don't get the support.

Many convenors and shop stewards attempted to overcome this potential disjunction between membership aspirations and concrete outcomes by forging a representative leadership style which was based more explicitly on honesty, trust and winning respect than might have been the case hitherto. Another convenor of lengthy experience summed this up:

> Very, very important good leadership. I had a debate Tuesday with my shop stewards about which avenue we should go down on the annual wage increase. A couple of the stewards said leave it to the factory and I said no, over my dead body. If you are going to make a decision, you are going to do it as a Joint Shop Stewards Committee and you're going to recommend it to these people. You're their leaders, they respect what you do. You don't say to them what do you want to do? You must lead and you've got to be honest. Don't ever lie to the workforce. It doesn't matter whether they want to hear the information, I won't lie to them. That's why you've got respect.

A case study of union victimisation and militant response at Smiths Industries best exemplifies this connection between effective workplace union organisation and a representative-member relationship based on mutual trust. The Smiths plant at Cheltenham suffered 18 separate redundancy programmes during the 1990s. The heaviest job losses occurred at the beginning of the decade and organisational changes were imposed during this time in an environment of fear when, as one steward described, 'people were too frightened of losing their jobs, we were fighting to keep jobs rather than fighting for anything else really and our people were frightened even to speak'. By 1994, the number of recognised stewards had been reduced from 38 to three. In the same year, the management issued a further compulsory redundancy programme and took advantage of this by sacking the long-standing AEEU convenor. The two remaining AEEU shop stewards, one the women's representative, responded to this victimisation by ignoring the threat to their own positions and organising unofficial overtime bans, go-slows and non-co-operation. As a result of plant-wide membership commitment to these actions the management was forced to re-instate the convenor. During our interviews the women's representative and the convenor both reflected on how membership commitment and respect for honest leadership – and plain courage – forged a new sense of solidarity and confidence within the beleaguered plant. The women's representative:

> I was frightened because I thought they were going to sack me and then I thought why should I bloody worry about that. Bollocks to them! I did stick in there and I'm still here. I just think you have to speak your mind and they don't always like to hear it, do they? That's why they reinstated Dave. Because the workforce wouldn't do any work, we didn't go on strike and we didn't do anything that they could prove we were doing illegally, but we just didn't work properly and the plant was getting desperate. I think that experience for the workforce, showing a united front, gave them a feeling of new solidarity, it let the company know that they can't do what they like. We had a good spirit here after that.

Dave, the convenor:

> I was the first works convenor in this country to get reinstated. It was because the workforce wanted me back. That was the happiest day of my life. I walked into that canteen and they clapped me in. That's what you call respect. That's what I've always said to this company, you'll never be able to touch me because this workforce won't let you. It was brilliant, it really was. £56,000 they offered me to go and I wouldn't go on principle. I'd sooner have got put out by them because I was no good.

MSF

In the previous sections of this chapter, we have shown how the white-collar MSF workplace unions generally failed to engage with the management agendas of organisational restructuring and labour process reform. However, some of the MSF unions did succeed in rebuilding their organisations by mobilising members around traditional aspects of the employment relationship, such as pay, redundancy and health and safety. A weaker trade union consciousness in engineering and technician occupations meant that this organising activity did not display the same consistency or tenacity as we observed with the AEEU. The nature of this MSF organising activity in the aerospace plants can be characterised rudimentarily as either 'strong' or 'weak'.

Those which are categorised as 'strong' tended to have the following characteristics. First, a good membership mass even though there was potential for further in-fill recruitment. Second, a disposition to systematically communicate with and involve members. Third, the senior representatives were more committed to an independent and assertive workplace unionism. The 'strong' MSF plants tended to use an array of different communications strategies aimed at mobilising members' commitment to the union's organisation and bargaining agenda. For example, at GKN-Westland and Rolls-Royce, mass meetings were held occasionally and more local 'sectional' meetings of members were held regularly; professionally produced newsletters and minutes of union meetings were frequently distributed to members; and two-way communications were encouraged by feeding members' views into departmental and site reps meetings. Such systematic approaches to communications enhanced the process of collectivisation of a traditionally fragmented and heterogeneous white-collar workforce. For example, at the time of the research over 1,000 MSF members at GKN-Westland's Yeovil workforce voted by 94 per cent to hold an all-out strike ballot in furtherance of their pay claim. The senior MSF rep commented on this:

> We make sure that we fully understand the psychology of the people we represent . . . We've probably communicated to death with our members, we will hand out paperwork throughout the factory, we're putting out a poster every week now as we move towards our postal ballot. We try very hard to keep our members involved, make sure they understand all the subtle nuances of all the issues that we are currently talking to the company about. I think then, when you come to a mass meeting and a vote, it pays dividends because there could have been very few people in the hall who didn't know what they were there for and they can, therefore, understand exactly how we got to where we got to.

The same principles of planning and strategy were applied to the recruitment process. At all of the 'strong' MSF plants, reps were expected to attempt to recruit non-members in their own vicinity, to practise the art of careful persuasion, often exploiting newsletters and leaflets as a means of catalysing a positive dialogue. At most of these plants MSF was taking a more strategic approach to recruitment, for example, by setting up site recruitment sub-committees, by establishing teams of recruiting activists and by completing workplace mapping exercises to highlight areas where membership density is weakest.

Much of this activity was occurring in large, well unionised plants where legacies of relative collective strength and confident leadership combined to maintain a durable organisational dynamic. By contrast, a more instructive example of the importance of independent leadership in *constructing* such a dynamic is provided by Bristol's Matra-Marconi Space plant.[3] This particular workplace did not obviously lend itself to trade union collectivisation. Although MSF had been established there since the early 1980s, the organisation was weak and membership density rarely exceeded 25 per cent. This was partly because the workforce comprised graduate space scientists and engineers working in a stable and highly individualistic, career-based environment. A process of MSF expansion commenced in 1992 when the firm, at that time owned by BAe, unilaterally announced fifty compulsory redundancies. At this point, a young graduate engineer decided to become involved because, as he put it, 'there was nobody to do it and I was pretty sure that what was going on was wrong, so somebody was needed to step in and start asking questions'. This activist immediately set about challenging management's failure to meet its statutory redundancy consultation obligations:

> We contacted our MSF colleagues at our Matra Stevenage plant and said, 'look at the time that they were putting out letters about voluntary redundancy at Bristol, they are claiming they started consultation. Did they start consulting with you because they didn't with us?' We met up together one night after work in Reading so that the company didn't know we were getting together, and we went back our separate ways and we both registered a 'failure to agree' with management. We told them, 'you put out this notice, we fail to agree because you haven't consulted'. They took a look and realised they were stuffed.

As a result of persistent union resistance the company was eventually forced to concede that the compulsory redundancy programme could just as easily be managed by calling for volunteers. Non-members started to take note:

> At the end of it, the union had been seen to be fighting for everybody and the result had been everybody knew the people who would have gone out on their nose didn't. We caught the company doing something illegal.

In 1994, Lagardere Groupe of France and GEC took over the BAe space operation. The MSF workplace leadership which was now growing in confidence strengthened its organisation around the employee uncertainty and insecurity which follows company mergers. The union was able to recruit further members on the basis of providing a collective enforcement of employee rights under the

TUPE (Transfer of Undertakings (Protection of Employment)) legislation. As a result of this sustained organising activity, the MSF membership at Matra-Marconi Space trebled over three years, reaching a density of over 80 per cent. This was not just a question of opportunistic exploitation of critical incidents, the MSF organisation also expanded on the basis of building a cadre of committed activists and systematic member communications.

By contrast, MSF organisation in the 'weak' aerospace plants had become merely reactive to management and even marginalised at the workplace. In different instances this was a function of relatively weak trade union consciousness on the office floor, processes of staff rationalisation and decollectivisation, work pressures on activists and an emergent psychology of defeatism. For example, at Matra-BAe Dynamics, Messier-Dowty and Smiths Industries, MSF reps complained variously of an 'organisation bumping along at the bottom', of 'work pressures, apathy and a fear factor' restricting activist and member recruitment. The following comment was typical:

> I don't know where half of the members are. That's why I need more reps and people who know other sets of people. The network has crumbled somewhat over the years. I think the direct approach to recruitment, the direct individual approach has fallen by the wayside. It's because it's down to a few people and you can't be everywhere.

These plants all contained the seeds for enhancing membership recruitment in terms of prevalent discontents and a large non-membership. But they had also been subject to severe labour – and activist – rationalisation over the past decade. In such conditions, the process of education, of building members' confidence and constructing an effective counter-balance to management's hold on material and ideological power resources required more dynamic networks of committed activists. In these 'weak' MSF plants such networks were either non-existent or in danger of atrophy. And so the few existing MSF representatives were caught up in a vicious circle of decline; their workplace organisation was unlikely to be salvaged without the injection of new blood (thus providing a new activist dynamic) but they lacked the necessary organisational resources to catalyse this.

Conclusion

At the national level, MSF has prioritised traditional organising techniques and membership participation at work in its current policy formulations (Carter 2000). However, the response of its different workplace unions to organisational restructuring in aerospace – the union's strongest membership sector – has been largely reactive and in many cases, passive. The data presented in this chapter show only partial success in rebuilding workplace union organisation in the aftermath of severe labour rationalisation. In four out of the eight plants visited, the MSF organisations enjoyed relatively high membership densities and higher member-rep ratios than their AEEU counterparts; however, in the remaining four plants the MSF workplace unions were severely undermined by membership densities well below 50 per cent and a lack of representatives. Moreover, in the context of the employers' ongoing strategies of securing additional labour flexibility and cheapening labour by use of outsourcing and sub-contractors, the MSF unions had verged on relinquishing their traditional regulation of the use of sub-contract labour. The MSF unions also failed to respond or adapt to the fragmentation of traditional departmental demarcations and managerial decentralisation caused by corporate restructuring, business unitisation and teamworking. In many cases, this inaction resulted in a weakening of union influence over non-economistic facets of the employment relationship, such as work reforms, and a weakening of union restraints over local managerial prerogatives in technical areas.

The general failure of the MSF unions to engage with, or respond to labour process changes cannot be solely attributed to brittle organisation or poor leadership. Indeed, as we saw in the last section, a number of the MSF workplace unions succeeded in mobilising members around such issues as pay and consultation rights, and this required sustained organising activity and independent leadership. Instead, the absence of a response to labour process reform was more a function of historical weaknesses in the unionisation of engineers and technical workers and the traditional forms of technical union organisation. Engineers' unions and professional associations have rarely exerted leverage over labour deployment and the organisation of technical work because their members have not been subject to the bureaucratic boundaries and demarcations that would facilitate such influence (Smith and Whalley 1996). And it may be no coincidence that one recent in-depth study of the impact of contemporary management practices on unionised technical workers contains no references to union engagement with the restructuring of work (McGovern 1998). Moreover, in the context of increased membership recruitment competition in the aerospace industry in the 1970s and 1980s, technical unions adapted their policies to a 'professional-scientific' ideology. As Smith (1987) observes, this involved eschewing a 'recruitment through militancy' approach in favour of 'recruitment through autonomy', an approach that stressed the autonomy of professional engineers and their separateness from more militant engineering workers.

These historical developments and traditions have constrained the emergence of new workplace union organising approaches that might facilitate MSF opposition to, or influence over, work restructuring. Both the traditions and current activity of the AEEU workplace unions stand in marked contrast to MSF. At the national level, the AEEU is one of the leading proponents of partnership with employers and government. Its 'productionist' policies concede that organisations need continually to seek efficiency gains providing the union and its members are involved in this process through teamworking, training and multi-skilling. One AEEU full-time officer summed this up:

> Our [partnership] policies are well developed and strongly pursued. We've actually got a situation where we would say to the employer, 'look, it's not your

prerogative to retrain for the pursuit of efficiencies, we can do it, our members can do it. But what we're saying in turn to you is that those efficiency gains when they are quantified, are shared.' We call that 'value share'.

In most cases, the AEEU unions in the aerospace plants took a quite different stance to this national policy. Rather than co-operate with the employers' agenda of securing efficiency gains through organisational restructuring, the AEEU workplace unions were mainly able to adapt their traditional forms of organising and member representation so as to 'engage with change' rather than embrace it (Stewart and Wass 1998). This approach placed significant constraints against the imposition of managerial prerogatives.

Compared to MSF, the AEEU workplace unions faced a greater severity of labour rationalisation and activist loss in the 1990s. Yet they were far more successful at rebuilding their union organisation and activist base, and as we saw in the last section, more adept at sustaining organisational renewal through communications, recruitment and assertive leadership. This reflects a stronger trade union consciousness on the engineering factory floor and also a resilient tradition of union participation. This new organisational strength has enabled the AEEU workplace unions to maintain opposition to on-site contractualisation, although like their MSF counterparts they have been unable to halt international outsourcing and consequent job loss. A resilient trade union consciousness in the AEEU areas has also maintained an egalitarianism supporting equal employment rights and conditions for all members irrespective of department or team. The employers' attempts to deregulate site-wide conditions through the introduction of both multiple, intra-site business units and teamworking posed a major threat to these principles. This constituted a particular form of 'company-specific employment regime' which requires unions to develop robust decentralised structures (Hyman 1997). The AEEU stewards responded by adapting the historical form of their workplace unionism to the new conditions. This involved recasting the traditional model of the engineering shop steward as an individual who is often primarily accountable to his or her immediate work group (Clegg 1970). With the current balance of power between employers and labour still favouring the former, the implementation of local managerial prerogatives at the point of production within teams and units can be facilitated by such fragmented work-group-based shop steward representation. The AEEU stewards adapted this highly decentralised structure by weakening steward accountability to local members (and line manager influence) and prioritising steward accountability to a central, cross-business unit union executive. And unlike the MSF workplace unions, the AEEU stewards engaged with the politics of teamworking. This was by reorganising its work group representation to ensure every team had steward representation; by either opposing or placing limits on the managerial functions of teamleaders and new supervisors; and by mobilising unofficial industrial action to place further limits on managerial prerogatives and maintain influence over work changes and working practices. These adaptations to the AEEU's traditional form of decentralised, group-based representation constituted what Fairbrother (2000a) has conceptualised as a 'beneficial sectionalism'; functionally, or team-divided members are organised by stewards who now act in concert with other stewards, a form of organisation which provides the basis for a more effective participative unionism.

4 Manufacturing change in an era of corporate instability

Introduction

Managerial strategies and tactics aimed at frustrating the ability of unions to struggle against multiple forms of exploitation in the workplace are particularly formidable in the UK manufacturing sector. Since the early 1970s, an extensive restructuring of industry has accompanied the increased internationalisation of production and intensified international competition. By examining work organisational changes, management–union relations and forms of union organised responses, ranging from 'militant independence' to 'respectable collaboration', in an eclectic range of South West manufacturing plants, this chapter weighs up workplace experiences in combating this new phase of capitalist competition and accumulation.

Capitalist restructuring has involved corporate take-over, merger, joint ventures and strategic alliance formation as individual capitals have sought to readjust their position within an expanding international product market. In its extreme version, the associated 'globalisation thesis' has become all-embracing, with footloose capital making national regulatory regimes irrelevant if not defunct. For labour the consequences of such a scenario are extreme. Trade union power is, according to this thesis, emasculated, as workers become powerless in the face of capital's threat to withdraw and relocate. The suggestion that organised labour is in the process of becoming completely marginalised in the face of the relentless drive of globalised capital has not gone unchallenged. For instance, McNally (1998) outlines the contradictions inherent in the globalisation thesis and illustrates how as an outcome of these contradictions new working-class struggles can emerge citing East Asia as an example. Yates (2001) contends (militant) unions are needed more than ever in the US to combat international capital. Dearlove (2000: 114), in his study of the British state and its relationship with the global economy, argues that 'the *determining* impact of the global economy is limited' as 'it can only work on and through domestic actors and institutions'. Nevertheless, whilst critics of the 'globalisation' thesis, such as Hirst and Thompson (1996), emphasise the overstated nature of the trends evident in the world economy they acknowledge that the UK is one of 'the most internationalised of the major industrial countries'. And within the globalised economy the UK is 'far ahead of the game' in terms of its dependence on overseas trade and investment (Hirst and Thompson 2000: 336).

Since the late 1970s there has been a marked liberalisation of the UK economy leading to an intensification of market forces. UK industry has been increasingly exposed to international competition and governments have played a proactive part in attracting foreign direct investment (FDI) in the belief that it must keep in step with the increasing integration of the world economy (Hirst and Thompson 2000). Foreign-owned companies supplied almost 47 per cent of manufacturing investment between 1994–97 (Great Britain Office of National Statistics 2001a). Even so, in respect to numbers directly employed the picture is less striking. In manufacturing, between 1990–97, foreign owned companies employed 17 per cent of the total (*Financial Times*, 10 July 2000), although this does not take into account indirect employment gains through multiplier effects. On the other hand, employment substitution resulting from FDI in some industries, such as aerospace engineering and clothing, has actually contributed to a decline in UK employment (Driffield 1999). In fact, Greenaway *et al.* (1999) have demonstrated that concomitant with the increasing internationalisation of UK industry, via trade and FDI, there has been a marked reduction of employment in UK manufacturing along with a significant rise in productivity.

The first point to make from these observations is that UK manufacturing industry is more prone to the decisions of foreign owners than most advanced industrial countries. As Child *et al.* (2000) related, major changes in domestic management practice have trailed foreign acquisition of UK companies. They identified US parent companies as more likely to centralise HRM issues, which can hinder local management in forming creditable relations with staff and trade unions. A second point is that with changes of corporate ownership and control having become commonplace a new corporate instability has emerged. Moreover, the 'short-termism' associated with relatively open and de-regulated financial markets which predominate in the UK has added to instability (Cosh *et al.* 1990; Marsh 1991). This has led in turn to an increasing divorce between patterns of corporate ownership as a legal entity and the everyday decision-making structures in individual enterprises. The increased dominance of holding companies, strategic alliances and joint ventures has further confused patterns of corporate governance, producing a high degree of diversification and divisionalisation of corporate structure (Edwards *et al.* 1992). Such instability leads Hirst and Thompson (2000: 352) to argue, *in extremis*, that the UK manufacturing sector at least 'is in danger of becoming a greater Canada, a branch-plant economy dependent on the decision of foreign owners'.[1]

The process of neo-liberal labour market and financial deregulation began earlier in the UK than in competitor nations and has been more intense in response to the high degree of internationalisation. As a result the impact on patterns and processes of managing the employment relationship has been severe. In addition to contributing to the decline in manufacturing employment since the late 1970s, as highlighted above, globalisation and deregulation have increased job insecurity (Standing 1997: 11; Capelli *et al.* 1997: 43–4). Moreover, driven by increased competitive pressures employers have initiated the introduction of new forms of work organisation to intensify work as a precursor to raising labour productivity and cutting unit labour costs (Casey *et al.* 1997; Gall 1998a; Danford 1999; Howell 1999). Recent studies, however, show that UK labour productivity still lags behind the EU and OECD average. In order to improve labour productivity the Labour Government supported actions designed to increase competition, including the prosecution of further liberalisation of the UK and World economy (DTI 1999).

For British trade unions these processes, lasting through the 1980s and 1990s, when combined with Government legislative attacks on rights to organise, have created a cold and inhospitable industrial relations climate in which trade union membership and density have declined and industrial stoppages have plummeted to an all-time low.[2] The 1997 election of the New Labour Government did not fundamentally reverse or alter the orientation on market internationalisation. Shortly after the election the New Labour Government authorised a strategy of creating 'strong markets, in which the stimulus of competition promotes innovation and the adoption of best business practices. To promote such markets, the Government has already introduced the Competition Bill and is encouraging further liberalisation in world trade' (DTI 1998). The signs are that New Labour in its second term of office, following its election success in June 2001, will resume its pursuance of neo-liberal policies. Patricia Hewitt MP, speaking at the AEEU conference in Blackpool, just after the 2001 election, gave strong pointers to New Labour's continued orientation to the free market:

> Government cannot and should not support lame duck industries or try and protect them from competition . . . There is no such thing as a job for life but there can be employability for life . . . Trade unions have a key role to play in helping their members become more employable in increasing their opportunities and strengthening their security in a changing world.

The decline in union membership and the associated 'crisis of representation' have for a decade or more been the focus of debate about the future of trade unions, which has thus been of particular relevance to British unions with membership in the manufacturing sector. The trend towards more insecure and precarious employment associated with both corporate instability and new forms of work has posed UK trade unions a series of problems (Heery and Abbott 2000).

Whilst analysis and research has focused on the response of trade union leaderships in the UK, little has been reported on workplace union response to industrial restructuring. In particular there is a need to address the particular problems for workplace unionism caused by the exceptional instability of corporate governance and control described above. Is it possible for British unions to establish partnership discourse, for example, when they are faced with unstable ownership patterns and more change than continuity? Furthermore, is it not the case that the decentralisation of industrial relations and the emergent 'mosaic' of management styles and ownership patterns make it difficult to generalise experience of UK union renewal on a sectoral or industry-wide basis? Could it be the case that the old certainties of centralised union approaches to recruitment and organising, based as they are on spheres of craft or occupational influence, are now becoming increasingly meaningless in a more unstable corporate environment with ever-changing employer initiatives on production methods and processes? The research presented in this chapter attempts to explore some of these questions with respect to different workplace unions with substantial membership in the manufacturing sector. Patterns of changing ownership and control of fifteen manufacturing enterprises are sketched together with their employment profiles. Continuity and change within management–union relationships and working practices are recorded before moving on to explore in more detail the resultant workplace union responses, providing further empirical evidence to inform the ongoing debate on prospects for trade union renewal.

The research base

AEEU, GMB and MSF union representatives in fifteen manufacturing establishments were interviewed between 1998 and 2000 (see Appendix). A profile of these establishments is provided in Table 4.1. As the table shows, the nature of products produced in the workplaces fall into multifarious Standard Industrial Classification (SIC) categories. Moreover, there were differences in the pattern of ownership of these workplaces. Four of the them were part of UK-based MNCs, four were US-based MNCs, two were Canadian-based MNCs, two German-based MNCs, one an Irish-based MNC, one a joint venture (Swiss/UK), and one was a UK private limited company. Most of the companies had experienced recent changes of ownership, and only the British private limited company, had a stable ownership history. Unions were recognised and had full bargaining rights in all of the establishments except one (OptoCo), where the AEEU had representative rights only.

UK and South West manufacturing in context

A feature of Britain's relative economic decline since the mid-nineteenth century has been the tendency of manufacturing jobs to contract relative to employment as a whole. Between 1966 and 1991, however, there was an absolute fall in the number of jobs across the manufacturing sector, of which the most significant losses were registered in the recession of 1979–82 (Glynn and Booth 1996: 280). Moreover, there was a further shakeout of manufacturing jobs in the recession of 1990–93. While a mini-recovery followed between 1994–98, the number of manufacturing jobs recorded in the first quarter of 1998 was still over 600,000 down on the corresponding period in 1990. Since 1998, employment in the manufacturing sector has fallen yet again. Between the first quarter of 1998 and the second quarter of 2000, 239,000 jobs were lost (Great Britain Office of National Statistics 2001a)[3], reducing the number employed in this sector close to the very low levels recorded in the 1990–93 recession and lower than any period

Table 4.1   Company profiles and employee trends.

Company	Union	Ownership	Employee trends
RubberCo	AEEU (60 members, 94% density), TGWU	UK-based MNC, auto and technical products	500 employed at site. Stable
PagerCo	AEEU (80% density)	UK-based MNC, computerised timing products (e.g. pagers)	67 employed at site, down by one-third after redundancy programme
CerealCo	AEEU (98% density)	Anglo-Swiss Joint Venture, breakfast cereals	Two-year-old site with workforce of 100
CheeseCo	AEEU (100% density) formerly TGWU	Irish-based MNC, cheese manufacturing	130 employed compared to 300 in 1972
BrakeCo	AEEU (50 members) TGWU	German-based MNC (formerly UK owned) Manufacture of hydraulic brakes	370 employed compared to 1,410 in 1989. Fears of plant closure with production shifted abroad under new owners
InjectorCo	AEEU (50% density) single union agreement	US-based MNC, manufacturing injector bodies	Ten-year-old plant with 450 employed compared to 700 nine months previously, compulsory redundancies
OptoCo	AEEU (300members) non-recognised for bargaining but recognised for disciplinary cases	Canadian-based MNC, optoelectrics	3,000 employed, an increase from 1,500 two years ago
CopyCo	AEEU (669 members), GMB (413), MSF (140) overall density 51%	US-based MNC document-processing systems	2,390 employed but only 897 have permanent contracts
AlloyCo	GMB (majority union), AEEU (100 members), MSF (small presence)	US-based MNC Nickel alloy manufacturer	900 employed, down from 1,100 one year previously with some compulsory redundancies
HydraulicCo	AEEU (180 members, 82% density)	US-based MNC, aircraft hydraulic systems	300 mainly production workers employed
Component-Co	GMB/APEX (80%:50% density)	Canadian-based MNC making auto components Formerly UK owned	250 employed on site with 40% women
PaperCo	GMB (65 members, 90% density on the shop-floor; staff non-union)	Ex family firm owned since 1995 by UK-based MNC, making high-quality security paper, e.g. travellers' cheques	140 employed, cut back by 10% following redundancies one and a half years ago

Table 4.1   Company profiles and employee trends.

Company	Union	Ownership	Employee trends
PlasticCo	GMB (90 members, 67% density)	Private limited company making plastic mouldings	135 staff, up from 125 two years previously. 40 women work in finishing shop
ValveCo	MSF (250 members, 50% density)	UK-based MNC making thermostatic valves and water control systems	Workforce reduced from 716 in 1996 to 661 in 1998
CarCo	MSF (430 staff members, 33 pattern makers and 18 craft)	German-based MNC owned (at time of survey) auto manufacturer Formerly UK owned	Staff, 800 Shop-floor, 1,500

between 1966 and 1992. While the data in the 1990s show some signs of job losses in manufacturing levelling out this should be looked at in the context of the almost continual contraction of employment in this sector since 1966 (Kitson and Mitchie 1998; Great Britain Office of National Statistics 2001a).

The trend in the South West reflects the national picture. In the recession year of 1992, 18.8 per cent of the total number of employee jobs in the South West were in the manufacturing sector. By September 1996, this figure had dropped to 17 per cent and by September 1999 had fallen again to 15.7 per cent. In absolute numbers, between 1981 and 1991, a total of 64,282 manufacturing jobs were lost in the South West,[4] although, between 1993 and 1997, a total of 31,930 were regained.[5] Since 1998, numbers of manufacturing jobs in the South West have again gone into decline (Regional Trends 1992–2000; Gripaios 2000).

Juxtaposed with the decline of manufacturing jobs in the last twenty years has been the expansion of foreign-owned firms operating in the UK. According to the WERS surveys, between 1980 and 1998 foreign ownership of British manufacturing workplaces engaged in metal goods, engineering and vehicles increased from 7 per cent of all private-sector workplaces to 19 per cent. In other private-sector establishments over the same period, excluding extraction industries, chemicals, minerals and metal production, foreign ownership expanded from 3 per cent to 20 per cent (Millward *et al.* 2000: 33). Another study (Industrial Management and Data Systems 1997) claims that in 1997 the extent of foreign ownership of UK manufacturing firms was even higher at 25 per cent. Foreign direct investment in the last twenty years has impacted on the South West region bringing in international companies such as Hewlett Packard in Bristol and Motorola and Honda in Swindon. But by the beginning of the new millennium, some of these companies were experiencing problems and were shedding jobs (Motorola and Hewlett Packard) although Honda was expanding.

Economic change has also taken the form of the break-up of long-standing firms through acquisitions and mergers. Changes in ownership of UK companies can impact on management–union relations, especially if as a consequence rationalisation occurs. The boom in acquisitions and mergers in the UK by British companies between 1986 and 1989 was running at an average of 1,311 per year. These figures have not been repeated in the 1990s, but at an average of 564 acquisitions and merger levels were still significant (Great Britain Office of National Statistics 2001b). Moreover, acquisitions of UK companies by overseas companies increased in the late 1990s. In the South West, as elsewhere, manufacturing firms with long domestic histories have been absorbed by multinationals and sometimes dissolved. For example the Pembridge Group swallowed the DRG Bristol-based company in 1989. The immediate break up of this company followed as different arms of the business were sold off to a number of concerns. As a consequence the distinct character of the firm with its roots in the local area was destroyed and many jobs were lost (Ollerenshaw and Wardley 1996). Similarly, changes in ownership in many of the companies visited in this research have frequently resulted in transformations in the organisation of work, changes in the nature of the relationships between employers and trade unions and rationalisation. Business planning decisions are increasingly taken at company headquarters, which are often based in other countries.

Ownership, control and restructuring of work

Ownership and control

All bar one of the manufacturing establishments researched for this study have been subject to a change in ownership in recent years, either through joint partnerships, acquisitions, mergers or disposals. This level of activity shows little sign of seriously slowing (Great Britain Office of National Statistics 2001b). While proponents of mergers and acquisitions may argue that the development of the capitalist global economy necessitates the continual reconfiguration of multinational companies to maintain dominance the big question is whether employees pay the price through poorer working conditions, work intensification and job insecurity. The separation of ownership and control changed class relationships in the twentieth century. Scott (1997) identifies the emergence of four different representations of capitalist exploitation in contemporary society, personal owners of entrepreneurial firms, rentier capitalists, and salaried executives or directors and finance capitalists. But as he argues this transition 'has transformed but not eliminated the capitalist classes' (Scott 1997: 275). The fact that financial institutions and corporate interests predominate does not alleviate exploitation but intensifies it particularly through transnational economic practices.

The 1998 WERS survey identified a number of distinctive features associated with establishments that have undergone ownership change in the 1990s, two of which are particularly relevant here. First, a change in ownership was cited as a notable cause for significant downsizing, although a reduction in product demand was the main reason given. Second, the WERS survey found that in a minority of cases a move to the centralisation of managerial decision-making followed corporate restructuring. This latter development was frequently accompanied by shifts in managerial attitude and behaviour in respect to industrial relations, especially in the private sector (Millward *et al.* 2000: 24, 27, 78–9).[6] Our findings show a similar pattern, although another variable, a fall in profits, was a further significant driver behind workforce reductions, restructuring the organisation of work and the transformation of management-employee relations. The regularity of corporate restructuring was often found to be destabilising, weakening employee morale.

Nearly half of the firms in our survey had been subject to job reduction in the 1990s. Notably newly acquired or merged organisations shed significant numbers of staff. For example, between 1998–99 AlloyCo cut 200 jobs, which amounted to 18 per cent of the workforce. This reduction trailed the disposal of the business by a Canadian multinational to an American multinational in 1998, a decision that was also influenced by severe financial losses in the subsequent 12 months. BrakeCo endured severe job losses between 1989 and 1999, under the direction first of an American and then a German multinational. Redundancies and natural wastage reduced the numbers employed from 1,410 in 1989 to 370 in 1999. InjectorCo has been subject to two take-overs in recent years, the first in 1996 by an Anglo-American engineering group and the second by an American multinational in 1999. At the time of research in 1999, InjectorCo employed 450 people. However, nine months previously staff levels were as high as 700 but due to the loss of a major contract all temporary workers were dismissed along with 96 permanent staff. It is too early to say what impact the recent change in ownership will have but in its wake jobs have been shed in two other UK plants in the group. Ownership change, job cuts and losses of £1.9m. were recorded at HydraulicCo. CopyCo experienced a reduction in the number of core workers following the American buy-out of its European partner and the transfer of some production work to a Greenfield site in Ireland. ComponentCo was acquired by a Canadian multinational in 1996 and has recently shed jobs. It slashed its workforce by 28 per cent in response to the fall in demand from Rover's Longbridge plant, which at the time was threatened with closure. Finally, two years after being taken over by a UK multinational in 1995, PaperCo restructured and rationalised its business reducing its shop-floor staff by 10 per cent.

Campaigning for jobs

A review of the union response to job cuts in the manufacturing plants is outside the remit of this chapter but worth recording are the forms of collective response to downsizing organised in two multinational subsidiaries. First, at CopyCo, the unions developed a campaign against job cuts that involved the local community. Manufacturing production at CopyCo supports an isolated single-industry community. It is a vital part of the local economy as well as an important source of local employment. Therefore, the announcement of significant job losses was of great concern to employees and the local community, which quickly turned to anger towards CopyCo. This collective community awareness of injustice was developed by MSF into a community campaign against shifting jobs out of the West of England plant to Ireland. Marches and demonstrations were organised in opposition, involving both the workforce and the local community. This 'external' campaign supplemented lobbying of local MPs and MEPs and the utilisation of the company's European Works Council. The strategy met with partial success in that the company conceded to making no compulsory redundancies of core staff but this protection did not extend to temporary workers employed by Manpower.

At BrakeCo fears of plant closure, following take-over by a German MNC, had prompted a narrower 'constitutional' campaign with the AEEU and TGWU jointly pursuing the issue, with the help of the local Labour MP and MEP, through the UK and European parliaments. The plant has faced constant redundancies in the last ten years. The site was split into four manufacturing divisions, which had been subject to some recent 're-unification'. Unlike CopyCo, BrakeCo was located in an urban area and was no longer the major employer it once was making it difficult to secure widespread support within the local community.

The German parent was clearly responding to tight product market competition in the supply of air brakes to lorry manufacturers. All low-tech (block braking manufacture) was in the process of being transferred to an Indian plant and all high-tech (new pneumatic specification) manufacture to French and Hungarian plants. Manufacturing was therefore to be concentrated in global production units despite the fact that the UK factory was once the world leader; not only was it profitable, it produced high-quality products and had over-full order books. Whilst the AEEU and TGWU unions were able to co-operate at UK level, the experience within the European Works Councils (EWC) has been less fruitful. The TGWU convenor, who was also the EWC representative, had recently been cold-shouldered at EWC meetings by representatives from the French and German plants, reflecting a more sectionalised response in the face of intra-national plant competition for jobs. As the AEEU steward explained:

> The last time [the TGWU convenor] went [to the EWC], they [his European counterparts] told him we're not interested in BrakeCo in Bristol, that's going. They've been told in their various factories that its closing. When he bought up the subject, he felt as though he was the odd man out, there was the cold feeling that – 'you're going, we don't need to talk to you'.

Such intra-national plant competition provides the multinational organisation with an opportunity to exploit divisions in the workforce by introducing 'coercive comparisons' between plants on a cost basis (Müller and Purcell 1992) and thus divide and rule with respect to employee relations strategy (Marginson 1994).

Challenging decisions

Turning to look at the impact of the examples where the centralisation of managerial decision-making clearly accompanied changes in ownership (at HydraulicCo, CopyCo, AlloyCo and PaperCo), our evidence suggests that in three of the four cases divisions opened up between 'old' and 'new' within organisational hierarchies. This development had serious implications for union organisation and strategy. The GMB senior steward at PaperCo, for example, noted that:

> There's been a lot of redundancies. There's been a lot of restructuring on a major level within the workforce right across the Group, right across the world where they are multi-national . . . What they [the company] tend to do . . . is leave everything to local management. They are basically telling them you have to cut this and cut that, and it's up to local management how they finance it and do it. They seem to be mill by mill or site by site negotiations.

Despite this apparent delegation of responsibility local managers had to work within strict financial parameters and a set of strategic goals. This was often the cause of antagonistic relations between management and the GMB representatives. Financial and strategic goals of the parent company took precedence over matters concerning industrial relations despite the destabilising impact this had on merger consolidation.

At AlloyCo, the AEEU senior steward was damning in his depiction of local managers' subjection to central control from the plant's head office in America:

> One of the biggest problems with this plant is that since it's been taken over, work is disseminated from this central position. R&D is carried out in America, product development is carried out here, but the basic structure . . . I don't even think anyone knows what the hell is going on.

In these two cases the extent to which the centralisation of managerial decision-making curtailed the authority of local managers impacted on the nature of industrial relations. At AlloyCo, this development frustrated attempts by AEEU to forge a partnership arrangement, as strategic decisions concerning HRM were made in America and two-way communication under this chain of command was non-existent. At PaperCo, centralisation of authority and power to the parent company was one factor in the creation of a more hostile industrial relations environment, which contributed to the outbreak, in February 1998, of a prolonged industrial dispute involving a positive strike ballot over bonus payments.

Table 4.2   Incidence of new management techniques.

Company	NMTs 1999–2000
RubberCo	Working time flexibility; teamworking; team briefings; *kaizen*
PagerCo	Functional flexibility
CerealCo	Functional flexibility; teamworking; team briefings; job rotation; working time flexibility (annualised hours)
CheeseCo	Teamworking; functional flexibility
BrakeCo	Teamworking; team briefings; functional flexibility; Just-in-Time working (JIT)
InjectorCo	Teamworking; team briefings; functional flexibility; continuous improvement; temporary employment contracts; performance related pay
OptoCo	Teamworking abandoned after worker opposition connected to peer assessment; temporary employment contracts
CopyCo	Outsourcing; teamworking; team briefings; quality circles; sub-contract labour, functional flexibility
AlloyCo	Teamworking; team briefings; functional flexibility; JIT
HydraulicCo	Teamworking proposed by union but opposed by management
ComponentCo	Teamworking; team briefings; *kaizen*; functional flexibility; sub-contract labour; profit sharing
PaperCo	Stalled attempt to introduce teamworking. Foremen still remain; Job and skill demarcation persists; profit related pay
PlasticCo	Traditional managerial structure; no teamworking; computerised systems introduced with no effect on work organisation; temporary employment contracts; payment by results
ValveCo	Teamworking; team briefings; functional flexibility; sub-contract labour; outsourcing; share ownership scheme
CarCo	Teamworking; team briefings; functional flexibility; JIT; single status; temporary employment contracts; outsourcing

Restructuring of work

Table 4.2 shows the incidence of new management techniques in the companies researched. The intensification of global competition and corporate restructuring in the manufacturing industry has caused many companies to reorganise their production processes. The South West manufacturing establishments visited were no exception, although divergent practices between (and within) establishments existed (see Table 4.2). The differing experiences are explored below beginning with the situation at the three manufacturing establishments where *kaizen* practice has been introduced. *Kaizen* as a practice rather than a philosophy operates as a mechanism of continuous improvement not dissimilar to the function of quality circles. Small groups of workers are organised to meet regularly to discuss and suggest improvements to resolve workplace production problems.

Kaizen

Testimony from the senior stewards from ComponentCo, RubberCo and InjectorCo revealed some contrasting reactions in regard to the implementation of *kaizen* as a specific practice.[7] At ComponentCo, GMB had all but reconciled itself to the changes in the way in which work was organised, the workforce had been subjected to more flexible working, labour discipline and labour control than most other manufacturing firms visited. The process of replacing traditional operational management practices and culture with new manufacturing techniques began in the early 1990s but a more systematic application of these techniques occurred in the late 1990s following a change in ownership. ComponentCo accelerated the process of change, drawing on a range of Japanese management techniques but with a particular focus on *kaizen* group problem solving. This change of strategy was based on the expectancy, suggested by influential commentators such as Womack *et al.* (1990), that benefits such as increased productivity and improvements in quality would follow. The GMB senior steward was in little doubt that the company used *kaizen* to reduce non-productive time and intensify the pace of production. He believed the company was able to achieve this because many of his members were beguiled by the 'work smarter, not harder' notion:

> Every time you do a *kaizen* the gap widens between the number of people actually doing the job and the amount of work they are supposed to do . . . Management says 'you give us suggestions on what you think should happen on your line'. People say 'we think that press should be round there next to that machine so we haven't got to walk across the room', so they move the press round and they don't need a bloke to walk across the room now, so they say 'he can go' [be made redundant] . . . Yes, and if anybody complains, they say 'it's not our suggestion, people on the line suggested this'.

Despite the senior steward's understanding of the 'dangers' posed by *kaizen* to his members, and the refusal of long-service employees to participate, new employees, under constant pressure from management, took part in *kaizen* activity. This undermined the senior steward's confidence in attempting to organise factory-wide union resistance to *kaizen* but hostility was still apparent as the senior steward revealed:

> What they now do, because the older employees have cottoned on to this, the older employee doesn't necessarily want to participate in the *kaizen*, so they get a new employee and then they say, 'these bloody old employees, they don't want to move forward, they're dinosaurs, they want to stay in the past'. The new employees want to move forward, but once they've been shafted as many times as the older employee, they won't be so keen to participate. This is what we find.

The reaction from the AEEU to *kaizen* practice at RubberCo was more effective, largely based on the fact that the union had secured a degree of involvement from the beginning in keeping with its traditional craft control. Since 1994, the company had employed a procedural type agreement with AEEU to ensure that a broad consensus was reached before any changes in relation to continuous improvement were introduced. This is how the senior steward detailed its operation:

> On our engineering team now, we have a document where we make modifications on the way we work . . . I make sure the changes are okay with the membership and we all go back and sign on the dotted line. We started with issue 1 going back a number of years, and now we're up to issue 9.

The fact that the union was able to sanction changes in work organisation reveals that it had maintained some influence at this plant and was able to restrict to some extent the way in which *kaizen* could be used as a tool of labour exploitation. According to the senior steward, *kaizen* was not applied in a deterministic fashion. Only the most practical and mutually beneficial suggestions received union approval.

Total quality management

Traditions of craft control were absent at the InjectorCo plant. Originally established in 1988, this plant moved to a Greenfield site in 1993. Union recognition was not secured until 1996. A year later, in 1997, a total quality (TQ) strategy was introduced as a process of continuous improvement. Notably, one of the AEEU shop stewards interviewed was an in-house TQ facilitator, which contributed to the emergence of conflicting views of TQ between union representatives. He remarked that 'at least now there's a formal structure by which people can suggest improvement ideas, that will be actioned one way or another'. The deputy convenor, however, had a different perception:

> Now they want you to make too many suggestions. Whether they want you to make two suggestions a day or week, I'm not sure. They can actually downgrade you on assessment if you haven't given enough ideas. I've had two or three people come to me on recent assessments, so this is something we've got to look into.

All employees had received basic TQ training, including a two-day course. Managers and TQ facilitators had received between four and ten days' tuition. A principal aim of this TQ strategy was to target the elimination of idle time or to be more precise to purge the effort, movement and use of time that did not add value. In contradistinction to those that hold the view that the implementation of TQ and *kaizen* is strongly associated with the intensification of work (Delbridge *et al.* 1992), the shop steward come TQ facilitator at InjectorCo argued that *kaizen* 'made work easier for people because they are having to do less unnecessary tasks.' Given his employee role of mentoring and monitoring TQ projects this conclusion is hardly surprising. Moreover, his office-based employment isolated him somewhat from the day-to-day experiences on the shop-floor. Factory-based shop stewards gave a more cautious assessment, although they acknowledged that in some cases implementation of TQ projects resulted in better working conditions.

Although *kaizen* embraces a number of methods and aims, after two years of operation the signs were that the workforce at InjectorCo was losing interest. Fewer suggestions were coming through despite the fact that workers' appraisals incorporated involvement with TQ, and team managers were assessed on the number of ideas that their teams generated. In fact this coercive attitude may well have contributed to alienating the workforce from proactively engaging with TQ, as implied by the deputy convenor's comment that the inclusion of TQ on appraisals was 'why we're seeing all the pitfalls from it'.

In fact the AEEU acknowledged that its members were on the whole becoming increasingly disgruntled with *kaizen* practice. The deputy convenor offered this explanation:

> I think it's frustration that people are being marked down on not giving enough ideas. The frustration is why should I come in to work, do my work and think up ideas to give the management when there's no reward. That's the way they're thinking.

However, despite these expressions of feelings of injustice towards *kaizen* no attempt was made to mobilise workers around this issue.

Overall then, unions' response to *kaizen* practice lies along a line of continuum towards passive acceptance, although this should not be seen as simple submission, unproblematic to employers. Employers at RubberCo felt it necessary to make significant concessions to AEEU in that its approval was sought before continuous improvement changes were implemented. At ComponentCo, GMB while recognising the negative outcome *kaizen* could bring, such as work intensification and redundancy, had not capitalised on the resistance shown by some of its members who refused to co-operate with *kaizen*. Lack of leadership was also evident at InjectorCo, which was compounded by the lack of awareness shown by the AEEU stewards. They seemed oblivious to the implications of *kaizen* practices. The resulting increases in labour productivity, often through labour intensification, enabled management to rationalise labour, increase the use of numerical flexibility and weaken trade union organisation.

Teamworking

Teamworking was present in all bar three establishments, PlasticCo, HydraulicCo and OptoCo. At PaperCo, teamworking was in place but, according to the senior GMB steward, was not fully operational. Apart from these exclusions the extent to which the implementation of teamworking could be described as fully autonomous (see Cully *et al.* 1999: 43) varied. Teamworking in most but not all of the establishments functioned to break down traditional demarcations in order to increase flexibility through the promotion of multi-skilling, multi-tasking and to a lesser degree job rotation and empowerment. Old lines of demarcation have been eroded exposing as inadequate the traditional workplace unionism organised along skilled, semi-skilled, white-collar, or blue-collar lines. At CopyCo, AEEU and MSF had taken cognisance of this by reorganising union representation so that each team had a shop steward, as teams had been empowered to handle a whole range of industrial relations issues. This reorganisation of union representation did not occur elsewhere. For instance, at InjectorCo, despite the existence of teamworking since the opening of the plant, union representation was still organised along craft and blue- and white-collar lines and union representation here was less effective.

The erosion of traditional demarcation lines and associated restrictive practices was the principal outcome of teamworking. This was evident at PagerCo, CopyCo, ComponentCo, ValveCo, CarCo, BrakeCo, InjectorCo, and CheeseCo. A few developed examples illustrate this point. At PagerCo, teams were cross-functional with labour flexibility operating between as well as within teams. The reduction of the workforce by 33 per cent in 1998, in response to a fall in profits, triggered an extension of multi-tasking and multi-skilling. According to the senior steward:

> Because of the low numbers of staff, it's a case of it's essential now for people to do other work . . . They [managers] are encouraging more self-development because it used to be one person would do one type of job all the time.

Experimentation with a new form of teamworking was under way at CopyCo. Based on a system employed at its sister plant in Holland all team leaders and managers were in the process of being replaced by a much smaller number of coaches. The idea was to 'empower' teams to manage themselves with a coach-cum-mentor to consult, guide and advise them. The AEEU convenor explained that teams were empowered to 'sort out everything, the day-to-day running of their section, they will run themselves'. However, there was an apparent contradiction in CopyCo's approach. Given the increased use of agency workers (see below), who did not enjoy job security guarantees, commitment to semi-autonomous teamworking may well have been weaker. And the success of management initiatives involving 'empowerment' depends heavily on procuring employee commitment (Wilkinson *et al.*, 1992; Guest 1992). Moreover, given the rationale for using agency labour – the reduction of labour costs – and the temporary nature of the employment contract it was less likely that investment in the training and development of these workers would have been at the same level as that given to permanent staff. These factors were potentially divisive in CopyCo's shift to team empowerment.

At ComponentCo, team leaders were appointed from the factory floor by higher management, rather than democratically elected by the workforce and supervisory line managers had been abolished. The GMB senior shop steward implied that team leaders were selected for their sycophantic qualities to switch loyalties and become the eyes, mouthpiece and defender of management. This is how he put it:

> [They] take ordinary people from the shop-floor and say 'you are now a team leader. You are now on the first rung of the ladder for promotion. But, you must report any wrong doings that are done by your colleagues'. We've actually had instances where union members are instrumental in another union member being disciplined . . . Yes and the managers justifiably say, 'hang on a minute, it's not me, it's one of your members that brought this to my attention'.

Such discipline by peers can be at least as coercive as more traditional ways of supervising the production process.

Conflict within teams was apparent at ValveCo, where teamworking had been operating for five years. Difficulties arose from the switch from individual to team bonus schemes. The upshot was that the maximum amount of bonus that could be earned under the individual performance related scheme was reduced in the new team-based scheme and the minimum increased. This caused friction between team members because those that worked at a faster rate under the old system and earned high bonuses lost out. This is how the senior steward described the situation:

> It caused massive problems in a round about way, problems which we didn't foresee. What you had was a situation, and the worst ones were women funnily enough, where they were earning 200 per cent working as an individual, but then you went into working in a team concept where you would be working at a set pace. The ones that were used to working at 200 per cent couldn't slow down.

Other brief examples capture a wider spectrum of problems associated with new working practices. Teamworking and continuous improvement was incorporated into an agreement at CarCo in 1992, an arrangement that continued after a change of ownership in 1994, as guarantees of job security given in 1992 were renewed. Subsequent disposal of the plant by its German owners raised new doubts on the agreements' future. At BrakeCo, JIT and teamworking had been operational for at least 12 years but the new management could not meet previous allied practices such as employee involvement, team briefing and so forth because its commitment to the future of the plant was again in doubt. This gave rise to rumours that the plant would close. To a limited degree evidence also emerged of an association between downsizing and a subsequent widening of functional flexibility. For instance, since redundancies at InjectorCo functional flexibility has increased although workers who demonstrated a special aptitude for a particular function were less likely to move from one function to another because team leaders 'know they're going to get output'. Similar findings emerged at PaperCo but at AlloyCo, despite significant job losses over many years, the use of multi-skilling has contracted rather than expanded as a result of worker reticence. This is how the AEEU senior steward put it:

> We've got multi-skilling... it was a brilliant idea when it was taken on, but it's never really come to fruition in so far as everybody wanted to do everybody else's job at the start because it was something different, now nobody wants to do somebody else's job, only their own.

Apart from AEEU and MSF at CopyCo, unions in the companies visited that employed teamworking had not adapted their representative structures to account for it. As a result some teams did not have their own union representative able to keep a close and critical eye on its effects. Therefore, where resistance to teamworking was present, grievances apparent or experiences negative then mobilisation of discontent was hindered by the absence of direct representation. Teamworking, as depicted above, had facilitated dramatic alterations in the organisation of work in the plants researched. These included the dissolution of skill demarcations, the replacement of chargehands with team leaders or coaches, the devolution of power over workplace tasks to employees, the replacement of individual with team-based incentive schemes and increases in flexible working practices. To varying degrees these developments around teamworking were unfavourably received by some workers. Therefore, teamworking presented an opportunity to unions to mobilise members around the attack on traditional work methods. However, there is little evidence of a coherent and co-ordinated attempt by AEEU, MSF and GMB to capitalise on the detrimental effects of teamworking by organising and generating activity in order prosecute members' concerns and build union confidence.

Flexibility

Extending the use of numerical flexibility, as well as functional flexibility, through the hiring of agency workers has been a particular mission at CopyCo, in order to maintain their international competitiveness. CopyCo has steadily reduced the number of its core permanent employees replacing them with agency workers, when it deemed necessary, to cope with fluctuations in demand. This has been achieved with the mutual consent of the unions concerned on the proviso that there would be no compulsory redundancies, although the unions showed some resistance to this strategy as agency workers came to outnumber direct employees. At the time of this research they comprised 62 per cent of the total workforce. However, despite this significant increase in the use of numerical flexibility CopyCo was contemplating reducing manufacturing costs further by outsourcing assembly and testing. According to the AEEU convenor, the worry was that given the change of emphasis from mechanical assembly to electronic modular assembly, work would be lost. He explained what could happen in the following words:

We could end up building a module, a processor, like your computer. We could build the processor, then someone else could build the screen and monitor, someone else could build the printer and it could all be assembled within your premises. Whereas today we assemble it all and we test it and then send it out. That is the frightening thing.[8]

Temporary workers were used extensively at PlasticCo, ValveCo, OptoCo and InjectorCo. In the latter instance this practice made it easier for the company to push through and manage the recent round of redundancies. Since the signing of a partnership agreement at CarCo, with its associated job guarantees, the company have outsourced a number of service functions such as road cleaning and taken to hiring temporary workers. As well as using temporary workers ValveCo was also outsourcing work and even though the MSF senior steward was consulted before this happened he was resigned to the belief that 'at the end of the day, you had no power to do anything about it'.

Overall, then, despite the evidence of some worker antipathy or concern towards new management techniques, unions failed to capitalise on this discontent in a structured form by mobilising its membership in forms of collective action. Lack of attention to such opportunities can only lead to the further disintegration of trade unions. Without a strong union organisation the chances of securing safeguards and benefits from work reorganisation are minimal. The picture here of union passivity hides the concerns of union members in respect to new management techniques.

Management–union relations

The characteristics of management–union relations in the fifteen companies varied reflecting past organisational strategy and culture as well as the entrenchment or otherwise of the trade unions in the process of job regulation and control. In most of the AEEU recognised workplaces, for example, union density was high and traditions of job demarcation and joint regulation had been established. However, in both InjectorCo and OptoCo recognition (or partial recognition) was recent and management maintained a hostile attitude to the unions. Differences could nevertheless be discerned on two dimensions – firstly, that of hardening/softening relationships and secondly, the degree of partnership implementation – and it is these differences and possible explanations for the differences which are explored below.

Hardening and softening relationships

Questions were asked during the interviews as to whether or not relationships between union and management at the workplace had improved (softened), deteriorated (hardened) or stayed the same in recent years. Responses were evenly divided, with some stewards reporting more antagonistic relations, some a 'softening' of relations including several reporting moves towards a 'partnership' agenda. At RubberCo a hardening relationship was linked by the AEEU stewards to a cultural change in the company involving a shift from a 'family firm' paternalist orientation to one where management had adopted a 'hard' strategic human resource approach (Storey 1992). As one steward explained:

> I think over the last few years, they've become less caring. If you were to take that as being harder, that's the way I would explain it. It used to be, once upon a time, if you worked at RubberCo, it was a very family oriented thing, you felt you were part of a big family. I don't think that is now in place.

The steward attributed the adoption of this new strategic focus to a shift in financial values within the company whereby shareholders had paramount importance above the needs of the workforce.

A similar hardening approach can be discerned from the GMB stewards at both PaperCo and ComponentCo. At PaperCo, there remained a strong tradition of job demarcation and attempts to introduce teamworking had previously stalled. The change in management attitude was claimed by the stewards to be a direct product of the take-over of the company by a British-based MNC:

> When [the British based MNC] took over, it was what I classed as welcome to the 1990s syndrome. All of a sudden you were going to get things that never happened before, would never have happened before.

Interestingly, this approach involved the British-based MNC bucking the trend to decentralise collective bargaining to divisional or plant level. It seems that rather than draw the association between increased productivity and pay closer the company actually favoured the elimination of local pay bargaining. Whether this was a conscious strategy in order to reduce the power of shop stewards and the rank and file at its individual sites is hard to say.

At ComponentCo, new control and ownership was accompanied with a less consultative management style. In contrast to PaperCo, however, it chose to decentralise pay bargaining, which had a deleterious effect on cross-plant contact between the union. 'Best practice' had not prevailed and combined union approaches to regulating pay and conditions appear to have weakened. One rare contact visit by the ComponentCo steward to a sister plant highlighted the differences. He explained:

> I couldn't believe it – fire exits with motorbikes stored in them. Horrendous it was ... When he [shop steward of the sister plant] came round here he couldn't believe it. He said, 'he just didn't believe the facilities we've got here'. I said, 'we weren't handed them. We bloody fought for them'.

The decentralisation of collective bargaining exposed a potential for re-igniting collective workplace identity. Devolution of collective bargaining to plant level provided an opportunity to develop workplace representation directly accountable to its members. This had yet to materialise but some sectional disputes broke out associated mostly with team-based targets or changes to working arrangements. The 'new collectivism' associated with teamworking and fractured collective bargaining thus had an impact on employees.

At InjectorCo, the shift towards a more hardened adversarial relationship was associated with a hard-fought recognition campaign resulting in the AEEU becoming the sole recognised union. The first ballot for recognition was lost but in the run up to a second ballot two years later the management had taken the opportunity with a move to a Greenfield site to tighten surveillance and control and to impose tighter work regimes. The existing staff association clearly could not cope with these attacks and in the second ballot the AEEU won on the basis of the ability to provide more effective representation.

In these plants, where a hardening relationship had been experienced, management–union relations were clearly adversarial. Whilst all of them had experienced recent changes of ownership the trigger for a more aggressive management approach to unions appeared to be different, suggesting that wider contextual factors than ownership change configure employer-employee relations strategies. Prominent among these wider factors were changes in the organisation of work, the demand for greater flexibility, shifts in organisation culture away from paternalism, and employer response to emergent union organisation. Mergers and acquisitions, however, often provided the catalyst for bringing about these changes and therefore the linkage between changes of ownership and a hardening of management attitudes is more marked than first appears.

Companies exhibiting a softening approach were PagerCo, CheeseCo, BrakeCo, PlasticCo, CarCo, CerealCo, CopyCo and ValveCo. In the case of ValveCo, the MSF reported an attempt by management, after changes in ownership, to introduce an open and consensus-based TQM programme to replace traditional hierarchical authority. The introduction of teams was used to replace foremen and a training programme introduced 'first in service' (FIS) to inject quality consciousness. However, there was a distinct fragility in this new consensus which was exposed as soon as management decided to implement immediate closure of the plant's toolroom. As the steward explained:

> The whole of 'first in service' was all about frankness and openness and all that. But when you had a situation where they shut the toolroom overnight and they'd been negotiating it for the last two years, FIS went out the window.

The other companies all shared the new discourse of partnership to a lesser or greater extent and it is to this second dimension of similarity and difference that we now turn.

Partnership

Of the fifteen companies researched, a total of seven recorded interviews with stewards referred to a partnership agenda. However, in two of the companies,

OptoCo and AlloyCo, partnership agendas and issues had been suggested by the unions and rebuffed or ignored by the management. The only actual written and jointly agreed partnership agreement was in one company – CarCo. In three of the other companies (CerealCo, CheeseCo and BrakeCo) partnership was claimed by the stewards to exist either in non-written form or as part of a new discourse between management and union. The final example, CopyCo, deserves special attention as two distinctly different responses to the partnership question emerged from the two separate sets of stewards interviewed (AEEU and MSF).

Attention here focuses on this range of 'partnership' responses and their contextual triggers. At OptoCo, the AEEU stewards had proposed a partnership approach against a background of attempts by management to increasingly marginalise the union and to exploit the use of temporary and contract labour. The union had not achieved full recognition at the plant but was given time to represent members in disciplinary and grievance hearings. Approximately 10 per cent of the 3,000 strong workforce were members of the AEEU. The union was clearly frustrated by the lack of progress in establishing working relations with management and had used a partnership approach as a strategy to bring management to the negotiating table. However, the rebuff by management clearly demoralised the union in a situation where 'partnership' may have been seen as a short cut to legitimacy by the union at the expense of building up membership by more traditional means. As the steward reported:

> Now we're getting more and more champing at the bit, we want to go forward now, we want our recognition. We've worked long and hard for what we've got and they won't give an inch. They just will not react to us.

At AlloyCo, the AEEU stewards were similarly proactive in attempting to introduce a partnership arrangement driven by the recent history of compulsory redundancies and substantial financial losses. As such it might have been responsive to suggestions for crisis management and partnership approaches as part of a 'survival pact' between management and union (see Knell 1999 for other such examples). The steward explained the strategy:

> We allowed our company to be reduced from 2,500 people and a world leader to 900 people with an infantry line trying to hold it back. What we're saying to you is we want to get involved with you in a partnership. We want to see arbitration instead of industrial action. We want to see flexible working patterns. We want to see lifelong learning and education. We want to see single spine structures. We want to see the ability to utilise the resource we've got within the plant to the best of its ability and to utilise best practice. The things that will make this company successful.

The lack of interest by the UK-based management led the union to suspect that it was acting on 'orders from above' and that one of the employers' strategies may have been to marginalise the unions in preparation for closure.

At CarCo, the original written and agreed partnership agreement was signed after ownership of the company passed from the public sector to a UK-based MNC. The national partnership agreement was narrowly accepted by the joint unions in a ballot and enabled management to tighten and extend the programme of continuous improvement first introduced in 1987 and remove lower-level management and supervisory tiers. Distinct changes in management style had preceded and followed the agreement. As the MSF senior steward explained:

> The old management style was totally confrontational. As soon as you'd got a shop steward's card the local manager was intent on dominating you and deliberately set you up for things . . . I think the idea was that the team leader would replace the shop steward and once they'd done that, they would have gone after the activist I think, no doubt about that. But I don't think the CarCo management really wanted to play that game.

The commitment to a partnership approach by the senior management was undoubtedly sincere and would involve disciplining lower-tier managers who continued to operate in the old ways. The employers' strategy was to seek to raise productivity at the plant by adopting a 'win-win' mutual gains partnership approach whereby new methods of working were traded for job guarantees and a more comprehensive benefits package. A downturn in the companies' fortunes and a corporate take-over triggered the opportunity. However, since the interview new German owners have sold off part of CarCo and the future of the West of England based plant (still currently owned by a German MNC) is uncertain.[9]

At CerealCo, where the AEEU had 98 per cent membership, a partnership 'arrangement' existed whereby some support was given by management to new entrants in terms of encouraging them to join the union. In this case the stewards saw partnership as little more than an attempt by management to develop a better understanding with the union hierarchy and to seek more co-operation. Differing interpretations of partnership were apparent at both PagerCo and BrakeCo, with no real substantive agreement attached to the claimed new or emerging 'partnership' approach. At PagerCo, the AEEU steward argued that he thought partnership 'was developing' whilst at BrakeCo the senior AEEU steward's vision of partnership included co-operation, transparency of decision-making and the harmonisation of working conditions. In practice, this had meant that a newly arrived Managing Director:

> . . . did away with private parking spaces' [and] 'did away with a lot of barriers and his door was always open . . . What he wanted from us, the workers, was our participation as trade unions in a joint venture of making this company profitable so we could keep our jobs.

However, the new German owners of BrakeCo later forced this particular British manager out of the company, following which the new management abandoned any partnership-type approach to industrial relations. Fears were expressed by the steward that corporate plans included the probable closure of the UK factory as work was shifted abroad to other plants owned by the parent German-based MNC.

The examples above illustrate that a wider corporate context predetermines the possibilities for partnership arrangements or agreements. In particular, if a remote corporate headquarters is seeking to run down operations then the prospects for a 'survival pact' approach with the unions are remote. Similarly, if corporate ownership or corporate strategy changes, then any partnership agreement becomes fragile and tenuous.

The divergent case of CopyCo

CopyCo is interesting in relation to the exploration of the 'partnership' experience, especially as its sister plant in the US, with about 4,000 employees, had a partnership agreement with the Union of Needletrades, Industrial, and Textile Employees (UNITE). In this case the union's attraction to partnership had been the commitment of the employer to providing job security. However, subsequently, the company was put under intense pressure to outsource more of its production to lower-cost manufacturers around the world. In short this meant that to sustain the partnership agreement the union would have had to deliver increased productivity, quality and flexibility over and above the levels demanded in the past (Kochan 1999).

In the UK, CopyCo provides an example whereby the lead given by the MSF and AEEU convenors, in keeping with the tradition, style and strategy of their respective unions, differed. The impact of these differences was not so great as to harm the operation of the combined activity of the MSF, AEEU, GMB and APEX on both the joint shop steward committee and the joint negotiating committee. However, if these variances are translated into a diagrammatic line of continuum between moderation and militancy (Kelly 1996) we would observe that the MSF held a relatively more militant perspective than the AEEU.

Contradictory accounts of management–union relationships emerged from the interviews held with the convenors at the plant. One concern of the ('militant') MSF convenor was that of the transfer of the Human Resource function to business councils, in regard to negotiating changes in working conditions, which enabled the company to circumvent convenors and senior stewards and reach agreements with inexperienced junior stewards within the divisional forum. The particular worry was that agreements made in isolation might prove to be detrimental to the interests of the membership as a whole. A second concern was that since the American arm of CopyCo bought out its European partner in 1997 higher levels of organisational decision-making had been increasingly subjected to central control. According to the MSF convenor contact with American decision-makers was difficult:

> You can get to them [decision-makers] if you kick up a stink. The one thing that this company doesn't like is any bad publicity. So it depends on how far

you are prepared to go on how much access you can get. But, the Americans do not like dealing with British trade unions. They totally detest it and if they can avoid it, they will do.

Given the misgivings expressed by the MSF convenor it is unsurprising to find that MSF stewards perceived CopyCo as a non-partnership establishment. Yet AEEU signified the contrary. This was reflected in the following deputy convenor's comment:

> We haven't got a formal Partnership agreement, but we have been referred to at various meetings as 'partners'. I believe we are partners in these ventures even though we haven't got a Partnership agreement.

CopyCo operated four business councils. These were consultative bodies made up of senior managers (including the human resource manager), accountants and senior and junior shop stewards. Non-union staff were denied representation. The aim of the business councils was to find ways of improving aspects of the organisation such as operations, strategy and so forth but their remit forbade encroaching on issues subject to negotiation between management and the unions. According to the AEEU deputy convenor, however, these councils were important sources of knowledge useful for negotiating purposes and developing union policy.

A further sign that AEEU stewards viewed themselves as tied into an informal partnership agreement was their willingness to withhold the release of information flagged up by the company as confidential. This seems to be a clear rejection of membership mobilisation in favour of greater dependence on the employer. The AEEU convenor revealed:

> It's given us the opportunity to divert some major decisions, to find some innovative ways between joining management that we can avoid some major confrontations . . . People come up to you and ask you what their future is and you know you can't say anything.

However, early in 1999 the company announced that it was to switch 500 jobs from the UK factory to a new plant in Ireland. The MSF convenor described the community campaign that took place in an effort to save these jobs: 'We've had marches through the village, mass meetings out there where we've invited all the local media, all the locals.' The European Works Council was involved and the issue was raised in the European Parliament. The MSF membership at CopyCo was balloted, voted in favour of taking industrial action and embarked on a course of non-co-operation. The AEEU was also involved with MSF and GMB in this campaign but did not ballot its membership or embrace any form of industrial action. The end result was that the company pledged $30 million investment and agreed to make no enforced redundancies among permanent staff at the plant. Ostensibly, by offering job security to the 'core' workers the company was edging closer towards a partnership agreement based on mutual gains with the unions, similar to the arrangement it had with UNITE at the company's manufacturing plant in America. However, CopyCo management only responded after workers, and the local community, were mobilised into action. It was demonstrations and the threat of industrial action that brought about an eventual settlement.

This 'partnership' example is a reminder that relying on 'partnership' at the expense of 'organising unionism' can be disarming. The fact that the MSF distanced itself from partnership and the AEEU embraced it resulted in a sort of an arranged marriage, of organising and partnership, which kept in place the capacity to mobilise workers to ensure agreements, particularly in relation to job security, were kept. However, events following our field research demonstrate the highly tenuous nature of 'partnerships' in an environment where large corporations are locked in combat for global dominance. A feature of this combat is that in their struggle to sustain global dominance (often through mergers and acquisitions and becoming leaner and meaner) large corporations can wreak economic and social misery on workers and their communities. Partnership arrangements with trade unions surely take second place as corporations argue that to survive, accommodation to global competitive forces is necessary. The announcement on 2 October 2001 that the company was to shed 1,350 jobs at its UK plant in addition to the 330 people already facing redundancy was part of a world-wide restructuring of its business to reverse its decline in profits by becoming more competitive.

Conclusion

The manufacturing establishments surveyed exhibited an exceptionally high degree of corporate change with fourteen engaging in recent partnership, acquisition, merger or disposal activity. Half of the establishments subject to corporate ownership change also experienced significant downsizing, confirming other evidence that corporate restructuring often involved job loss. Associated with corporate restructuring were the significant introduction of new methods and ways of organising work, such as continuous improvement (*kaizen*) and teamworking. One particularly striking aspect of this has been the implicit and explicit erosion of job demarcation lines and a shift away from 'traditional' working practices. Such changes have, as would be expected, posed enormous challenges for trade union organisation at workplace level. However, there is only sporadic evidence in the survey that the unions have managed to retain some control and authority. For example, in one case (CopyCo) one union (MSF) had re-organised itself at the workplace to encourage the election of union representatives within each team. At PaperCo, the GMB had successfully tempered the introduction of teamworking by retaining existing job demarcation patterns. This contrasts with other examples (e.g ComponentCo) where management had replaced line managers with appointed team leaders from the factory floor, selected, according to the GMB, on the basis of the personality trait of 'servility'. With continuous improvement programmes our evidence shows that in some cases (e.g. AEEU at RubberCo) the union has negotiated the schemes and has become actively involved in their implementation whilst attempting to 'soften' their impact on workload. In other cases (e.g. ComponentCo), no union strategy had evolved to either oppose or co-operate and consequently schemes have been introduced which have been clearly detrimental in terms of work intensification. Our evidence on union response to changing work organisation has therefore been mixed, with examples of emergent pro-active, but mainly re-active or passive union strategies.

An obvious consequence of intense corporate change has been instability in corporate culture and management employee relations' strategy. Evidence of 'remote control' appeared in a number of establishments, particularly those with US ownership, which is in line with the findings of Child *et al.* (2000). Responses were evenly divided as to whether management had 'hardened' or 'softened' its attitudes and relationship towards unions in the workplace. In those workplaces where a 'hardening' relationship was exposed, a variety of contextual factors had acted to trigger the change, suggesting a complex interpretation involving issues other than corporate change. However, clearly acquisitions or mergers acted as a stimulant for change making it difficult to separate out other issues impacting on organisational, managerial and cultural adjustments. In the 'softening' work-places there was some evidence of emerging 'partnership' discourse, although a written partnership agreement was found in only one establishment (CarCo). What is interesting is that the driving force for partnership agendas came from different sources. In two cases (OptoCo and AlloyCo) the issue had been raised by the union and rebuffed by management. In three other companies it was a joint initiative whereas in the divergent case of CopyCo management had accommodated the issue with one union (AEEU) whilst at the same time the other union (MSF) had distanced itself. In these latter cases there emerged a tendency for the union side to become involved in partnership discourse either as an extension of a moderate (as opposed to militant) approach or alternatively, as a perceived need to establish a 'survival pact' framework to negotiations when the individual plant was faced with potential closure or a financial 'crisis' (either real or perceived).

Finally, the issue of job insecurity was also widespread and in two cases (CopyCo and BrakeCo) had led to union-led public campaigns to save the plant. However, the nature of these campaigns was different. In the former case a 'community unionism' approach had emerged with the unions going outside the plant and union structure for help, whereas in the latter case a more 'con-stitutional' approach was used by concentrated lobby support from the local MP and MEP and through the parent companies' EWC. In both these cases the more threatening aspects to organised labour of 'globalisation' were apparent, with, in these instances at least, the 'community union' approach proving more successful as a strategy to preserve jobs.[10]

Our research suggests a high degree of corporate change and a variegated union response to the effects of that change in UK manufacturing. There is undoubted resilience of union organisation from which the possibilities of union resistance remain. Yet, the general picture is of union passivity. Despite the positive sounding rhetoric of 'partnership' preliminary evidence from the South West manufacturing sector does not suggest this as an attractive way forward for unions but to do nothing is not an option. The examples of CopyCo and PaperCo are small but important signs that actively organising and mobilising shop-floor workers can produce results but it can form only part of a much bigger struggle against the effects of global capitalism.

5   The insurance industry – back to basics

Introduction

If trade unions in Britain and elsewhere are to revive under New Unionism then a key area for attention must be the private service sectors. Trade union density has been historically weaker in these sectors, yet in terms of employment its weight within the economy has been growing. In addition it is a prime area for new information technology and is staffed by younger workers and females to a greater extent than manufacturing. The purpose of this chapter is to explore the experience of one union, the MSF, in its attempt to unionise within the insurance segment of the financial services sector.

The pattern of industrial relations practices and issues in the finance sector in general is extremely diverse, reflecting in part major changes in the regulation of the industry and new competitive pressures, as well as the nature of the sector in terms of products and services. The finance sector is defined in broad terms as SIC92 Groups 65–67 and embraces banks, building societies and insurance companies as well as some business services attached to financial intermediation. More specifically SIC92 groups 65 and 66 refer to banking, finance and insurance accounting for 1.065 million employee jobs in March 2001, representing 4.2 per cent of the UK workforce. This represents a slight fall from 1990, when jobs in the sector peaked at 1.1 million. Currently there are 231,000 jobs in the insurance and pensions sub-sector (*Labour Market Trends*, July 2001). In the past, divisions between the three sub-sectors (banking, insurance and finance) were fairly well established but since the 1980s boundaries within the sector have become blurred as they have undergone the 'financial services revolution' (Moran 1991). The finance sector in general has since been prone to mergers, acquisitions and take-overs alongside deregulation of related financial markets and the de-mutualisation of key players within the sector. This process has been a response to increased competition, as organisations seek to develop economies of scale and secure and increase market share (Hasluck 1999). In insurance this has meant an increase in product competition from banks and other finance providers as well as from new entrant organisations as diverse as Virgin and Tesco. The restructuring and rationalisation of the industry has also meant potential job loss as cost efficiency or capital concentration has taken its toll. New forms of delivery emerged following the telephone-based creation of Direct Line in the 1980s. Internet and digital television access is now further increasing the range of consumer and producer options (Tailby 2001). Because of the nature of the product, the provision of insurance services tends to be more home-based and less globalised than banking. The industry remains predominantly UK owned (with increasing numbers of exceptions) and is currently the fourth largest in the world after the US, Japan and Germany (Woodward *et al.* 2000).

The finance sector in the South West of England

The finance sector has seen a disproportionate growth in the South West when compared to other UK regions. Growth has been concentrated in the Bath-Bristol-Gloucester triangle. The sector now has a relatively high proportion of employees in the sector compared to other UK regions, with Bristol now the largest employer in the sector of all UK cities outside London. A high proportion of growth in employment (40 per cent in the 1970s, for example) was in insurance (rather than banking) and this was particularly concentrated in Bristol. The first jobs were essentially clerical based and labour intensive, but this was later followed by the relocation of head offices. The 1970s was an important decade of growth and relocation as a result of a combination of industry expansion plus the Bristol area's increase in attraction after completion of the M4, M5, M32 and upgrading of the rail link. Land prices were cheaper than the London area and Bristol was perceived as a nice place to live, and not too far from London, by affected staff (Boddy 1986). Between 1972 and 1983 four UK companies – Phoenix, Sun Life, Clerical Medical and General, and London Life all relocated their head offices to the Bristol area, and the NatWest bank established its insurance subsidiary. In the same period Northern Star also relocated its head office from Croydon to Gloucester.

The employment growth of the 1970s and 1980s continued into the 1990s. Even during recessionary periods for the sector the region went against the national trend and expanded employment. In particular Lloyds Bank chose to relocate its retail headquarters from London to harbourside Bristol in 1987, and Eagle Star relocated to Cheltenham in 1991. Endsleigh Insurance opened in Cheltenham in the summer of 1998. The importance of the Bristol-Bath-Gloucester triangle for the sector is reinforced when placed against a comparable regional centre such as Cardiff. Bristol-Bath now has 29 insurance company head offices, seven banks and seven finance companies against Cardiff's seven insurance companies, two banks, and six finance companies (Gripaios 2000). The region is home to, among others, Stroud and Swindon Building Society and the Chelsea Building Society headquarters at Cheltenham; the Cheltenham and Gloucester (now part of LloydTSB Bank); Ecclesiastical Insurance in Cheltenham; a large Friends Provident centre in Salisbury; London and Manchester Life Assurance in Exeter; Bristol and West Building Society (owned since 1997 by the Bank of Ireland) and the UK head office of the German-owned DAS Legal in Bristol. As a spin-off from the insurance presence, Bristol has also developed a reputation for specialist underwriting and brokering. Approximately 250,000 people now work in the region in the finance sector, representing 17 per cent of the total workforce.

Industrial relations traditions and practice

In terms of staff representation the insurance industry exhibits the complete range of relationships from non-union (or indeed anti-union), through recognition of dependent staff association, independent staff association, to independent trade union. The degree of 'unionateness' of the independent unions has been relatively low, with a low dispute level and non-affiliation to the TUC and Labour Party in evidence. This has been explained in the past, with reference to banking, as a reflection of the conservative organisational culture of the industry setting banks apart from the 'more vulgar occupations of industry and commerce' (Nevin and Davis 1979). Banking was considered to be a secure job with prospects if not a 'job for life'. The physical closeness of the manager to staff in everyday branch life, together with the relatively good pay and conditions tended to preclude the development of collectivism amongst the staff and a 'them and us' approach to the management-worker relationship. However, as other commentators have pointed out, banks were more accurately characterised by a division of staff into career and non-career grades with women being mostly left behind in the more routine jobs (Egan 1982; O'Reilly 1992; Storey *et al.* 1997).

The development of staff associations in the general finance sector was particularly rapid in the 1970s and mirrored the emergence of white-collar unionism in the wider economy. The closed nature of the sector and its distinct culture, together with some hostility to the perceived militancy of the TUC, helped ensure that independent TUC affiliates were kept out. In the building societies this process was undoubtedly employer-driven with the BSA (Building Societies Association) acting to co-ordinate employee relations strategies to resist independent unionism. Within the banks the National Union of Bank Employees – NUBE (forerunner of BIFU, the Banking, Insurance and Finance Union) conducted a series of campaigns from the 1940s onwards to challenge the hold of the staff associations. Recognition was gained in Barclays in 1941, TSB in 1947, the Royal Bank of Scotland in 1960, and National Westminster in 1969. In insurance a more hybrid pattern emerged, with interest expressed by the National Union of Insurance Workers (NUIW) and ASTMS as well as NUBE/BIFU.

A new issue in the industry emanating from EU (European Union) Directives concerns worker representative forums in relation to redundancy consultation and the establishment in appropriate cases of European Works Councils. Worker representative consultative forums need to be established by employers where no existing trade union consultative machinery exists and so this is particularly significant in those companies where unions or staff associations are absent. Many companies in the industry can now be categorised as European-based multinationals (with a total workforce of at least 1,000 and more than 100 employees in each of two or more offices in EU countries and so at some level, senior union or worker representatives need to be elected.

Industrial relations in the sector in the late 1990s

Despite the difficulties presented by employer substitution strategies, union density in the finance sector as a whole has been relatively high. Total union density reached 49 per cent in the late 1980s and rose to a peak of 54 per cent in 1994 before falling back to 48 per cent in the late 1990s (Waddington, 2001). This comparatively high density means that a critical mass of union activists were often present to form a springboard opportunity for further union growth by deepening membership profiles in individual organisations. MSF has a long presence within the sector having represented staff in the insurance industry since the beginning of the century. The first Guild of Insurance Officials (GIO) became first the Union of Insurance Staffs (UIS) and then part of ASTMS in 1970. MSF currently has approximately 80,000 members in the industry in both the UK and Ireland across a large range of insurance companies. The occupations represented are quite diverse including sales staff, surveyors, managers, insurance specialists, actuaries, accountants, lawyers, computer specialists and clerical and administrative staffs. In most companies where MSF is recognised it is the single union.

The upheaval experienced by the wider finance sector in recent years has been accompanied by shifting alliances and mergers between the numerous unions and staff associations. The TUC co-ordinates a Confederation of Insurance Trades Unions (CITU) and there was in addition in the 1990s a partnership in the Financial Services Union (FSU) embracing MSF, the National Union of Insurance Workers (NUIW), BIFU, UNiFI (the union for Barclays staff), Eagle Star Staff Union, Nationwide Group Staff Union, Scottish Equitable Staff Association and AXIS (AXA Sun Life Staff). The above unions and staff associations also belonged to the broader based Alliance for Finance (AFF) which had 24 affiliates. In May 1999 this alliance was consolidated into a new merged union (UNIFI) embracing BIFU, The NatWest Staff Association and UNiFI. MSF at the time of research had a working relationship with the NUIW whereby the NUIW remains a completely independent union sharing full time officers with the MSF. Sixty per cent of the NUIW subscriptions were paid to the MSF under this arrangement. The main employers' bodies include the Association of British Insurers (ABI) which is the main trade association for the insurance industry, and the Building Societies Association (BSA).

Questions for research and research base

The nature and pace of changes within the insurance industry and wider finance sector raise a number of questions for industrial relations transformation and trade union response. First, the rapid introduction of new technology is likely to have been associated with changes in the organisation of work which would have proved a test for the preservation of existing skills and job descriptions. Management control over the labour process was likely to be re-inforced with the introduction of 'new' jobs at the expense of 'old jobs' and the associated drive for cost efficiency. Second, the deregulation and de-mutualisation of the industry has clearly been associated with a shift from a conservative and sometimes paternalistic management style to a more entrepreneurially based approach where value added per worker has become the *Leitmotif.* Both these tendencies are prime inducers of work intensification either through material means in the form of increased work targets and through ideological means in terms of attitudinal restructuring and the 'need' to accept the new performance-based culture. As such, exceptional challenges to union workplace organisation are raised, which, when set against a background of low-level militancy and union combativity in the industry, pose severe tests for the future of trade union collective approaches. These questions frame the core of the research inquiry.

The research base

Interviews were conducted with MSF workplace representatives in seven different companies in the region. In addition 26 workplace representatives from the seven companies also returned a completed survey questionnaire. Short profiles of the individual workplaces, together with details of the MSF presence, are given in Table 5.1.

Management practices and organisation of work

Changes in work organisation began to occur in the 1980s relating to the impact and diffusion of new technology and the deregulation of financial markets. New computer advances were an additional reason for the relocation of many functions outside London as information could be stored on mainframe computers and accessed from remote terminals. The establishment of specialised centres handling routine computer linked tasks went hand in hand with a restructuring of the sector and a move to distance staff from face-to-face customer contact. These processes had a direct impact on industrial relations as they created new types of jobs in which contact between manager and staff became more psychologically and physically distant. In the insurance industry a similar pattern emerged as call centres were established in the wake of the creation of Direct Line in 1985. More 'individualised' jobs were also created as the direct sales force in insurance companies was often replaced with 'independent' financial advisers with direct computer access to intelligent software and databanks. It would be fair to say that a polarisation of skills between routinised jobs and 'information rich' advisory work can be discerned throughout the sector (e.g. Hasluck 1999). The changing nature of work organisation enables some reassessment of the sector as a focus of trade union activity. In effect, unions within the sector (especially banking) were forced either to respond in a more traditionally collective fashion and become more 'unionate' or to collaborate with the employer in the hope of retaining a foothold in the sector. Morris *et al.* (2001) argue that unions generally chose the former path under new leaderships incorporating policy changes and new values. The general experience of restructuring and routinisation of many jobs has been argued by Gall (1993, 1999), for example, to be a prime cause of the

Table 5.1 MSF membership in the South West insurance industry (1999–2000).

Company	Union membership	Potential membership and current density (%)	No. of MSF reps. and member-rep. ratios	Membership trends	Comments
Das Legal	130 (Bristol Office)	195 (67%)	4 (1:33)	Static. Past threat to derecognise union	UK head office of a German company Motor insurance and legal expenses claims
Friends Provident	100–150 (Salisbury)	600–800 (18%)		Static	Company founded by Quakers in 1832. Friends Provident nationally has its own MSF section
London and Manchester	250 (Exeter)	900 (28%)	7 (1:35)	Static	Partnership agreement exists Company taken over in 1998 by Friends Provident
CompanyA (name withheld for confidentiality reasons)	285 (Bristol offices)	1600 (16%)	12 (Bristol) (1:21)	Membership increased due to merger and 'cold' recruitment campaigns	Result of a 1996 merger and associated 5,000 job cuts
Prudential	51 (Bristol office)	120 (43%)	3 (1:17)	22 in February 1997	Small Bristol office. Recovering from a pensions mis-selling case with large compensation claims
Northern Star	30 (two offices in Gloucester)	250 (12%)	4 (1:7.5)	Grown from zero in nine months Membership began from external 'cold' recruitment	Office relocated from Croydon Company now Italian owned. MSF is unrecognised
Norwich Union	68 (one office in Bristol)	100 (68%)	2 (1:34)	Increase from 35 one year before recruitment campaign achieved 80	Company founded in 1792 and now one of the largest institutional investors in the UK. Longer tradition of union membership and representation

increase in militancy and unionateness of the banking-based unions throughout this period. It needs to be tested whether the same processes drive up levels of 'unionateness' in insurance.

The process of change also had gender implications, reinforcing the inferior position of women in the sector who tend to be concentrated in data entry and call centre operations as opposed to men who tend to be in managerial or specialist adviser posts (Gallie 1991; Waddington 2001). The shift towards direct selling over the telephone has also raised the demand for aurally aesthetic 'skills' which are predominantly 'supplied' by women (Nickson *et al.* 2001). In 1997, women's share of employment in the insurance industry was 47 per cent. In contrast to the banking industry only 14 per cent of women in insurance worked part time (cf. 60 per cent in banking), and this was a decline from 1993 when 16.4 per cent worked part time (Association of British Insurers, Insurance Statistics Yearbook 1987–97). However, only 1.6 per cent of men in insurance worked part time in 1997, reflecting a different occupational working time pattern.

Deregulation and de-mutualisation, according to Cressey and Scott (1992) was also a prime reason for the emergence of a new management 'model' in the sector whereby the old model based on paternalism, conservatism and bureaucracy gave way to a new model of sales and performance orientation and technocracy. This signified a new approach to the desired organisation culture and hence a new approach to employee relations. Although relatively ripe for the introduction of individualised HRM techniques the application of many HRM methods has had mixed fortunes within the sector (again with special reference to banking). This is because they have been introduced against the background of staff reductions and low trust of management motives by many staff (Storey *et al.* 1997). Job reductions have been a dominant feature since the 1980s. Computerisation has led in many instances to the centralisation of many functions involving the move of jobs to Bristol and the South West (Boddy *et al.* 1986). De-layering has been accompanied by the break up of the whole business into separately accountable business divisions. Where rationalisation has taken place it has more often than not been a cost cutting exercise whereby existing workloads are redistributed to fewer staff. In some instances redundant employees have been re-recruited on temporary contracts. The pace of mergers and acquisitions must be placed in an international context whereby deregulation and de-mutualisation has opened up opportunities for increased international movement of capital and raising of funds beyond domestic markets. New global business divisions are now commonplace in the sector as well as new patterns of ownership reaching outside the UK. Eagle Star (Cheltenham), for example, is now owned by a Zurich-based company having been transferred from British American Tobacco (BAT).

New substantive issues

These combined forces for change have created new employee relations tensions as job security has been replaced by fears of job loss and new skills have often been

Table 5.2   Incidence of new pay management reported by MSF representatives in selected sectors, $n = 196$.

MSF sector	Job evaluation (%)	PRP/merit pay (%)
Insurance	81	89
Aerospace	46	52
Manufacturing	80	50
NHS Trusts	30	11
NHS health visitors	43	0
Universities	67	13

necessary for personal survival. Performance orientation has meant that performance related and/or competency pay has been introduced alongside, or instead of, seniority-based incremental pay that was long associated with a more stable and rule-bound career environment. Performance appraisal schemes have also become widespread in an attempt to link performance and targets to pay. Job evaluation is also common within the sector (see Table 5.2) as a response to the introduction of new technological skills and as a result of rationalisation of pay and grading structures following mergers and acquisitions. The spate of mergers and acquisitions also creates problems for continuity in pension arrangements with in some cases a multitude of schemes running in any one company (for example in the merged *CompanyA* there are thirteen different pension schemes covering all employees).[1] Since the advent of more intense commercialisation some concern has also been expressed at the lack of formal training initiatives from the employers. For example, the insurance industry has failed so far to implement the national vocational qualifications (NVQ) framework, with only 250 NVQs being awarded in 1998.[2] Similarly, in the past employers usually took responsibility for employees' training and education for the Chartered Institute of Insurers examinations but increasingly this is being left to individual employees to arrange and finance in their own time.

Union response

Having described the various contextual influences, the union responses to change are now recorded. These are grouped in three areas. First, are responses to organisational restructuring, second are responses to work intensification, and third are responses to the new entrepreneurialism.

Organisational restructuring

The whole rationalisation process, together with the spate of mergers and acquisitions appears to have been fraught with problems. In particular it would appear that the cultural shifts in the industry – from stable bureaucracy to entrepreneurialism – have led to the now somewhat familiar problems of culture clash between 'old' and 'new' within organisation hierarchies that is particularly severe in cases of merger and acquisition. This has had some consequences for union organisation and strategy as activists have spoken both of obvious changes in management strategy when one chief executive replaces another and of different (and sometimes contradictory) strategies of different divisions in the same company. Changes in organisational design and culture have also involved a rethinking of relationships between head office authority and that of divisional or line management. The changes have not been uniform across the industry. In some cases authority has been centralised at head office for many functions whilst in other cases a clear process of decentralisation of decision-making can be traced. At Friends Provident, for example, decentralisation has occurred and the role of personnel appears to have been downgraded and reduced to a servicing-only role from the centre. Personnel remain the 'guardians' of correct procedure but in reality the power given to divisional or line managers allows them to stretch policy to its limit, even to the extent of running the risk of losing employment tribunal cases if it means that staff can continue to be 'successfully' dismissed for operational reasons (authors' interview notes). The divisionalisation of businesses has also allowed scope for inconsistencies in the treatment of unions by management. Such a process of division and competition can be part of an overall corporate employee relations strategy or it may simply be either the case that divisional or local managers have had no previous experience of dealing with unions or there is a lack of effective trade union presence. Whichever is the case there is a need for clear monitoring of differences by centralised MSF organisation within each company.

In contrast, at Das Legal, decision-making within the organisation is very centralised. Each regional office manager in offices in the UK must report to the senior manager or the 'Human and Systems' manager at the Bristol head office who then makes key employee relations decisions. This degree of centralisation may be a cultural product of the parent ownership (German) of the company or it may be a reflection of the (relatively) small scale of operation that Das Legal has within the UK. However, it does mean that employee relations strategies within the company can be traced to the senior management and consequently some regularity and transparency can be established. After an earlier threat to derecognise the union, relationships between the union and management have stabilised, with regular quarterly meetings attended intermittently (so far once a year) with the management. However, the line between consultation and negotiation remains blurred. As one representative reported:

> I think they consult us when they think they have to. Sometimes we don't hear anything for months on end, even when things have happened, Other times they tell us things that aren't really of much concern to us. We were in dire straits a couple of years ago, but it has improved in leaps and bounds since then. It's just that we're secondary to the business. They make their business decision, decide what impact that has, whether it will impact on Union members or non-Union members. If it's Union members, they will usually consult, but it's a *fait accompli*.

London and Manchester has experienced considerable decentralisation which has particularly affected the personnel function. Formerly the HR division was well staffed and covered a variety of functions (including the employment of a specialist industrial relations officer) but since reorganisation has been cut back and the role of personnel has become one of client HR consultant with vastly reduced staffing. Combined with major changes to terms and conditions (the move to 'market related pay' and annualised hours) this has meant the trade union has felt disadvantaged in terms of negotiating rights and access to management decision-making structures:

> Recruitment was always done through Personnel. They are HR. They used to do all the recruitment. Now they are very much consultants. Managers have to go through structures if they want to replace someone, there is a process that they have to go through. But it is up to them, they have to write the job description, they have to go through the job matching exercise with HR, but every job has to be approved by our Chief Executive, if they even want to employ a contractor, it has to be approved by the Chief Executive

The shift towards a consultant-client HR model has been combined with the devolvement of a limited degree of decision-making powers to line managers for a range of personnel-based functions. To react to this new organisational structure the union is faced not only with the prospect of becoming remote from key decision-makers at the top (on strategic issues) but also with the need to be more proactive with line managers at the bottom of the management hierarchy. The old certainties of knowing who and at what level negotiations can take place have been removed and the union must adapt to maintain its voice.

Such partial decentralisation of management functions can be an opportunity for unions implying a shift towards a 'participative unionism', dependent more on membership level activism and providing a stimulus to branch organisation (Fairbrother 1996). Such a shift would, of course, dovetail into the philosophy and practicalities of a successfully operating 'Organising Works' model of trade unionism. The tailoring of MSF organisation of branches to workplaces would, however, aid the process of participation, an experience confirmed by the representative interviewed at Prudential:

> I think [when membership improved] it was when we got our own branch in January. It does make you feel more positive about things. We used to be assigned to Cardiff. I'd never been to a branch meeting over there in about eight years and they do a completely different job to us now . . . When I went to last year's conference, I put forward a motion that we should have our own branch and we had the people willing to take on the official roles, so we did it.

To summarise, the disorienting process of organisational restructuring therefore poses many threats to trade union organisation as management authority either disperses or centralises within new structures. The process of dispersion creates inconsistencies in employee relations strategies with the consequent need for the union to pursue best practice agreements at both formal and informal levels. This is a hard task and there is some limited evidence from only one of the case studies of this being achieved in practice. Centralising tendencies create the risk of accelerating remoteness and reducing transparency of management decisions. This problem can be observed in other industries and organisations subject to constant restructuring. The union response is inevitably a frustrated one, dependent for any success on a double strategy of engagement with both top management and local line managers.

Work intensification

The case study interviews provide evidence that the shift towards computerised information and word processing has intensified work in relation to such areas as claims and insurance applications. Paper applications for claims and premiums are usually scanned in post rooms and distributed electronically to workers staffed at monitor screens. Rather than the paper forms being dealt with directly by the staff concerned, work speeds, inputs and outputs can thus be governed centrally and continually monitored. In addition the scope for the individual worker to create 'down-time' between work batches is reduced, as the next batch of work can appear on screen immediately the last one is completed. Porosity is reduced and work is intensified as a result.

At Friends Provident the evidence is starkly expressed:

> Instead of you picking and choosing which bit of work you want to do, when you finish the piece of work and you press a button to say I have finished this piece of work, it just brings up the next bit. There's no question of you having a break . . . and we have all sorts of health and safety arguments about natural breaks and people not taking their breaks.

In addition to the routinisation brought about by computerisation there is added pressure from the system whereby claims work is caseload based and the number of cases per worker is given a set time-based ratio. The need to complete so many cases per day (a form of measured day work) creates problems for union organisation as simply touring offices talking to people with a view to recruitment becomes a problem when the union representatives concerned are under such constant pressure as individual workers. This pressure places limits on the ability of some MSF representatives to find time to satisfactorily complete or start any serious union work. One representative at Das Legal, for example, who was himself a 'claims' worker, clearly suffered if he was away from his desk on union work as this led both to pressure from the line manager and to pressure to clear up the backlog of claims work on his return. Facility time, however generous, in these instances is not enough unless it is also accompanied with a corresponding reduction in assessed work loads.

> What needs to happen really is if we are going to have the time off we are entitled to, we need to see a reduction in the amount of workload we are expected to do during that week. The only time when it's easier to get time off is when it's for a pay negotiation because they have a vested interest in that! Then they are quite happy to send me off for the day!

Again at Friends Provident, the representative reported:

> ... the work is now scanned into a machine, everything's much more regulated, everything's much more controlled and the teamleaders who don't actually know how to do the job are there now just to monitor whether the staff are doing enough cases in a day. There's much more pressure on these people which has several effects. It means that their job is their life in the sense that that's the only thing they can really concentrate on. The second thing is it makes them very difficult to recruit and get active, if any of them really wanted to, and I don't think we've got any reps who actually do this particular job, because they simply wouldn't be able to do it.

In one case, at Norwich Union, the office was in the process of undergoing preparation for the introduction of new computer systems and the work was in the process of being reorganised in advance. Interestingly, these new procedures will mark a shift away from team-working to a Taylorised system of division of tasks and labour. The pressure of routinisation and measured day work does raise an important question for union organisation. As already discussed it has been argued routinisation is an explanation for increased membership and 'union-ateness' within the banking industry. It is also the case that in other clerical related areas, such as the Civil Service and local government, the impact of clerical work measurement has for a long period provided an organising focus for such unions as the CPSA (Civil and Public Services Association, now PCS, the Public and Commercial Services Union) and NALGO (now UNISON). However, both these examples have been set in a context of higher union densities and more localised union organisational structures. Nevertheless, the potential for union organisation is clear. Despite this potential MSF in these insurance case studies does not appear to have mounted a challenge to the new workload models implied in the new technology-based work regimes. This is a major area of weakness in trade union organisation, demonstrating a lack of engagement in the process of work regulation and control.

Union membership in the industry also embraces the more specialised worker for whom knowledge is at a premium and for which different criteria of organising potential apply. The ability of MSF to organise such staff is also of interest, given contemporary interest in such workers outlined in Chapter 1. In reality the range of experience in organising IT and computer specialists varies considerably across the survey. At Das Legal membership amongst the computer specialists is zero, with comments from the representatives that the computer specialists 'do not feel that MSF is specialist enough to protect them'. There was also a clear feeling of job security in the section related primarily to the imminent (at the time) millennium debugging and high premium rates of pay for the work. In contrast, at London and Manchester, membership in the IT section is close to 100 per cent but problems exist in other specialist areas such as customer services (mainly underwriters). The likelihood of routinisation is much less in these specialist areas of work, even though these areas have been subject to rationalisation pressures in recent years which has created the feeling of increased work pressure. In other offices any occupational split in membership density is dwarfed by sectional divisions that reflect different traditions of trade union membership. For example at Norwich Union there is a division between those working in General Insurance, where membership is high, and those in Life, where membership is low.

In summary no clear pattern of 'knowledge worker' union organisation emerges across the study. It can only be commented that the existence of high union density levels in some areas would suggest future possibilities for membership in other, less unionised areas. From comments obtained it is possible to suggest that many specialist workers see their personal destinies dependent on trends within national organisational labour markets. As such they have less affinity with a need to express their voice within the organisational context over collective issues, at least not alongside less specialised workers. The task of the union here is to place itself not only as a defender of interests against the individual employer, but also to act as representative of the individual's professional interest in the wider economy.

New entrepreneurialism, individualism and collectivism

Part of the process of focusing insurance organisations on the customer in a more competitive environment has been a concerted attempt to relate individual performance to pay. As already discussed in the introductory chapter this trend is not confined to insurance, but our quantitative data would suggest that the process is more advanced in the industry than in the research comparators. As Table 5.2 shows, the incidence of both job evaluation (often a precursor to new methods of pay determination) and performance related and merit pay has been more prominent in the sector than in other areas where MSF representatives were surveyed.

The higher incidence of new pay determination in insurance can be explained not only by the more pronounced shift to entrepreneurialist values but also by the relative weakness of collective bargaining and joint pay regulation as an embedded alternative in the sector. The net result has been a discernible trend towards a range of types of performance related pay and a dilution of the importance of centrally negotiated pay.

In Prudential this process has been further obscured by the divisionalisation of pay which has further weakened the trade union position and opened the door for separate treatment of sections of staff. One representative stated:

> Each different business area within the Prudential Corporation has a different attitude towards the union. Unfortunately ours has a very poor

attitude towards the union. It's been a case of 'This is what we are offering and it's not negotiable and, by the way, we'll do a joint statement about it.'

In Norwich Union pay banded gradings were replaced by individual performance related pay in 1993–94. Individual merit pay is awarded by the regional manager over and above any nationally agreed and negotiated basic increase. In addition there are possibilities for a team bonus payable in February of each year which is company profit related. At London and Manchester this process of dilution has gone further with a secondary shift away from individual performance pay to a system of market related pay. This process of individualisation has allowed management to engineer a situation where pay rates are 'hidden' from staff and where MSF would find it extremely difficult to re-establish a strong negotiating position. As a representative said:

> Market related pay is very much a job matching exercise. It starts with a job description, it's matched in the market. Then the company places itself into the market so they have a range of salaries for the job. They do try and pitch themselves as a medium-sized company so they try and pitch themselves as a medium employer, but they don't publish the salary ranges. There's no grades anymore, so instead of having a grade 1–15, we don't have any grades.

In other companies new systems of payment have retained more scope for union involvement. Das Legal, for example, has retained a banded pay scale but with the bands set according to skills by Hay Management. The total 'pot' of money is negotiated at a national level together with yearly overall increases. Individualisation is a core component of the system with every employee receiving information of their allocation within scales via a letter. The fact that bandings are related to skills by job evaluation allows scope for the union to take on individual grievances for individuals and so the union can be shown to have some effect.

Recent employer discontent with the outcomes of individual performance related pay has led some employers to look to competency-based pay as an alternative. At *CompanyA* competency pay has been introduced linked to job evaluation in the aftermath of the merger. Job evaluation itself has been criticised in the past by unions both because of its pseudo-scientific nature whereby existing inequities are legitimised by the skill definitions and its potential discriminatory bias. One of the criticisms of performance-related pay has also been that of lack of transparency in establishing and implementing targets. Competency pay is even less transparent in this respect and places much authority in the line manager to 'judge' competencies on an almost entirely qualitative (and hence subjective) basis.[3] When this is combined with the traditional concerns over job evaluation the potential for employee discontent is considerable. As a *CompanyA* representative reported:

> We're also now looking at job evaluation and linking it to competency-based pay [all jobs being re-evaluated with new descriptions]. The trouble here is

that the jobs people are applying for bear no resemblance to the jobs they're doing. All of the jobs have grown because there aren't the people to do it. You take on more roles, more workloads.

One consequence of the introduction of competency pay is that it creates an opportunity for the union to reopen the issue of training and development linked to the defined 'competencies'. In many instances the developmental aspect of performance-linked appraisal has been ignored and systems have been discredited as a result. The creation of a competency system linked to job evaluation thus poses unions with a decision as to the desirability or otherwise of agreeing to joint management-union efforts to define the competencies and link them to the job evaluation exercise. The dilemma here is that if the union co-operates it may legitimise the outcomes and undercut opportunities for disputing either the criteria applied or the final linkages established with pay. At *CompanyA* the potential dangers of legitimisation appear to have been minimised by MSF representatives avoiding formal involvement but reserving the right to suggest alterations to the scheme and placing demands on the management for improved training. As one representative said:

> Competency-based pay is very much a training issue. We get involved not so much with writing the competencies and the training required but having the final say as to what's included and putting suggestions forward.

The individualisation of pay within the employment relationship poses starkly the potential problem of creeping attitudinal individualism at the expense of collectivism. In some respects, as the above examples have shown, the union has managed to focus on individual pay grievances as a way of maintaining union involvement. However, there is little evidence of MSF generalising from the individual grievances and pressing for collective dispute over pay.

At London and Manchester a perceived decline in collectivism was felt to be a particular problem. One representative reported:

> I think it's more individualised. I don't think we have that same collective outlook. As soon as you go into the realms of differentiated pay, you lose a lot of the collective bargaining issues anyway. You start focusing on the individual. Therefore, every individual is looking at themselves and it's very difficult to get them to think about the collective.

The problem with validating such a premise is that employers' attempts to individualise the employment relationship over the last two decades have run parallel with other external forces for change that are likely to be detrimental to trade union organisation and hence to likely trade union attachment. Recent research by Heery (1997) also points to the conclusion that individual performance-related pay (IPRP), for example, can provide the conditions for more positive trade union attachment rather than less, as employees seek help from the union in cases of perceived unfair treatment. The potential for individual case work has thus expanded as a result of IPRP, and this in itself raises problems of the ability of the union to service such a potential number of personal cases.

In general the problems facing MSF in the insurance offices visited tended not to come from feelings of declining collectivity but rather from other factors relating more to either management intransigence or conventional difficulties of organising fairly disparate groups of employees across a range of occupations. In some instances, however, 'cultural' difficulties associated with the South West (or parts of) were mentioned as a barrier to the development of collective attitudes. At London and Manchester (in Exeter) the representative reported:

> This is a very Tory area. I'm a card carrying member of the Labour party but this is very much a Liberal or Conservative area ... that believes trade unionism has caused all the problems that the workforce has got.

The challenges to union organisation so far described need to be met with a cohesive and strategic union response if union renewal is to take place. The question here is whether or not the participation and self-reliance implied in the 'organising model' would either be sufficient in itself or be capable of being applied in such a potentially hostile environment. These problems are now assessed.

Organising in insurance: back to basics?

Most of the workplaces surveyed had experienced a static or falling membership against the background of job cuts and redundancies (see Table 5.1). Recruitment was often necessary merely to maintain membership levels, and overall MSF has recorded more absolute recruitment gains in insurance than in other sectors, both nationally and in the South West.[4] Problems of low density have nevertheless had a negative effect on the perceived effectiveness of the union, thus making it harder for it to recruit. In such circumstances reliance on full-time officers, or full-time seconded lay officials was seen as a condition for both membership renewal and constructive engagement with management. As such the likelihood of dependence on officials was likely to create a barrier to the devolved participation necessary for an organising approach. So despite a number of successful initiatives or experiences, the context of recruitment – hostile management, low existing densities, lack of time, etc., has made progress particularly difficult.

Membership participation and recruitment

In one case, Prudential, there had been a surge in recruitment albeit from a relatively low base. The methods used were a mixture of the traditional and new, with particular emphasis on targeting of individual non-members, arguing with them the benefits of membership and 'bothering' to ask them to join. The representative reports:

I actually went on an MSF training course and it made you feel yes there are people out there who have the same views as you and it made me feel a little more positive about things. I came back and everyone I worked with at the time, I called on them to join. Then we had our AGM the next morning, five people came up and asked to join and it was a case of going round and hassling people.

In fact most of the recent rise in recruitment is a result of simply asking (sometimes 'hassling') people to join:

I do rely on S. and J. as well to do their bit to recruit and we try and set little target groups of people to work on. I move around the office quite a bit doing different jobs so I tend to centre on one little group and try and recruit them.

The process of asking staff to join may sound obvious yet it is a basic task that may often be neglected by union activists in many workplaces. The process of mobilising members also goes hand-in-hand with recruitment and central to the modest but positive experience at Prudential has been the provision of information about what the union is doing for members and non-members alike. The same representative reports:

Every time I do Branch minutes, then I do a desk-drop to everyone with an application form on the top . . . If they bin it, they bin it, but someone might read it. It instigated the part timers getting together about their salary bandings after the last meeting and that was successful. One had been at the meeting and had raised it. It was an issue that had been brought to me a year ago and no-one had come back. I thought it had been resolved, no-one had said anything and it was raised again. I put it in the minutes and they all came up and said, 'what's going on?' I helped to get them organised. Three of them are already now members.

A similar story can be told at Norwich Union, where membership increased from 35 to 80 over a twelve-month period as a result of a recruiting drive linked to general feelings of low morale. Management wished to issue everybody with headphones (which would have intensified monitoring and reduced individual scope for pacing workload) and it was this 'critical incident' which sparked off a positive attitude to the union.

There was a real feeling of injustice. They'd all had headphones to wear. People were a bit cheesed off. We just went round and spoke to them and asked if they wanted to become a member. They said yes, basically there was no hard sell.

Different experiences came from other offices. At London and Manchester union membership is large (although relatively low in density) and the workplace is larger. Problems of communicating information and recruiting suitable union representatives are of paramount importance, and this was done by devolving responsibility to specialist teams of representatives. The senior representative reports:

> Everybody had their own areas of expertise, they had their little teams. They elected a spokesperson from each of the teams. I was the senior negotiator, but they elected a spokesperson from their team to actually come on the negotiations with me. Then we fed back to the whole team and we fed back to all the members.

The difficulties of finding volunteers from amongst the membership in a situation of intensifying workloads often proves very difficult. At Friends Provident the representative felt this to be more of a problem today than it has been in the past. As was reported:

> What tends to happen is we have had reps experienced in union activity or who want to be experienced because they've got some sort of political background, etc., but they often eventually leave the company. We are just not getting the people coming through who have the same views, or the same opinions or the same desire to get involved. It's very difficult. Basically we can only get people into the Union by promising that we won't ask them to do too much.

The utilisation of publicity material such as newsletters as a tool for recruitment and retention varied considerably. The time taken to produce professional looking newsletters (as well as to determine content) has been considerably eased with offers from MSF nationally (via organisers and officials) to supply proforma and, if necessary, laptops with dedicated union software. Newsletters and other forms of written communication are likely to be vital, especially where there are management-imposed restrictions on union representatives moving around the office on union as opposed to 'official' work-related business. A good example of a membership awareness programme came from *CompanyA* where a relationship between members and union representatives has been deliberately nurtured to include constant feedback and information dissemination. Attendance at mass meetings is argued to be high as a result, although on pay issues attendance is poorer, possibly as a result of the amount of information members are already receiving in other forms. The representative reported:

> We do have a system where we call all our reps together who have gone out to collect feed-back from the members and that's fed up to senior reps and this is used to set agendas. Information is fed back down in the same way . . . works well with pay, so much that attendance at pay mass meetings is poor. But mass meetings over other issues get 'a huge attendance'.

At Friends Provident management were distinctly hostile to union activism and as a result even the distribution of literature was difficult and there was negative pressure on the establishment of union awareness. The representative said:

> We are not supposed to walk round and actually recruit people. The only way you can do it is to send literature. Occasionally you will get someone in this way. Send literature, arrange meetings, call meetings to which hardly anybody ever turns up, try to get them at lunchtimes and things like this.

It is in such a situation that there is a link between 'perceived union ineffectiveness' and the lack of legitimacy given to the union representatives from the company management. Strategically it is then necessary to take an opportunity to mobilise members and recruit from a situation where there is some common grievance, however small or insignificant it may seem. In such a way 'perceived union inneffectiveness' may be converted to 'perceived effectiveness' and the local union can enact a 'take-off' or surge in recruitment from a low base (Upchurch and Donnelly 1992). Part of this process also allows their justified grievances to be progressed efficiently by a collective agency (Klandermans 1997). Some branches and workplace representatives had instigated such recruitment by responding to an individual critical incident within the workplace. For example, at *CompanyA* a new direct retailing section has been targeted for a recruitment drive following breakdown of staff confidence in a management inspired staff forum. 'Bread and butter' issues of personal protection have been used successfully to recruit where union success is apparent (and perceived effectiveness is increased). At Das Legal this approach has been used over disciplinary cases. The representative reports:

> It doesn't happen so much now, but when people were laid off or made redundant, especially in an area where people don't think that sort of thing happens. Especially if we've had a result out of it, where somebody has been sacked for gross misconduct and we've turned it round to redundancy with £15,000 payout. They're not employed, but they get a bit of money out of it.

In some offices, particularly Friends Provident, there is a constant battle to prove to non-members (and members) that the union can be effective at all against the background of low density and hostile management. Often recruitment initiatives, where they take place, have the effect of stopping membership from falling rather than that of increasing the total. As the representative said:

> We have had initiatives where we have offered stereos and things like that and that's generated about another 20 members, but what we have to do, we have to do these very small things and we have to do these things which generate a very small number simply to even remotely keep to our numbers.

In absolute terms the potential for recruitment in Friends Provident is very large, and partly for this reason the office has been targeted by MSF for a recruitment campaign involving the use of a dedicated full-time organiser for a period of six months. Attempts to mobilise the membership have had some success in the past within Friends Provident and this tradition is important as it represents accumulated knowledge and experience crossing a psychological barrier in the workplace for the staff which legitimises the concept of industrial action. However, the representatives feel that a sense of militancy apparent in the 1970s went into decline in the 1980s, and this has adversely affected willingness to act in the 1990s

In many of these workplaces MSF representatives had to operate at a basic level of trade union organisation, both in terms of challenging management and convincing non-members of the benefits of joining the union. Ironically this 'back-to-basics' approach meant that some of the aspects of the organising approach were integral to the unions' everyday life in a way that it may not have been in workplaces where the union was more established as part of joint regulatory processes. Nowhere was this more evident than in the case of Northern Star, where a cold recruitment campaign had been organised internally by a small group of activists. There are two main offices of the company in Gloucester and early in 1998 a leafleting campaign outside the office was begun resulting initially in one person (now a representative) attending a local meeting. Membership quickly grew to 30, meetings were held regularly in a local pub, four representatives volunteered and union material was distributed (covertly) inside the buildings. Senior management at the company was extremely hostile to union activity, having earlier withdrawn financial support from the staff association when discussions of approaching an independent union materialised. As the representative explains:

> As far as I know, we had a staff association some time ago and that was leading up to a union organisation and as soon as the management found out about it they cut off the funding and they decided to call it a sports and social club.

The relative success of the initial recruitment campaign stemmed from the personal leadership of one or two individuals inside the offices who were motivated to become active in the union coupled with general feelings of the lack of 'voice' of staff within the company. Again, as the representative explained:

> There's always that threat of redundancies laying over us, because we've had so many different computer systems coming through at the moment and you can see the down-sizing all the time. And working conditions as well, there's no real voice. We haven't got a voice, that's what it is. You can talk to your supervisor but nothing much will happen.

The initial phase of recruitment (to 20 members) was quite easy. However, recruitment beyond that became more difficult both because of management hostility and because while the union remained unrecognised staff questioned the effectiveness of the union and measured this against the personal risk and the cost of subscriptions before joining. Together with MSF organisers the representatives developed a plan of action in order to try to raise the union's profile, centred around the European Works Council (EWC) and the emerging Fairness at Work legislation. Two of the representatives' names were put forward by MSF to attend a Works Council for two days in Italy, where the Northern Star representatives would participate alongside others from offices in other EU countries in the Italian-owned Generani insurance group. As one representative explained:

> The Personnel Manager spoke to the Managing Director, the Managing Director spoke to someone in Trieste (that's where Generani are based) and I got a letter back saying I can't go. So something happened between Northern Star and Generani. They said in the end it was a misunderstanding. They put forward that there should have been an election [ballot] of all employees.

The fact that representatives are required by law placed the company with a strategic dilemma, either it needed to establish its own worker representative forum and utilise this as an electoral base or recognise the right of MSF to conduct elections as workforce representatives (thus *de facto* implying recognition of the union by the company). This management dilemma could be used by the union to its advantage and, combined with the representative rights enshrined in the 1999 Employment Relations Act, presented an opportunity to raise the profile and potential perceived effectiveness of the union to enable further recruitment success.

Widening and deepening agendas, and employee voice

Within the framework of union organising of the model presented in the introductory chapter (Figure 1.1) it appeared that only limited evidence was available to suggest that MSF within the insurance workplaces had managed to extend the scope of bargaining beyond basic pay and conditions. This finding is confirmed by the quantitative analysis gathered from the survey of all union representatives across different sectors, where in insurance there was generally less evidence (apart from the issue of maternity/paternity leave) than elsewhere of widening bargaining. Table 5.3 compares the reported incidence of new bargaining agenda issues by MSF representatives in insurance compared to all union representatives in all sectors.

Two reasons may explain the relatively low incidence of new bargaining agendas in insurance. Either the insurance companies themselves were 'better' or more benevolent employers than in the other sectors or the union was less able to develop new agendas within insurance due to other internalised factors. The analysis would suggest that MSF in the insurance industry is still struggling to establish itself as a bargaining agent with management on basic issues of pay and

Table 5.3   MSF representatives in insurance reporting negotiations on 'new bargaining agenda issues', compared to all union representatives and sectors, $n = 356$.

	All union representatives, all sectors (%)	MSF representatives in insurance (%)
Skill training	34	11
Sex discrimination	16	11
Race discrimination	9	6
Sexual harassment	14	10
Maternity/paternity leave	26	38
Childcare facilities	15	13
Stress	39	22
Bullying	27	17

conditions, and has not emerged in the majority of cases beyond the traditional core of bread and butter bargaining agendas as a consequence. Lingering employer paternalism within the industry has in some cases undoubtedly preserved an authoritarian atmosphere, whereby challenges to management authority are relatively rare and transient. One notable exception was at Das Legal where one of the representatives was motivated to campaign over flexitime for return-to-work mothers. As was explained:

> At the moment, we are trying to change the flexitime. We are trying to get them to do something on maternity, ahead of the new legislation and also adoption leave. Basically their answer to that is that they will do statutory minimum and no more. They are not very flexible for returning mums, it's been a bit of a problem, getting them to agree to put mums that were full time on to part-time working

The motivation of this particular representative raises the issue of leadership and the question of why and how individual workers wish to become union representatives, what inspires them, and how this is reflected in union organising activity. The articulation of such employee voice is, of course, a fundamental motive for union activity, going beyond any personal self-interest that would be assumed in any rational choice theory (e.g. Olson 1971). The representative at Das Legal explained why she became a union representative:

> I originally worked for the civil service and was a union member there, but not very active. I came to DAS and joined the union immediately. I came back, I was the first working mum to return to work and I had quite a struggle, because I wanted to come back part time and they said I could, but when I returned they wouldn't – it was full time or nothing. So I decided when the secretary and treasurers role came up that I would play a much more active role, predominately to help other working mums.

In contrast her fellow representative wished to have more involvement in company affairs and enjoyed this extra involvement:

> I initially started just for the involvement in what the company is doing. The job I had at the time, I wasn't involved in anything, it was at a very junior clerical level. I initially got involved to get myself on panels and committees. My job's changed now but even so, I have more meetings with the management now as a union rep than I ever would with my job. Of course I enjoy it, I enjoy meetings, trying to make some sort of difference to the whole company.

At Northern Star, the need for employee voice within the organisation was again an important motive for engaging in union activity. The representative states:

> I suppose being 38, I've seen what happened with the unions in the '70s, but I just see that Northern Star is very dictatorial, you don't have a voice at all, the staff don't. They impose certain things all the time and we haven't got any say in how things are run or how things are done. I've seen how they treat people and I thought 'can we do something about it', so when the MSF came along, I thought I would go along and speak to them.

There was some evidence of representatives having wider political inspirations to their trade union work although from the interviews undertaken this would appear less important than motives seeking greater involvement in company affairs. At Prudential the representative (female) explained her Labour Party background:

> My dad used to be secretary of our local Labour Party in Bristol South. I used to go out delivering leaflets when I was about seven! Child labour! I'm not active any more. I don't like Tony Blair. Anybody that smiles that much is a bit dodgy to me!

And, in the case of London and Manchester:

> I'm a Scottish socialist, I feel very strongly about representation and individual rights, and I agree with the changes (partnership) now, because we are now recognising the way that they can work together with companies. I feel that this is very much the right way and I do believe very strongly. I have seen it work, and it can work and I think that just being honest goes a long way. And being business aware.

At Norwich Union both representatives interviewed had a previous history of union activity but neither claimed to have come from a socialist or labour oriented background (one describing himself as middle class and having been to a private school). One had been a union member in the insurance industry for over 40 years and was active in wider MSF activities such as regional committee and conference attendance. The other representative was also active in the Bristol-based FSU (association of finance industry unions).

From these limited examples we can discern a combination of factors which led to union activism. They range from a simple desire to become more involved in company affairs to a commitment to challenge corporate injustice involving some personal risk to the individual activist. The survey did not seek to test the political affiliation or orientation of those union representatives who were interviewed or surveyed, and as such the evidence remains anecdotal rather than scientific.

Conclusion

The insurance industry has experienced major changes both in patterns of governance and product market environment in the last two decades whereby competition and entrepreneurialism have replaced a more regulated and bureau-cratic environment. Work has also changed, the injection of new information technology has predicated new internal structures and relationships to customers. The evidence would suggest that a routinisation of much work has occurred, coupled with a rise in job insecurity as corporate restructuring takes its toll on job totals within the industry. Some specialist jobs remain, and there has been skill enhancement of these jobs as they embrace the new information-based age. These changes have posed a major challenge to trade union organisation. The divisionalisation and fracturing of organisations into discrete business units has confused lines of communication, while the new entrepreneurialism associated with the service culture has obfuscated pay, performance and reward within the industry. In such a fragmented environment collective responses have been difficult to maintain or establish, especially given the relatively low level of union density, the history of management paternalism (which as Blyton and Turnbull, 1998: 251, suggest, can be translated as authoritarianism), and the relatively weak history of joint job regulation within the industry. In many ways the above scenario carries with it many of the pre-conditions expected for a breakdown of collectivism described in the introductory chapter. Yet in reality we can trace a contradictory process whereby the new entrepreneurialism which characterises the industry has been accompanied with an intensification of work, rising job insecurity and a routinisation of tasks. The felt need for employee voice in this new harsh corporate world has risen as a result, and some potentially fertile soil for the reinforcement of collective attitudes may have been provoked as a consequence.

The trade union response to this challenge has been mixed but does exhibit some evidence of innovative effort to recruit and retain members. In some cases the workplace union is enacting a traditional approach to union recruiting which is described here as 'back to basics', with an emphasis on one-to-one recruitment, the isolation and targeting of non-members and the imaginative use of newsletters and other such material. This basic approach reflects both low density and the associated need to establish a critical mass of union members in an often hostile environment. Similarly in some workplaces the union has successfully appealed to staff to join the union around small-scale critical incidents. This process has been described as one where the union has attempted to move from a situation of perceived ineffectiveness to perceived effectiveness, dependent again on establishing a critical mass of members and the ability to confront management authority and power. However, the filtration of new organising agendas in the industry appears to be weak, with limited evidence of widening or deepening the scope of bargaining. There is also a relatively high dependence on outside support for organising, either from full-time or seconded lay officials, coupled with difficulties in establishing and sustaining membership involvement and negotiating facility time for union activity.

The overwhelming task of the workplace unions in the survey has been simply to begin to establish a position whereby the union can engage with management on their agenda for change, while preserving or creating some sense of collective solidarity among a sometimes disparate group of staff. In reality, the prospects for union organising in these new private service workplaces are especially dependent on the action of key individuals in providing the leadership needed to begin to establish a voice for the collective worker.

6 The paradox of partnership in the public sector

Introduction

This chapter explores the inherent tensions in the TUC's variant of 'New Unionism' by investigating trade union responses to the restructuring of workplace relations in the public sector (see Chapter 1 for a discussion of 'New Unionism'). We compare and contrast the organising strategies adopted by different GMB and MSF workplace unions in local government and the NHS. We focus on the contradiction between on the one hand, New Unionism's support for partnership relations at work and on the other, its promotion of a more aggressive approach to grass roots union organising (Heery 1998; see also TUC 1999).

British unions still have a relatively strong presence in the public sector although this has been subject to recent decline. Aggregate union density in 1998 stood at 57 per cent; this represented a significant fall from the 84 per cent density registered in 1980 and 72 per cent in 1990 (Millward *et al.* 2000). This decline is not surprising given the hostility of respective Conservative governments both to public-sector services and organised labour between 1979 and 1997. This government hostility manifested itself through cuts in public spending, marketisation processes, new public management techniques borrowing from the private sector, and managerial decentralisation (Carter 2000; Carter and Poynter 1999; Fairbrother 2000b; Foster and Scott 1998; Lloyd 1997; Nichols 2001; Winchester and Bach 1995).

During the last decade, the public-sector unions' response to this unfavourable climate derived from a political choice based on social partnership and this coincided with concurrent shifts in the policies of the Labour Party. The neo-liberalism and managerialism of New Labour which took hold after the defeat of the Labour Party in the 1992 general election involved a process of recasting the party's relationship with the unions in order to break free from what it perceived as one of its main electoral handicaps. Out went traditional ideas that were predisposed towards weak corporatism; instead, the trade union movement was to be marginalised and treated as just another supportive pressure group, albeit a major donor (McIlroy 1998: 539, 546). By the 1997 general election, most national union leaderships had acquiesced to the industrial relations implications of New

Labour's political mutation by supporting enterprise-level social partnership placed within a unitary framework. Inherent in this was an acceptance of the requirement to minimise industrial disputes, improve corporate performance and protect the public (McIlroy 1998: 548).

Yet despite the union leaderships' adaptation to New Labour little seemed to have been given in return to public-sector workers themselves. Some legislation was introduced in response to union campaigning but tempered to assuage employers. The introduction of the minimum wage of £3.60 per hour for adult workers in 1999 was much lower than the unions' demands and while statutory union recognition procedures were also introduced in the Employment Relations Act 1999, they were diluted in response to intense lobbying by employers. The result was new union rights that promoted co-operative forms of trade unionism rather than independent rank and file activity (Smith and Morton 2001).

The New Labour government did sign up to the EU social chapter and reinstated trade union rights to the Government Communications Headquarters (GCHQ) workers; otherwise continuity with previous Conservative policy prevailed. This was particularly apparent in Labour's economic policy. Public spending was kept within the tight limits set by the preceding Conservative administration for the first two years that Labour held office. Moreover, in spite of union opposition the Private Finance Initiative (PFI), introduced by the Conservatives in 1992, was continued and extended under New Labour.

The portrayal of the state as a 'model employer' has rightly been subject to much qualification. Yet with some justification this tag continued to have some resonance until the late 1970s. However, the Conservative Governments of the 1980s and 1990s finally destroyed this 'model employer' image as control of labour costs in particular and public spending in general were tightened. Unions no longer had the ear of government. The transparent process of outsourcing public-sector services to achieve 'economy, efficiency and effectiveness' under Compulsory Competitive Tendering (CCT), and the reorganisation of work and implementation of new labour control techniques all revealed the change in public-sector managerialism. This new ground has altered the pattern of industrial relations in the state sector to correspond more closely to the unionised private sector (Carter and Fairbrother 1999). Trade union responses to this restructuring of workplace relations in local government and the NHS are explored in this chapter.

The research base

GMB and local government

Interviews were carried out with GMB full-time organising and recruitment officers based in the union's South West region, and with lay representatives in two urban local authorities. These are referred to as CityA and CityB.

CityA, a Labour-controlled authority located in the South West region, employed 20,000 staff. The GMB membership, primarily working in low-skill blue-collar occupations, totalled 718, comprising 211 male and 169 female full-time staff and 72 male and 266 female part-time staff. Overall membership density stood at 50 per cent but the potential for recruitment was much higher in the non-teaching occupations. Two senior shop stewards were employed full time on union work; eight lay representatives and additional 'communicators' supported them.

CityB, a hung council (the Liberal Democrats were the largest party) employed 6,500 staff. Membership density stood at 60 per cent though again the teaching unions accounted for much of this. Six GMB shop stewards represented around 600 members in CityB, although records of the make-up and location of these were at best imprecise. However, the GMB convenor imparted that there was a significant number of female, part-time staff in social services (home help), education (school assistants, catering, cleaning) and traditional male-dominated manual occupations such as ground maintenance, road repair and school caretaking.

MSF and the NHS

The analysis of MSF qualitative data used for this chapter focuses upon interviews with senior and lay representatives in three NHS trusts located in the same urban areas as the local authorities CityA and CityB. The three trusts are referred to as TrustA, TrustB and TrustC. Interviews were held with representatives in the departments of Pathology, Medical Physics, Microbiology, Chemistry and Clinical Psychology. TrustA is a general hospital employing 4,200 staff. MSF had 30 workplace representatives and 250 members. The main occupations represented were Medical Laboratory Scientific Officers (MLSOs) and Medical Laboratory Assistants MLAs. TrustB was a general hospital employing 4,000 staff. MSF had nine workplace representatives and 250 members. Again the core membership comprised MLSOs and MLAs although many ancillary workers such as porters and health care assistants (HCAs) held MSF rather than UNISON membership. TrustC was a general hospital employing almost 5,000 staff. Unlike TrustA and TrustB, a partnership agreement had been signed between management and unions. The trust's MSF representatives complained of their inability to provide total MSF membership figures as no branch or head office data were available. MSF had six workplace representatives and its membership is concentrated in clinical psychology, health visitors, and in MLSOs and MLAs.

GMB and MSF: variations in strategy

The introduction of marketisation and private-sector management techniques into the public sector can engender two new dynamics in industrial relations. The first is based on the resulting potential for trade union mobilisation around new employee discontents (Kelly 1998). Linked to this, the second results from managerial decentralisation and a concomitant shift in bargaining and power relations which raises the prospect for greater trade union activity and renewal at the workplace level (Fairbrother 1994b, 2000a, b). However, as Lloyd (1997) observes, mediating factors such as local management policy, lay leadership style and organisation, and full-time officer relations with the workplace union can bring about significant variations in union responses. In this chapter we explore these variations by considering the following three dimensions of workplace union organisation:

- *Management–union relations* (from 'partnership' to 'adversarial')
- *Different activist leadership styles* (from 'detached' to 'inclusive')
- *Activist–full-time officer relations* (from 'dependent' to 'independent').

We use these categorisations to provide a framework for the discussion of our interview data. The evidence suggests that different management attempts to develop partnership relations with local unions highlights a dichotomy in union organisational practice and outcomes between the pro-partnership workplace unions at CityA, CityB (GMB) and TrustC (MSF) and the MSF unions at TrustA and TrustB, which employed an alternative organising approach. This calls into question notions of a complementarity between partnership and organising. However, before analysing the evidence for this it is necessary to refer briefly to the alternative orientations of MSF and GMB to partnership.

The GMB is one of the key trade union protagonists for partnership in the UK. Its national policy document, *The GMB and Employers – Partnerships for Success* (GMB 1998) argues that employers and unions have to develop the strengths needed to succeed in a competitive global environment. By utilising a partnership approach (meaning that unions work with employers in building the business by developing a skilled, committed workforce), co-operation rather than conflict becomes the foundation for change at work. This policy of collaboration with employers is quite consistent with the union's previous approaches to 'modernisation' over the past two decades. Under the leadership of David Basnett (1973–85), and then John Edmonds, the GMB embarked upon a programme of modernisation. This comprised organisational restructuring to make it more merger friendly (Undy 1999); support for the ideology and business rhetoric of HRM (Kelly 1996); and the development of a managerial servicing relationship with its members, a kind of 'consumer-responsive unionism' (Heery 1996). The latter involved surveying members' aspirations at work and designing union services accordingly. The union's current support for partnership is a corollary of this modernisation process. One GMB regional officer interviewed for the research summarised this as follows:

> One of the things that has separated the GMB from other unions is that we don't believe that you could form a picket line and force the issue – what we want is a caring boss, what we want is satisfaction coming to work. These aren't the kind of issues that are normally seen by trade unions as the ones you would fight for. I think we are trying to pick what our members want and come through with something different. I think that does separate us from a lot of trade unions (GMB regional officer).

In contrast, although MSF has signed a number of partnership deals with employers, particularly in the finance sector, its leadership has displayed a more cautious and pragmatic approach. This is due in part to the critical stance taken by some groups of activists and full-time officers. For example, one ex-TASS officer based in the South West region had this to say about the issue:

> You can only have partnership if you share the ownership of industry or commerce. You can have a partnership, but where you are talking about the distribution of wealth, you have to recognise that people will have different interests and what we are about is to ensure that we maximise the fruits from the result of the labours of our members ... It's interesting looking through the agenda of the union's conference this year. There's clear concern amongst members at the way it's going. I think there's a concern that we are too much involved with collusion and collaboration with employers. It's the same debate that took place in the 1930s. With Mondism. (MSF full-time officer).

MSF's pragmatism may also be a function of the lack of coherent strategy since it was formed in 1988 from the merger between ASTMS and TASS. The difficulties stemming from the diverse core traditions, organisational structures and political orientations of the two unions have been well documented (Carter 1991, 1997, 2000; Smith and Whalley 1996). Eventually, with the exception of the better organised workplace unions in engineering, the ASTMS form of unionism prevailed with the adoption of a 'servicing approach' to organisation. However, this strategy failed to stem the new union's membership losses and concomitant financial crisis. In this context, the MSF national leadership took the decision to embrace the organising model and launch its own 'Organising Works' initiative in 1997. This seeks to promote a vibrant workplace activism through membership participation in organising and recruitment campaigns. The new organising approach has clearly not been easy to carry amongst some sections of the membership and full-time officer machine, involving as it does a 'cultural' change and a redirection and redefinition of full-time regional officers' priorities (Carter 1997). Neither has the process of organisational change been helped by the leadership's failure to initiate a debate throughout all levels of the union. As one full-time officer commented:

> The only way you will build up an organisation is from the grass roots and the problem is that the 'Organising Works' ethos is top down. What has to take place is a ferment, an intellectual ferment, debate, so that people have ownership of the union. If it is your union, our union, we want to change society, then you'll get that enthusiasm. (MSF regional officer).

In practical terms the union has appointed a number of regionally based recruitment organisers responsible to the national office. It has attempted to address cultural change by integrating the 'organising culture' into educational courses at the union's national Whitehall College; the union's regional councils have been allocated additional education budgets for arranging 'Organising Works' training sessions; courses have been specially designed for lay activists in the NHS and finance sectors where the servicing culture is prevalent; and Organising Works articles appear recurrently in the union's various journals and newsletters.

GMB organising in two local authorities

For the past two decades, local government has been subject to a combination of increased centralised control by national government, new managerialist approaches to control at the workplace and marketisation through such techniques as compulsory competitive tendering (Fairbrother 1996; Winchester and Bach 1995). The impact of these changes on local government employees has been uneven. Whilst budgetary control, pay restraint and departmental restructuring have significantly affected the job content and employment conditions of both white-collar and manual workers, the latter group, which makes up the GMB's key member constituency, has been more adversely affected by privatisation, job loss and labour intensification (Fairbrother 1996; Kessler 1991; Laffin 1989).

In the two local authorities investigated, CityA and CityB, the GMB's shop stewards were still having to respond to member discontents arising from these changes. However, three new salient issues had emerged since the election of the Labour Government in 1997: workplace partnership; 'Best Value'; and harmonisation. Trade union incorporation into the management structure has traditionally characterised management-union relations in local government (Laffin 1989). And despite attacks on employment conditions and sporadic episodes of worker militancy, critical issues such as CCT have often been managed by union 'co-optation' and weak processes of consultation at the workplace (Kessler 1991). In this context, and that of a potential re-emergence of the pre-Thatcherite 'model employer' tradition in the public sector (Stuart and Martinez Lucio 2000), local government constitutes a prime site for the implementation of New Labour's workplace partnership agenda. Management at both CityA and CityB supported partnership policies aimed at providing greater trade union input into managerial decision-making and fostering a sense of 'employee voice'.

CityA was particularly proactive in experimenting in new partnership practices that were utilised in addition to existing consultative committees. The council's 'positive flexibility' project provided an example of this. Positive flexibility is a clear manifestation of the 'mutual gains' approach to partnership (Kochan and Osterman 1994) where innovative patterns of managing working hours should enhance employees' ability to balance their paid work with personal/domestic commitments whilst also enhancing the quality of council service provided. Working in partnership with the TUC and the Local Government Employers' Organisation, the council secured EU funding for implementation and evaluation of different pilot projects. The partnership processes utilised for developing these projects consisted of: (i) establishing a Project Steering Group which consisted of the TUC, employers, elected members, management, policy officers, trade union reps and academics and (ii) establishing Service Steering Groups for affected services composed of some of the above representatives. These groups then developed surveys and focus group techniques to investigate staff working patterns and aspirations. The surveys highlighted low staff morale, low trust in management intentions but support for some new working patterns. At the time of the research, the one concrete development to emerge from this partnership process is that despite 70 per cent staff opposition, Sunday opening in library services had been introduced by using the surveys to fragment the initial opposition (staff are employed on Sunday shifts on a voluntary basis).

Despite such tensions, the GMB senior stewards at CityA strongly supported workplace partnership for both ideological and job security reasons. One commented:

> Really it's about survival, isn't it? If we don't provide these services efficiently, then down the road, there will be someone else who is waiting in the wings to do that. In the old days, you worked for the Council and you had a job for life. But we've gone through so many changes, so many upheavals, that now most of us realise that is not the case. It used to be that although local authorities didn't pay terribly well you did have that security. That's gone, no-one has security in local authority work any more. It's a general awareness that if we want to survive, we really have got to work together.

Partnership practices were not so well established in the Liberal Democrat-run CityB authority. However, in 1998 its Chief Executive issued instructions to managers that the trade unions should be consulted prior to the drafting of policy documentation rather than seeking discussions on final implementation and that line managers should hold monthly briefing sessions with employees. As a result, representatives of the GMB and other authority unions took up places on Joint Consultative Committees, a Joint Consultative Forum and have also been offered positions on new working parties to discuss policy implementation. However, unlike their counterparts in CityA, the GMB's (and other unions') stewards took a more cautious approach to partnership and declined to become too involved with management through the working parties. Instead, out of a sense of self-defence, the senior steward sought to negotiate policy implementation at the point of service:

> There's always a danger in not getting involved with negotiations at the early stage. On the other hand, there's a danger in flying with the management. Because you might end up agreeing to something but then you realise you made a booby and you'd get the blame. I've had enough kickings in this job over the last few years. I don't really want to get any more. So the strategy at the moment is not to get involved with implementation but to be kept informed, to get the overall picture and the local picture which we will need when the negotiations eventually come.

The second issue currently confronting local government unions was 'Best Value'. The Labour Government's approach to the control of local authority organisation ostensibly prioritises service quality over cost reduction. However, the Government's Best Value agenda, embodied in the Local Government Bill, November 1998, hardly mentions quality *per se* (Gaster 1999) but instead signifies a continuation of local government managerialism. Best Value employs a classic TQM approach to cost control focusing upon measuring current service performance, incorporating benchmarking to compare performance with best practice elsewhere and using workstudy/continuous improvement techniques to enhance external customer service at minimal cost. It also incorporates the principles of partnership by emphasising consultation with service users, service providers and their trade unions. Both CityA and CityB were adopting Best Value practice but CityA was more advanced in this process since it was chosen as one of the Government's key pilot authorities for early implementation. The adoption of Best Value is generating new discontents as local authority employees become subject to greater management control, labour intensification and staff rationalisation. The research uncovered a number of examples of this, none more stark than the experience of CityA's homecarers.

Well before Best Value appeared on CityA's policy agenda cuts in spending had reduced social services budgets and squeezed staffing levels and resources. As a result, remaining staff in all occupations had been forced to take on significantly increased workloads and new responsibilities. Work had got harder, stress levels had increased and both the quality of care and the quality of working life of the carer had declined. The Best Value agenda merely 'continuously improved' this process of labour intensification by employing Taylorite principles of surveillance and time control. One homecarer's steward explained this:

> You go to a client and you write down the time you get there and the time you leave and the client has to sign it. This is supposed to be for the purposes of audit for social services . . . But this really is to manage staff. They can say if you are in with one client for half an hour, then within an hour you can cover two clients, with five minutes between each call. And that's how they've been working it out. At the end of the day, the client's not getting good service, and you are breaking your neck in the mornings to cover as many services as possible. It's just ridiculous . . . I mean, how can that tie up with Best Value?

> . . . I went to one client near here who's husband is dying of cancer and I was having a chat with her, she's in her eighties and he's in his seventies, and it turned out that their grand-daughter was dying of cancer. I started there on the Monday and the grand-daughter died on the Wednesday, she was twenty-six. It was good for her to talk to someone about it. It's for this sort of thing that you don't just rush around and go. You need to have that bit of time as well, it's really important.

The impact of these Best Value principles of 'effectiveness', 'economics' and 'efficiency' on the quality of life of the careworker was one of increased workplace stress and in some cases depression. The same shop steward:

> We had a staff meeting last Wednesday, the first meeting we've had since just after Christmas. It could have lasted the whole day because there are so many problems. Girls who might be having problems with their clients, they phone up for something and it's not been dealt with. Everybody was trying to get it out. One girl who was at the meeting – and another who rang me yesterday – they told me they cry before they come into work, because the role has changed so much, they are put under so much pressure, the expectations are so great now.

Best Value, even in its early stages, was therefore generating new discontents within the GMB membership that demanded a forthright collective response.

The third salient issue in local government industrial relations was harmonisation. A new national single status agreement was incorporated into the 1998 annual pay negotiations following acceptance in principle in the National Joint Council's 1997 National Agreement on Pay and Conditions. It was regarded by some activists as a 'pay pressure safety valve' that might lessen public-sector pay demands on the New Labour Government (Brown 1999). The eventual 1998 NJC settlement confirmed this: a pay increase of just 2.7 per cent, a new integrated pay and grading structure for all council workers (single spine, 49 grades), and a harmonised thirty-seven hour week by 1999 (manual workers worked thirty-nine hours). The GMB's lower-paid manual workers, whose grades were being integrated into the non-manual grading structure, were supposed to secure the most pay (and hours) gains from the single-status agreement. The national agreement required local authorities to embark upon local grading reviews based on systematic job evaluation.

Although the GMB's senior stewards were confident that their partnership approach would secure significant gains for their predominantly manual worker membership (at CityA the GMB had secured a full-time seconded position on newly formed job evaluation panels), shop stewards at both local authorities displayed a degree of unease. CityA and CityB had acquired unitary authority status in 1996 as a result of the restructuring of county councils. Accompanying job evaluation and regrading exercises had generated extensive job and pay cuts. In both authorities the GMB's strategy had been to attempt to service a mountain of individual grievances rather than mobilise a collective response. A failure to resolve many of these grievances satisfactorily had resulted in some member resignations. In the context of the employers' ongoing cost-cutting agenda the implementation of the single-status agreement was likely to generate new employee discontents. For example, a senior steward at CityB described how management refused to concede any financial compensation for refuse collectors who would not gain from the harmonisation of manual workers' hours from thirty-nine down to thirty-seven hours per week. This was because the service was contracted out and refuse collectors were compelled to work until all refuse tasks were completed. This normally involved working in excess of thirty-nine hours. Similarly, the management was demanding a cut in school caretakers' pay and a withdrawal of the dinner assistants' school holiday retainer in order to pay for the shorter harmonised working week.

Kelly (1996; 1998) has argued that although partnership-based union approaches do not deny a conflict of interest between employers and labour they nevertheless incorporate a belief that the new workplace agendas hold the prospect of forging common interests and co-operation around such issues as health and safety, work organisation and working time. The above analysis has suggested that the new workplace agendas in local authorities may in fact contain many points of conflict around such issues as labour intensification, multi-tasking, workplace stress, pay cuts and extended hours. The GMB's organisational response to these problems in many ways reflected the inherent tensions of 'New Unionism'. It relied upon intensive recruitment campaigns by full-time officers following which new members were supposed to be integrated into a partnership-based workplace union and an extant GMB servicing culture.

The GMB did indeed secure impressive membership gains in local government in its South Western region (which included South Wales). Between 1996 and 1999 membership rose from 12,700 to 17,500. This was achieved primarily through the targeted campaigns of the union's full-time recruitment officers with minimal lay activist involvement. Prior to this period, the regional bureaucracy of the GMB comprised regional secretaries and industrial officers (now designated as 'organising officers') who were responsible for both recruiting and servicing a region's membership; the leading South West organising officer referred to these as 'servicing officers'. During 1994 the GMB altered this structure by augmenting servicing officers with new recruitment officers. By 1999, all new recruits to the GMB's officer teams started as probationer recruitment officers who served a lengthy apprenticeship in membership recruitment campaigns before they could be considered for an organiser's position. The new officers were normally recruited from GMB branches.

Recruitment campaigns were recurrent events and targeted to specific groups that were identified by a 'senior management team' of organising officers. A senior organising officer described this:

> The overall strategy is this. The senior management team meets once a month to review the whole activities of the region. The regional secretary and organising officers meet the recruitment officers once a month and we target a campaign. Or we designate that they work with a certain officer that produces recruitment. That's how we are focusing everything now and not having a scatter gun approach. We are targeting and going where we want to go.

Utilising this more systematic, planned approach to recruitment the GMB succeeded in securing significant membership gains at CityA and CityB. In the context of increasing employee discontents the recruitment officers seemed to be knocking at an open door. Paying regular visits to such workplaces as schools and local authority homes they recruited significant numbers of caretakers, cleaners and other low-paid manual workers. The campaigns were also promoted by use of local radio advertisement broadcasts. Moreover, the union recruited additional numbers of part-time workers by offering fifty pence per week subscriptions to workers on ten hours per week or less (such as school crosssing 'lollipop' patrollers). Those working up to twenty hours per week pay just half of the full subscription rate.

Whether or not these membership gains could be sustained or at least consolidated in the longer term is a moot point. There were a number of problems here. First, the GMB's managerialist approach to organising meant that senior stewards at CityA and CityB were neither involved with recruitment nor aware of the location of new members and prospective activists (field notes). Second, to varying degrees, the senior stewards' incorporation into the processes of partnership and their assumption that a passive member/officer servicing relationship would be maintained effectively distanced new members from the union. For example, some local stewards felt that despite the partnership rhetoric of 'collective voice' both management and the senior stewards were not prepared to listen to the concerns of staff:

> If they really wanted to be aware of our concerns they could just sit down and have a meeting with us. Sit down and say how do you feel about the work place now and what sort of pressures do you think you're under and things like that. (CityA shop steward)

The processes of partnership and traditions of servicing discouraged the emergence of forms of participative trade unionism as an organisational response to local government managerialism, marketisation and decentralisation (Fairbrother 1996). At both CityA and CityB the senior stewards described difficulties in recruiting new activists in the context of the pressures placed on staff by labour rationalisation, labour intensification and line management assertiveness. The GMB full-time officers had responded to this in 1997 by organising local government stewards' workshops. But rather than provide activists with new skills in building a workplace organisation the workshops instead emphasised techniques in individual member servicing and representation in order to reduce the increasing servicing workloads of full-time officers. For example, at CityA the GMB union organisation comprised a core of two senior stewards and eight shop stewards plus a network of additional communicators. The shop stewards attended monthly stewards' meetings but few attempts were made to involve or systematically communicate with members. Communications tended to rely on informal channels such as occasional discussions between a shop steward and his/her group of members. No workplace newsletters or minutes were distributed to members. At CityB the situation was worse, where the development of a more dynamic organising culture was severely constrained by a lack of young activists and a reliance on older 'union patricians'. The GMB's six shop stewards rarely held meetings, no attempts were made to communicate with members and again the emphasis was upon servicing passive, individual members. A senior steward commented:

> The members participate in the union if they have a problem on their section. They just write to their shop steward. The steward goes into management and gets it sorted one way or another, or doesn't get it sorted, whichever. I don't get too much involved in that unless they can't handle it and then they come to me.

At both local authorities these constraints against mobilisation were compounded by the senior activists' non-political style of leadership. This suited the GMB's well embedded servicing culture which at the workplace level was essentially based on individual representation of members. For example, during discussions on the nature of workplace leadership the following typical comments were elicited from senior stewards:

> I suppose it depends upon how you look on your role as a steward. I look upon it as being someone who people can come to when they've got problems, or if they want something sorted out, trying to be the link. I don't tend to use the role for political reasons, or anything like that. (CityA)

> [No there's not much possibility of members acting on these discontents], as I say we have regular meetings with management so we cut the need for that. Also, it's individual problems more than anything else now, so we put an emphasis upon individual representation, the member comes to the rep, the rep comes to us, and we take it to central personnel, human resources. And we usually sort something out. (CityB)

As a result, these GMB workplace unions lacked the organisational dynamic required to build upon the membership gains secured through external targeted campaigns. Interviews with local shop stewards also highlighted an increasing feeling of isolation brought about by the union's failure to adapt its organisation to departmental fragmentation and privatisation. In summary, the GMB organising approach in CityA and CityB was characterised by a dependent, detached partnership. To varying degrees, the senior stewards became incorporated into management processes through partnership relations; as a result, their activities became increasingly detached from the needs and discontents of their members; and their relationship with full-time officers remained a dependent one.

MSF organising in three NHS trusts

As in local government, workplace relations in the NHS have been subject to significant change over the past two decades. The previous Conservative

Governments' implementation of 'marketising' reforms in the 1980s and trust-based management in the 1990s caused a divisionalisation of employer units, the introduction of new managerialist approaches to cost control and labour utilisation, and a decentralisation of industrial relations (Carter and Poynter 1999; Lloyd 1997). Although to date the process of local pay negotiation has stalled due to trade union opposition, the lack of provision of information to local pay bargainers and failed management attempts to impose pay offers (Carr 1999; Thornley 1998), significant changes in the management of local industrial relations have taken hold. The requirement to maintain tight budgetary controls and efficiency targets has prompted local trust managers to introduce staff reductions, longer hours, compulsory rotating day and night shifts, casualisation, downgrading through skill-mixing, pay-cutting and attacks on overtime premia, sick pay and holiday pay (Carter and Poynter 1999; Corby and Blundell 1997; Fisher 1999).

MSF's representatives in the three NHS trusts (TrustA, TrustB and TrustC) reported increasing levels of employee discontent over these issues. Problems associated with work intensification, low pay, long working hours, workplace stress and bullying were frequently raised during the interviews. In the context of previous and current government demands for ever greater efficiency and labour productivity, the processes of marketisation and decentralisation had engendered new working practices where employees were expected to take on more tasks and responsibilities, but in the interests of meeting tight staff budgetary controls, were also expected to accept lower grades and salaries (Thornley 1994). One senior MSF representative at TrustA commented on this:

> But have you ever noticed when any politician or official talks about wanting to spend more money on health care? Have you ever really thought about what that actually means? When you go into hospital, what happens is people do things for you, or people do things to you, in other words it's all people. So if you want more health care, what it really means is you want more staff doing things. It's never really appreciated by anybody. So if they want more work done they won't pay for it, instead they look at even more imaginative ways of paying the staff less to do that same amount of work! So the magic trick is always reorganisation. Which is to say when they announce, 'right, we are going to reorganise Surgical Services', what they really mean is that they are going to downgrade all the staff ... and they save megabucks on that.

In the absence of staff increases, raising patient throughput and referrals has intensified work processes within trust institutions not merely by increasing the pace of work but also by catalysing a recomposition of work through a process of multi-tasking, or 'skill mixing'. In the absence of real increases in resources, rather than enjoy compensatory salary enhancement and upgrading, many groups of NHS staff have suffered the opposite. As one representative put it:

I think staffing levels haven't gone down in the NHS really very much but what has happened is there have been reorganisations where, there's been a lot of, not so much de-skilling, because people have still got the skills, but there's been a lot of rejigging grades which doesn't reflect these skills if you see what I mean. There has been a lot of downward pressure on the grades of staff, and obviously their pay, whilst still expecting them to actually do the same professional work.

The new trust managements were also increasing capital equipment and labour utilisation at minimal cost by introducing flexible shift systems and extending the working day in the MLSO areas. For example, at TrustC the working day for MSF's technical staff was recently changed from a nine to five shift to a form of rostered double-day shift allowing laboratory facilities to stay open from six o'clock in the morning to eight o'clock at night. Under this arrangement, a skeleton staff was always available and individuals took turns to start early and finish late. The effect was an extension of hours through a redistribution of existing labour – the number of staff available at any one time decreased. The trust management gained two advantages from this. Firstly, the porosity of the working day was closed up as the same number of staff were expected to provide the same service for an additional six hours per day. Secondly, management was able to gain control over its on-call budget, since the on-call period was now significantly reduced.

Increasing managerial aggression and bullying at work were also widely reported by the MSF representatives. For example, at TrustB, bullying was a common complaint. In one area fifteen members of staff had left in a period of six months due to problems with a head of department. MSF's senior officer recalled:

We had a member who, when introduced to the department, was brought into the office and told, 'if you work properly and you behave yourself, you will find I am very good to work for, if you are not, you will find that I am a right bastard.' Those were the exact words used. This was the first day this person started. He and others like him joined up with MSF on their first day because they came out and spoke to other members of staff saying is this really what it's like here?

The MSF workplace unions at the three trusts were forced to respond to these discontents. As Fairbrother (1996, 1994a, b) has argued, the shift in the locus of bargaining to the local level following organisational decentralisation in the public sector may provide the conditions, and in some cases the discovery, of local trade union activism and renewal. This potential of decentralised bargaining to overcome the 'democratic deficit' of the centralised Whitley bargaining system by activating a formerly passive and unheard rank and file was well summed up by one senior MSF representative at TrustA:

This is a big one for us. In actual fact, I think the changes in the NHS paradoxically gave us a big impetus here for more grass roots regeneration of the
unions, because effectively before we had Trusts, the union framework for
industrial relations was, effectively, completely moribund. We had members,
but there were only a few people that were interested in it and they were
doing absolutely everything. But everything wasn't really very much. It was
just a little bit of liaison between us and national officials, because everything
was national negotiations for every single thing that impacted on us. So there
was a 'disempowerment' problem there.

However, the local response was not uniform in character. As Lloyd's (1997)
analysis of union responses to decentralisation in the NHS suggests, there can be
significant variations in union organisation and strategy at the workplace level as
a result of, *inter alia*, such factors as the role of full-time officers, management
policy towards trade unions, the strength of shop steward organisation and the
style of local leadership. At the three trusts investigated these factors influenced
the emergence of contrasting strategies in the form of an organising approach at
TrustA and TrustB and a partnership approach at TrustC. These will now be
compared.

TrustA and TrustB: independent, participative, adversarial

Of the three trusts, the MSF workplace organisations at TrustA and TrustB were
stronger in terms of representatives' organisation, membership participation and
recruitment performance. This was particularly the case at TrustA. Although this
trust's management was not hostile to trade unions, and indeed, at the time of the
research was making overtures to partnership, the style of the local MSF
leadership was characterised by independence, an awareness of the need to take
a militant stance on certain workplace issues and a determination to forge a
democratic accountability to the rank and file. Two senior MSF representatives
articulated this:

> I think you have to accept responsibility as a trade union steward at some
> point or other. It's a careful balance. You always have to be mandated to do
> things by your members. I've always been very careful never to be sitting at
> a meeting where the only opinions being expressed are mine. I've seen that
> happen time and again with other Unions. I've seen people where I know for
> a certain fact that the only person's opinion being expressed was theirs and
> I've always been pretty mindful of that. You should never do that. You are out
> on a limb and it's just a crazy place to be. So, you must always been mandated.

Another:

> ... So I think leadership is important. I think so. It's a very careful line
> between the old days of the shop steward, where the shop steward says 'I

didn't like this so we're going out'. It's come down to perhaps a more democratic leadership.'I think this is wrong, let's chat about it and let's make a decision.' I think that's the correct way to do it. But I think as a rep you've always got to give a lead, otherwise you cop out.

This style of local leadership was partly a function of the emergence of particular individuals with coherent political views on the role of trade unions and an awareness of the links between internal workplace politics and external political activity. The fact that some of these activists were left-wing Labour Party and SWP members highlighted how political affiliation can sometimes be significant for the emergence of independent and oppositional leadership positions (Darlington 1998; Gall 1998).

Since the creation of TrustA in the early 1990s, the MSF senior representatives had implemented a conscious strategy of building the local workplace union by recruiting a large mass of activists. By 1999, the union had 40 activists serving 240 members. Although one MSF senior representative played a full part on the trust's joint union JNC (Joint Negotiating Committee) emphasis was placed upon devolvement of the responsibilities for membership communication and representation to local activists in order to foster a more dynamic, participative union. And in the context of the pressures arising from processes of work intensification, this approach required less time commitment from any individual activist. It also meant that the workplace union was much less dependent upon the servicing function of local MSF full-time officers.

Union communication techniques were also regarded as essential instruments for building a more dynamic workplace organisation. TrustA's MSF reps organised bi-monthly open member meetings to provide briefings on current negotiating issues. Attendance averaged around 40 members and some of these were categorised as 'communicators' from key areas who had agreed to attend all meetings and report back to their local memberships. About four times a year, larger mass meetings were called, and attended by the majority of members, to discuss single-issue agendas such as pay and trust reorganisation. The reps also produced regular newsletters which provided a further means of representative accountability and catalyst for discussion. Membership surveys on specific workplace problems such as health and safety were used to mobilise supporting evidence to reinforce negotiating strategies with management.

At TrustB, the MSF workplace union employed a similar organising approach. Its activists sought to maintain an independent stance, to mobilise members around specific workplace issues and to recruit new members on this basis. However, compared to TrustA the efficacy of the organisation was impaired by its reliance upon a lesser number of activists (nine accredited representatives) and the organisational constraints imposed by the dispersion of departments across a 30-mile radius from the centre of this particular trust hospital. This meant that if self-activity was to be sustained it required continuing external support from full-time officers, implicit in the following remark from the senior MSF representative:

> People are getting dead stroppy. We've been working at getting people stroppy, because management have pushed them for so long... [but] I'm anti Organising Works and I have been all along when it gets to the stage where we are doing a full-time officer's job, which is what it has become here.

Nevertheless, like their colleagues at TrustA, the MSF activists at TrustB placed much emphasis upon workplace organising, systematic membership communication and involvement. For example, at the time of the research these activists took a leading role in mobilising staff opposition to a series of workplace problems: regrading exercises that were perceived as unfair; management attempts to impose annualised hours; and cases of management bullying. The activists also employed systematic communications techniques both to enhance membership interest and participation in the union and to maximise recruitment. Newsletters and staff surveys were often designed explicitly to engage in a dialogue with non-union staff to convince them that they were not immune from the consequences of the arbitrary decisions of management.

The MSF workplace organisations at both TrustA and TrustB secured significant membership increases by constructing an infrastructure for participation and mobilisation. For example, at TrustB, MSF membership rose by 50 to 250 in 1999; and at TrustA, the MSF membership more than doubled between 1992 and 1998 (from 105 to over 250 members). Although no systematic recruitment campaigns were employed, new members came to the union because MSF enjoyed a perception of union effectiveness and legitimacy. At both trusts, MSF also exploited the critical workplace incident or 'specific stimulus' to arouse local interest in unionisation (Snape 1994). One representative described this:

> We've organised vocal opposition to Trust proposals to make cuts to save money, which is the first time I've seen it go beyond passing resolutions... I think the management aren't as confident and as cocky as they used to be. There used to be several things where, when the Trust was formed, they just imposed them, they didn't even consult. So it's gone from a process of no consultation to a kind of consultation, I think an improvement. People are having the confidence to say, 'hang on, I don't agree with that, that doesn't make sense. That's based on control of budgets really, not based on the best care of the patient.'

> And this has affected recruitment. For example, recently in one particular department we had six people join in one week over a grading issue. So yes I think people are joining the union.

In summary, the organising approach adopted by the MSF workplace unions at TrustA and TrustB was characterised by independent leadership; a disposition to mobilise members around critical incidents at work and at times, antagonistic relations with the employer. The two groups of activists also maintained a relatively independent relationship with their union full-time officers although this did generate tensions around workload for the much smaller cadre of activists at TrustB.

TrustC: detached, dependent partnership

In contrast to TrustA and TrustB, a formal partnership agreement between management and MSF and other trust unions was in place at TrustC. During the period following the creation of the trust at the beginning of the 1990s the relations between the new local management and site unions were antagonistic. Management tended to treat trade unions with some disdain and regarded local industrial relations as a process of, at most, consultation rather than meaningful bargaining. At the same time, the local MSF representatives' organisation failed to recruit new activists and was unwilling to depart from its reliance on a servicing culture. The representatives found themselves unable to cope with the increasing level of discontent and conflict that arose from trust decentralisation, organisational restructuring and new managerialist processes of control. Staff morale and discontent deteriorated through the 1990s as increased demands were placed on healthcare services and staff, a fact certified by TrustC's chief executive. He stated in the trust's annual report for 1995–96 that the rise in workload had resulted in 'overstretched staff, rising sick levels, high use of agency nurses and a steep escalation in our costs'.

These antagonistic relations did not change until 1997 when a dispute over the imposition of staff car-parking charges prompted calls from both managers and senior representatives for a more co-operative approach to industrial relations. As a result of detailed discussions a partnership agreement was signed which enshrined the principles of sharing information and elements of joint decision-making. The agreement established a local bargaining structure comprising staff and management-side representation on a Joint Negotiating Committee; frequency of meetings with the HRM department and the trust board; the provision of a new Joint Union Committee comprising representatives from recognised trade unions and professional associations that were committed to working in partnership both with management and each other; and a working definition of what 'partnership negotiation' entails. A senior MSF representative at TrustC described this as follows:

> It means that we expect management to be as transparent as they possibly can, given that there's no longer a market or the need for that rather dubious secrecy. So we've got access to documents, to finances, we've got access to the stuff sometimes at the same time or before it's released to the board. We've got an opportunity to go in and comment on and respond to policies even before they have been offered as a formal paper. We can contribute to drafting them and I think that's what partnership means. It means taking full account and giving full weight to the staff side and their views before you can get that far.

Management take notice of what we say. We often propose stuff that finally does end up as a policy and the MSF policy models are found to be extremely welcome. The managers welcome them. We ought to send them a bill really, because we are doing their job for them! But we get the policies we want at the end of the day. It's justified.

MSF's leading representatives felt that these partnership arrangements catalysed a shift in their role from that of mere passive recipients of management consultation to (reactive) bargainers on such employment practices as staff recruitment, redeployment and training. It was also felt that the union secured some input into management decision-making processes on such strategic questions as trust merger policies and the development of primary care groups. MSF's leading negotiator – and the union's main protagonist for partnership – summed up the perceived benefits for the union:

I actually feel positive about the MSF organisation. The reps have put in a tremendous amount of work in terms of building up a partnership relationship with management. But not for it's own sake. We've done it in order to make sure we get a major input into the Trust policy-making process. And that's not just on matters concerning pay, terms and conditions, but on major policy decisions.

Don't forget our reps and their members are not just service providers, they are service users. We all have families and relations who use the NHS and who want a decent, quality service. So, for example, as trade unionists we will demand a major say over the siting, funding and quality of the Renal Dialysis Unit. To put this another way, Renal Dialysis is a union issue.

This process of partnership-based bargaining, which incorporated the principles of legitimate interest and 'collective voice', was also marked by the same constraints against workplace organising described in the above analysis of GMB activity in local government. MSF had six accredited representatives at TrustC. Two of these were senior representatives who devoted all of their time spent on union business to Joint Union Committee (JUC) partnership activity. The remaining representatives plus a few additional 'communicators' merely distributed material that was generated at MSF's head office; no newsletters, member communications forum or committee structure for MSF representatives existed at the workplace level. In other words, no infrastructure was in place that enabled rank and file participation or mobilisation, instead, it was assumed that increasing employee discontents, formalised in grievance and disciplinary issues, should be serviced by a 'professional' regional officer. One senior representative summed this up:

. . . I don't agree with Organising Works in principle. I think there is too much emphasis on reps doing too much and I really think that members' expectations are that they should have access to the skill and expertise of regional officers . . . I really do feel that the bottom line is adequate access to regional officers and I think if the union is getting healthier financially, it's priority should be to increase the access to regional officers. More importantly, to develop proactive input from regional officers. We are constantly given stuff from the centre, but it's very difficult to translate that into real action or effective action unless you've got very close contact with the regional officer.

As a result, the leading MSF activists at TrustC confined their activity to policy formulation and involvement in high-level committee structures; they made little attempt, indeed they had little time to link this activity with member participation and mobilisation. As we saw in the local government case studies this raised the likelihood of the rank and file becoming distanced from the partnership process and even the union itself. One local MSF representative commented:

> No. I don't think partnership is having a positive effect on getting people interested in the union. I don't think it makes any difference to the majority of people out there at the end of the day. Who really looks at a redundancy policy until they are going to be made redundant? Who really looks at a sickness, absence policy until it actually affects them?

Like their GMB counterparts in the local authority case studies the emphasis upon partnership and servicing rather than mobilisation meant that MSF's activists at TrustC did not involve themselves in recruitment campaigns. Different informants conceded that they had no precise idea of the size and location of non-members (or of many current members) whilst they assumed that new staff would approach the union rather than vice versa. They also believed that membership levels had been static for a number of years. At the time of the research, and this also mirrored GMB practice in the local authorities, as part of its Organising Works initiative MSF had allocated a young regional organiser to the workplace union with a view to increasing recruitment. As a result, at least 300 potential recruits had been identified. However, without a combination of sufficient full-time organiser resources and a cadre of workplace representatives committed to change through self-activity then the objective of reinvigorating union organisation at the workplace level may not be fulfilled (Carter 2000). In the case of TrustC, and unlike the actions of the GMB officers in the local authorities, the full-time organiser only had time to complete a simple mapping and leafleting exercise, with limited recruitment results, before moving on to new workplaces elsewhere in the region.

Conclusion

We have attempted to characterise industrial relations in the five public-sector workplaces by considering the following three dimensions of workplace union organisation: management-union relations (a continuum from 'partnership' to 'adversarial'); activist leadership style (from 'detached' to 'inclusive'); and activist-full-time officer relations (from 'dependent' to 'independent').

To differing degrees, the GMB workplace unions at CityA and CityB (local government) and the MSF union at TrustC (NHS) became incorporated into management through the *partnership* process and its consultative structures. Although the senior stewards believed that they articulated the separate interests and concerns of their members they maintained that these interests were best defended by working with management and influencing management policy rather than by mobilising against it. The upshot of this was that senior stewards became intensively engaged with processes of consultation but secured much less scope for hard bargaining on concrete membership concerns. Discussions with departmental stewards highlighted how this approach acted to distance the senior stewards from the rank and file and undermine any collectivisation of discontents. In the context of work restructuring and decentralisation, the failure of the senior stewards to establish a robust, decentralised activists' organisation – and consequent absence of any infrastructure for membership participation – meant that their leadership style tended to be of a '*detached*' nature. That is, senior steward activity focused solely on the time-consuming partnership processes of reactive bargaining and consultation without linking this to the needs and discontents of members. Consequently, despite the different policy orientations of their national unions, the GMB and MSF senior representatives at CityA, CityB and TrustC shared a belief that these members' needs should continue to be serviced by professional full-time officers rather than through self-activity at the workplace. This required the continuation of a *dependency* relationship between the rank and file and union full-time officers.

In contrast, although management did employ a partnership rhetoric at TrustA and TrustB, the MSF workplace unions maintained an independent relationship with the employer and where necessary adopted *adversarial* strategies involving membership mobilisation around critical incidents. The MSF workplace representatives at TrustA and TrustB also displayed a more '*inclusive*' leadership style compared to the above partnership unions. The creation of an infrastructure for member participation in the form of systematic and extensive two-way communications between members and activists provided lines of democratic accountability which were felt to be essential for maintaining a cohesive workplace organisation. Moreover, in TrustA in particular, activists had responded to managerial decentralisation by establishing a robust shop steward organisation and devolving union responsibilities to a large mass of activists. Finally, the emergence of a more dynamic form of workplace unionism at the two trusts inevitably shifted the relationship between the activists and their full-time officers away from one of 'servicing' and towards one characterised by relative *independence*. Again, this was particularly the case in TrustA where MSF had built up an organisation of 40 activists to represent 240 members. However, in TrustB, where the hospital organisation was more fragmentary and widely dispersed, the MSF union was at a more rudimentary stage of development. Although the union representatives emphasised the importance of organising and mobilisation their success in heightening the legitimacy of the union and attracting new recruits had resulted in the need for continuing external officer support.

The 'pro-partnership' workplace unions investigated in this chapter highlight certain contradictions in the 'New Unionism' project. The incorporation of senior stewards, a detached leadership style and the consequent lack of an infrastructure for member participation together run the risk of weakening employee support for the union. As Claydon (1998: 190) has argued, if member participation is low there is a likelihood that in their desire to consolidate relations with management through partnership unions may concede greater flexibility and labour intensification in return for job security, despite employee opposition. This may result in disillusion and eventual membership decline. This does not deny the potential for immediate union recruitment, however. Recently, the GMB has secured substantial recruitment gains in local government as a result of well planned and targeted campaigns executed by its full-time officers. But as we saw at CityA and CityB, the lack of activist involvement or even awareness of these campaigns and their distancing from the membership through partnership-based processes of incorporation raises the possibility that the union will not be able to consolidate these gains in the longer term. This possibility is reinforced by the implications of Waddington and Kerr's (1999) large-scale survey of significant membership turnover in the public sector. This found that retention is impaired by employee disillusion with union structure and organisation. Factors such as insufficient help given to members with problems, insufficient union communications and insufficient contact from activists – which were found to be associated with partnership 'distancing' in our local government and NHS case studies – constituted salient reasons for employees leaving their union.

Finally, if union renewal is to be conceptualised as involving more widespread democratic and participative union activity at work then our public-sector case studies suggest that the 'partnership' and 'organising' approaches to union activity are not complementary strategies on the road to renewal. When the material interests of trade union members themselves are considered – rather than the interests of the union bureaucracy, or management concerns to secure stable, trouble-free industrial relations – then it becomes clear that accommodation through partnership may both constrain and undermine the rank-and-file self-activity that is essential for workplace organising.

7   Negotiated privatisation in public utilities

Introduction

Privatisation of the public utilities was the most radical change to state policy in public ownership since the Second World War. Gas was privatised in 1986, water in 1989, electricity distribution in 1990 and electricity generation in 1991. The neo-liberal Conservative policy of 'rolling back the frontier of the state' was a central platform of the 1979 Conservative Government, and the programme gathered pace in the 1980s. Exposing the public sector to market disciplines became central to this Conservative project. This included privatisation, deregulation, commercialism and industrial relations reform all set against the framework of a desire to reduce the levels and proportion of public spending, lower direct taxation and weaken trade union power and influence (Pendleton and Winterton 1993: 1). The formulation and evolution of business strategies based on commercial competition, the establishment of new patterns of ownership, new strategic alliances and mergers and acquisitions have in turn led to further change in business strategy and managerial style in the privatised utilities. The aftershocks of these reforms form the backdrop to unions' response to change in the 1990s. The uncertainty over corporate governance produced a new feeling of job insecurity as a trade off emerged between shareholder dividend, consumer price, external regulatory constraints and wage costs. In addition, shifts from national to local business-based bargaining contributed to curtailing the power of public-sector unions and called into doubt the former certainty of 'model employer' pay structures, whilst new management techniques such as flexible working have acted to disorientate long-established work demarcation (Ferner and Colling 1993; Ogden 1993: 135).

Since the election of the first Labour Government in 1997, there has been continuity with previous Conservative Governments in respect to privatisation policy. New Labour accepted the prevailing financial and market disciplines introduced into the public sector in various guises, and is intent on further privatisation through public-private partnership schemes. Hence a reversal of the privatisation programme looks unlikely. The privatisation process is part of a global transitory shift towards neo-liberal capitalism that developed in Britain from the ideological programme of the New Right in the late 1970s and early

1980s. It was driven by the purposeful intervention of the state to 'commercialise' the public sector through tighter financial controls and the introduction of private-sector management practices, of which the restoration of management prerogatives released a 'willingness of management to force through change in the face of union and workforce opposition' (Ferner 1989: 5). The advance of privatisation on a global scale is such that even centre and centre-left governments see no alternatives to privatisation, New Labour in Britain being a prime example. Increasingly, this has become a subject of tension between trade unions and the Labour Government and therefore research on the impact on the labour process and management–union relations of placing public monopolies in private hands is particularly germane. Moreover, the passing of time since the transfer of gas, water and electricity to the private sector provides an opportunity to assess how unions in these workplaces have adjusted to their new environment.

Most of the 'new' reshaped workplaces deliver the same public services in an environment where shareholder value and the disciplines of the market, supplemented by state economic regulation and the maintenance of management control, now predominate. Even those enterprises that have retained their public-sector status have undergone radical change in the way they are managed. Downsizing, commercialisation and organisational restructuring are now common features of enterprises still in the public sector.

Pendleton and Winterton (1993), in a study of privatisation, argue that the most significant changes in work organisation and management–union relations were introduced prior to, and in preparation for, privatisation. But in the electricity and water industries, Ferner and Colling (1993) and Ogden (1993) suggest that the restructuring of work did not radically impact on the form and character of industrial relations, which remained much the same as they were in the 1970s and 1980s. It was argued, in part, that this was due to union officials and many senior managers resisting major changes to centralised bargaining structures, despite the shift from industry bargaining to single employer bargaining.

In her study of the impact of privatisation on work organisation and industrial relations in a water company, O'Connell Davidson (1993) placed as much emphasis on post-privatisation changes as those preceding privatisation. She argues that privatisation, concomitant with the wider political anti-union climate, severely weakened the union's ability to defend its members from the impact of work reorganisation. In particular, she observed the greater use of contract labour and the de-unionisation of unskilled manual workers whose work had been outsourced to civil engineering contractors. She argued that the impact of privatisation had been uneven. For skilled workers there was little change in the form and character of union representation but for unskilled manual workers the outsourcing of their work resulted in derecognition of the union and the loss of a collective representative voice. Moreover, O'Connell Davidson places greater prominence on the impact of the break-up of the national pay bargaining machinery on industrial relations in the water industry than Ogden (1993).

Fairbrother (2000b) has examined workers' experience of privatisation in three core utilities – telecommunications, gas and water. He argued that decentralisation and the reorganisation of management had radically altered the management-union terrain in utilities. Limited lay-union membership involvement had increased in the context of post-privatisation. These changes in the water industry resulted in the development of a workplace steward system that stimulated greater membership participation and involvement (Fairbrother 2000b: 229). Membership participation and involvement was encouraged, by GMB in particular, in the gas industry. This development formed the basis of Fairbrother's argument that union renewal could be built.

By examining workplace union responses to changes introduced as a consequence of the privatisation process this chapter sheds further light on the industrial relations implications of restructuring the organisation of work by focusing on management–union relations and employee discontents.

The research base

Interviews were carried out with GMB and AEEU senior and departmental union representatives in the gas, water and electricity utilities in the South West region (see Appendix). The occupations that these shop stewards represented covered mainly skilled and non-skilled manual workers. Five organisations were visited; from the public sector two of British Nuclear Fuels' (BNFL) power stations at Oldbury in Gloucestershire and Hinckley 'A' in Somerset; in the private sector, one electricity company, Western Power Distribution (WPD) but on three separate sites (two in Bristol, one in Somerset); one gas company, British Gas plc, and two water companies, Wessex Water and Bristol Water.

The changing organisation of work

Patterns in the public-sector Magnox power stations

Ferner and Colling (1993) indicate that the nuclear industry, which had remained in the public sector, was subject to much the same pressure as the energy industries in the private sector to restructure the labour process. The difference being that market forces compelled private-sector energy companies continually to improve the organisation of work to remain competitive while the pressure for change in the public-sector nuclear industry came from governments as custodians of the public purse. This was particularly meaningful in that the private sector considered the take-over of Magnox stations as unfeasible without government incurring the cost of decommissioning. During the 1990s, the Conservative Government, therefore, set in motion the incorporation of the Magnox Generation Division as part of the publicly owned British Nuclear Fuels (BNFL), seeing this as the only viable alternative. This integration was completed in January 1998 under a new Labour Government, which, however, threatened to sell off 49 per cent of BNFL as part of its public-private partnership policy, once again placing the future of Magnox power stations in jeopardy. These developments were the key drivers behind unions co-operating closely with the employers in bringing about changes in working methods. As the senior AEEU steward at Hinckley 'A' commented: 'It was decided that we must start to work in partnership, it's the only way forward for the company. If BNFL had not taken us on board, this station would have been shut in 2002.'[1]

Our evidence suggests that the implementation of new ways of working in nuclear power stations was kick-started after BNFL took over the responsibility of running Magnox power stations in 1996. However, in contrast to some public-sector organisations the momentum for bringing about changes to working practices was centrally driven. The long established and formal negotiation and consultation body, the Magnox Joint Council (MJC), forged a national agreement on flexible/generic working covering all Magnox power stations in 1998–99, following 18 months of negotiation. According to a lay delegate to the MJC, the concept of generic working was 'health and safety staff, maintenance staff and operations staff all coming together and becoming a production technician. There's a mix and match of duties'. Breaking down distinctions between jobs and teamworking played a central part in this new structure. One common problem was the organisation, evaluation and monitoring of training. Although BNFL was committed to investing more in training its workforce to the level and range of competencies required for generic working, in some extreme cases qualifications could take years to obtain. One case in point was a GMB steward who was 'about to start the fourth year of an HNC programme' which he said was 'a prerequisite for going back in the control room'. The shift towards generic working whilst apparent could in some cases therefore be rather slow but training was not the only factor hindering the rate of progress.

Apart from training, there was some variance in union and employee response to generic working between and within power stations. For instance, at Oldbury power station the resistance of day-workers to the removal of lines of demarcation slowed the pace of change.[2] One GMB steward observed:

> What has happened in reality is that the shift fitting staff are not being allowed to do any proper fitting work. Anything mechanical or electrical that comes up with any slightly more intricate nature, they are prevented from doing it. That's not necessarily by management, it's by the colleagues on the day side of it. If the feed pumps are stripped down, shift fitters are not allowed to touch it. I know two shift fitters recently that got a ten hour night shift going around changing eye wash bottles and little else due to these restrictions.

Nevertheless, the Oldbury stewards felt that demarcation lines were breaking down and it was only a matter of time before day-workers would be compelled to comply. As mentioned above, agreement on generic working was made between senior management and national union officials through the MJC, which was binding on all parties.

Hinckley 'A' power station was also covered by this agreement and, like the situation at Oldbury, generic working had yet to be introduced to day-workers. However, according to the AEEU senior steward, day-workers at Hinckley 'A', unlike their counterparts at Oldbury, were 'champing at the bit' to take on new flexible working because of the opportunity to earn higher salaries. Financial encouragement to accept flexible working practices was welcomed by day-workers at Hinckley 'A' but not at Oldbury. This was partly because of differences in the leadership style and the extent of involvement in the decision-making process between the AEEU and GMB at their respective power stations. The AEEU senior steward at Hinckley 'A' was a lay delegate to the MJC and was party to the flexibility agreement and active in its implementation at his place of work. Each Magnox site had a joint implementation team comprising trade union representatives, the production manager, shift charge engineer and a spokesperson from human resources. At Hinckley 'A' this team met regularly but its mandate was to oversee the agreement. This could be seen as an imperious approach. By contrast the GMB stewards at Oldbury felt detached from the decision-making process. One union steward put it in these words:

> Everything comes down from the MJC to the LJC [Local Joint Council] as a *fait accompli* – this is it, you are having it. We get very little input into what's going on. We tend only to get called together once a decision has been made, which I think is poor.

In summary, BNFL nuclear power stations in the public sector had only recently begun to push through significant changes to the organisation of work in co-operation with the trade unions via the centralised bargaining machinery. This was possible because the old Whitley-based negotiating machinery, in the form of National and Local Joint Councils, remained intact. Opportunities for negotiated rather than imposed change had thus been possible. Decisions made at the MJC level were disseminated down to LJCs, which were charged with executing agreements made at the higher level. The fact that unions co-operated with public-sector management's drive to introduce new methods of working, including the removal of job demarcation, has been attributed to four main factors (Fairbrother 1996), and all were evident in our study of Magnox power stations. First, there is a long history of good relations between the union hierarchy and senior management, albeit infused with senior management values of paternalism and benevolence (Salama and Easterby-Smith 1994). Second, strong consensual centralised bargaining procedures existed. Third, local bargaining procedures were relatively weak. Fourth, union organisation at the workplace was largely non-participatory. Our research also uncovered another factor for acceptance of change in the nuclear power industry – the threat of closure. Unions and power station management held a common view that they needed to keep govern-ment(s) on side to avoid power stations closing, for as well as being concerned about costs different governments were under constant pressure from environmental bodies to shut and decommission all nuclear stations.

Patterns in the private utilities sector

Common to all privatised utilities was the shift of collective bargaining from national to regional level as new management structures based on business units were put in place. However, despite the more active involvement of senior lay union officials in the bargaining process the pattern of industrial relations based on the Whitley model still predominated. This was a system that was not conducive to the involvement of rank-and-file union members. Thus largely traditional forms of unionism faced new management structures and strategies in a new competitive environment. This was the context in which changes were introduced to reconstitute established employment practices.

Changes to the organisation of work in utility companies prior to and immediately after privatisation were largely focused on raising productivity through financial incentives and reducing staffing levels (Ferner and Colling 1993). To sustain competitive advantage the pursuit of productivity had to be unremitting. Increasingly this demanded organisational change and radical revisions to working practices. This development was reflected in our survey. For instance, the AEEU stewards at Western Power Distribution (WPD) reported significant changes in the organisation of work between 1994–99 in electricity distribution. New ground was broken through the negotiated introduction of teamworking. This involved, somewhat controversially, the removal of demarcation lines. Jobs of the Engineering Managers Association (EMA) were lost as most of the higher-grade engineer duties were transferred directly to members of the AEEU. As a consequence around 25 per cent of the AEEU members most affected were upgraded. However, one shop steward commented:

> If you ask the majority of individuals who have to carry out those working practices and go through all the changes, . . . you would find that a lot of the staff are unhappy within their working environment through the added pressure that people are under now which they weren't years ago.

Unsurprisingly the higher-grade engineers fought tenaciously to retain their jobs but to no avail and inter-union relations were seriously impaired. One of the external drivers for acceptance of change was the AEEU's fear of losing jobs to outside contractors. AEEU stewards remarked that whilst understanding the bitterness and resentment of EMA members 'you've got to recognise that we had to move away from "that's not my job, that's Harry's job". We had to move otherwise we would have gone under and an outside contractor would have got the job.'

Ownership changes since South Western Electricity Board (SWEB) was first privatised reflect the growing corporate internationalisation of the world energy business, whereby foreign investors seek to buy up subsidiary concerns to match their core business interests. However, the resultant instability of corporate ownership and culture create enormous problems of consolidating worker 'voice' within the organisation. The process of organisational fragmentation has been driven down the organisation as contracting out has taken place leaving only the 'core' business of power distribution and data collection (meter reading) intact.

The AEEU used to represent workers engaged in such work as cable laying, tree cutting and digging. These members were lost when the company placed what they perceived as work not of central concern with outside contractors as part of the organisation's strategy of pursuing flexibility. This outsourcing of work triggered a parochial rearguard action by the AEEU. The reaction to the suggestion that they could take responsibility to organise these contract workers was:

> We don't want them. I don't want anything to do with them; I don't want to represent them. I want them out . . . First and foremost, I represent the people here.

The dangers of this approach have been articulated on numerous occasions since the formative years of trade unionism. Craft unions in the nineteenth and twentieth centuries utilised exclusionist polices in their attempts to control the labour market by imposing exacting standards of entry that gave rise to what some commentators dubbed as an aristocracy of labour (Gray 1981). Thus trade unionism has always been of a fragmentary nature and the recent increase in the outsourcing of work in utility companies has provided fresh opportunities for employers to exploit the differences of status, occupation, skill and earnings. Divisions between unions and between workers have, as in the past, been utilised to weaken workers' solidarity to the advantage of employers both in the public and private sectors; but managers did not create these divisions (Friedman 1977: 53).

At British Gas, substantive changes to the organisation of work following privatisation were not initiated until after 1995, in the run up to the demerger of British Gas plc in February 1997 when Centrica was created. Then a radical transformation in the organisation of engineer's work was introduced. First, work was conducted from home rather than an office. All engineers received job instructions by fax or phone and via a laptop computer. Second, and more significant, new technological developments broke down the previous demarcation of jobs between the gas engineer and the technician. A computer laptop is now an essential part of the engineer's equipment. It is used to run CD-ROM software detailing technical specifications and directions for all the work engineers are likely to encounter. Consequently, computer software programmes have to a large extent replaced the higher-graded work of the technician. The GMB senior representative expressed this development in these words:

> In the past the technician would come on the job and help you. You've now got a computer with a CD-ROM in it; it's got every aspect of your job in it. It's got an expert system in there . . . The technician is your CD-ROM. The computer will guide you through fault finding. At the end of the day, the company was going to stand down technicians to bring them down to the same level, or bring up the engineers.

Moreover, engineers have had to become multi-skilled as the company have moved into retailing and installing electrical as well as gas white goods. Even selling products direct to the customer has become part of the engineer's job. They are organised on a team basis and bonuses are calculated on the number of jobs a team completes plus extra sales a team generates.

One implication of home-based working in the gas industry was that because engineers no longer met on a daily basis, as they did before, the opportunity to discuss work-related matters was lost (Fairbrother 1996). This was confirmed by one GMB representative interviewed who said:

> That [home based working] does have an impact on the collective feeling, you don't always realise it when you come in the morning just talk, have a couple of moans and then go off. All that's gone.

However, home-based working and the introduction of teamworking triggered a change in union communications and the input of senior shop stewards. Meetings of shop stewards in the South West were easier to organise because they could meet bimonthly after company-arranged team briefings. Moreover, since 1997 regional senior shop stewards had taken on a more active role in dealing with workplace issues. The GMB senior representative in the South West had a time-off allowance of one day a week to deal with union matters. He sometimes organised 'breakfast' meetings with his members, although for those living in Cornwall this is a problem because of travelling time.

The drive towards teamworking, multi-skilling and the breakdown of job demarcation appeared less advanced in the water supply industry. To a certain extent water supply remains a 'natural monopoly' and less subject to competition than gas or electricity (O'Connell Davidson 1993). This may help to explain the slower pace of work organisation reform. Nevertheless there is evidence of change. Multi-tasking rather than multi-skilling characterised increases in flexible working at Bristol Water, a company that has been in the private sector since its foundation in the nineteenth century. Interchangability and flexibility within grades had increased but lines of demarcation between craft workers, mechanics and electricians, remained. Changing working patterns had enabled the company to secure 24-hour cover seven days a week. Although this negotiated arrangement had been in place only a short time, according to the senior GMB representative the new way of working, combined with financial compensation, was well received by the workforce. This is how he put it:

> They [the company] called it a win-win situation, which in effect has worked that way. The company's got the cover they've got, our people now have got a better wage packet, they are more settled, they are only putting themselves out one week in eight now, whereas they were doing a standby one in three, one in four, and they could get called any time.

However, the financial rewards that went with this package only applied to existing staff. Any new employees hired were expected to do the same work and adhere to the same shift pattern for less money. An example given by one GMB shop steward revealed that the yearly salary of a new shift attendant was £2,500 less than that received by a day attendant, which he thought would increasingly lead to bad feelings between staff.

In common with the practice at WPD, one flexible staffing technique utilised by Bristol Water was that of outsourcing work. Although not new to the armoury of management practices, the senior GMB representative reported that since the privatisation of the water industry Bristol Water has resorted to outsourcing work that has long been performed by its own employees.[3] Although the renewal of mains and associated tasks had long been contracted out, responsibility for repairing leaks and household plumbing services, jobs that had always been dependent on in-house labour, was also contracted out following water privatisation.

This expansion in the outsourcing of core manual work resulted in GMB losing negotiating rights and most of its membership in pipe-laying, pipe maintenance and domestic plumbing services. Unlike the AEEU at WPD the senior GMB steward at Bristol Water regretted this because

> These guys [manual workers] . . . were probably more outspoken and more militant, because it was hard physical work and in the old days of bonus schemes, they were never happy with that. Probably there was more togetherness with the old-fashioned physical manual workers than there is today.

Thus the growth of outsourcing served to weaken unions' collective spirit and undermine workers' solidarity making it increasingly difficult for unions to organise and service its membership.

There was little sign, however, of resistance to outsourcing as craft workers abandoned any attempt to keep non-craft workers within the boundaries of union leverage in the face of what was at the time an authoritarian management. The company had successfully divided craft from manual workers. Morale was at a low ebb which was not helped by the high-profile sacking of over 100 print workers after a long-running dispute in close proximity to Bristol Water's main depot.[4] Soon after, in 1994, for the first time in the company's history compulsory redundancies were announced.

Experimentation with new management techniques was more apparent at Wessex Water. Here a range of new human resource methods was tested in the run up to and aftermath of privatisation. In particular, teamworking, team briefing, attitude surveys and quality circles were introduced along with performance related pay. Performance related pay has since been abandoned in favour of a system likely to rest on basic salary plus incentives. This American-owned Company[5] seemed more proactive in initiating change, frequently utilising outside management consultants, and less tied to traditional ways of working than the British-owned Bristol Water. There was little evidence of organised resistance from workplace unions. Activity at shopfloor level was minimal with no workplace meetings. A shortage of union representatives around the region was evident, although there were signs of change. Members at various sites scattered around the region were beginning to show interest in representative positions because they wanted to improve channels of communication and get access to more information (interview notes).

To sum up, all the companies surveyed had been subject to change of ownership (apart from Bristol Water), structural adjustment and new methods of working since deregulation and privatisation. Rigid job demarcation lines were dismantled with multi-skilling and multi-tasking becoming more common as a result of negotiated change. This was controversial as the jobs of technicians in the gas industry and higher-graded engineers in electricity distribution were eroded. The extent and pace of change varied between the companies researched. Paradoxically, it was the long-standing private company, Bristol Water, which was slowest off the mark. Here multi-skilling and multi-tasking was yet to be fully developed. However, like that practised at WPD, outsourcing lower-skilled manual activities proved attractive in securing a tighter control over labour costs and met with little or no union resistance. The fragmentation of the organisation of work as a result of teamworking, flexible working, outsourcing and commercialisation of the business had left the traditional steward system of representation struggling to adapt. The unions have become more parochial and defensive in their outlook and apart from a few minor adjustments have on the whole stuck to hierarchical and remote forms of representation even in cases where national bargaining has been replaced by regional or local bargaining.

Management–union relations

The public sector Magnox power stations

At the time of our survey management–union relations in Magnox power stations were in the process of undergoing important changes. Hinckley 'A', together with Dungeness, was piloting an initiative designed as a step towards forging a 'partnership pact' between BNFL and its workforce. The decision to move to partnership arrangements was taken at the MJC in October 1998 as part of the BNFL plan to establish a BNFL Partnership Council. Given that Oldbury was not included in this pilot scheme it is not surprising to find that some differences in management–union relations at these two sites existed. At Hinckley 'A' (and Dungeness) the framework for the repositioning of employment relations was based on a shared vision; shared obligations and responsibility for problem solving; early involvement of trade unions and staff; regular and open communications; and changed behaviour.[6]

The 'behavioural' changes, in this pilot run, were targeted at managers and trade union representatives and were engendered by a training programme conducted by consultants following a pre-training 360-degree personal assessment. The intended 'behavioural change' is actually a process of attitudinal restructuring with a concentration on key concepts centred on the notion of 'working together in true partnership'. The senior AEEU steward strongly believed that conflicts of interest between employer and employees could be resolved through psychoanalytical methods that were able to recreate organisational structures and relationships along harmonious lines. Following the training programme the steward advocated the new approach to other Magnox stewards at Hinckley. He explained:

> Yes, I've convinced the rest of my shop stewards across all the five unions, when we're meeting as a local joint council or committee, we must use the words 'working together in a true partnership'. Keep using the words, they are there to be used, say we've got to do this together in partnership. At one time it was a bit difficult, but now most of the people are starting to use these words. You have to work in partnership. Now you see management have started to use them as well.

The AEEU was confident that its members could be 'coached' to accept the merits of partnership by convincing them that their jobs were secure and their terms and conditions of employment safe.

Although Oldbury power station was not part of the pilot partnership, increasingly the term was integrated into management language in its dealings with union workplace representatives. The GMB senior representative reported that while a formal partnership arrangement did not exist, management 'would certainly consult and seek agreement on everything'. No jobs or posts were lost or changes made without full consultation with workplace union representatives but this in practice did 'little to deflect' management from imposing change. Strong formal industrial relations mechanisms were a feature of Magnox power stations, Oldbury being no exception. The establishment of Local Joint Councils (LJCs) in the late 1980s enabled engineers, clerical staff, and industrial staff to discuss workplace problems with management collectively rather than meeting as separate little committees as practised previously. Moreover, a single spine agreement was introduced so that all staff came under one set of terms and conditions.

These changes helped to sustain co-operative relations between management and unions but against the backdrop of many union members perceiving management as all-powerful. There was still a sense of 'them and us' but the view of some that management was indomitable created an atmosphere of inevitability leading to passive acceptance of change among some union members. That this attitude was not shared by all is evident in the resistance of day-workers to the removal of demarcation lines described above. However, the senior GMB steward's stance in negotiations with management was very much driven by this sense of inevitability:

> You dilute the change rather than stop the change, you'll never stop it because unless the membership are prepared to do something, there's very little we

can do . . . It's amazing that station management actually do us the courtesy of informing us of some of these things, because I think that the state of play at the moment is that they could impose what they liked and nobody would do a thing about it.

The private utilities sector

Since privatisation our data suggest that management–union relations have become less adversarial in electricity distribution. The harmonisation of employment conditions have helped to bring this about but the restructuring of collective bargaining procedures has resulted in a reduction of bargaining at plant level and the abandonment of many local agreements. A new single-spine grading structure evaluated by Hay Management replaced the old one based on craft lines of demarcation. The introduction of single-table bargaining through the formation of one joint committee for the whole of the company, the Electricity Business Forum (EBF), comprising of management representatives, full-time union representatives and senior shop stewards, replaced the previous multi-committee negotiating structure. This joint committee had the authority to negotiate changes to the Electricity Business Agreement (EBA); thus centralised machinery for negotiating changes to pay and conditions not only remained intact but was strengthened.

At EBF level more co-operative attitudes have replaced the adversarial 'them and us' climate that previously existed. At shop-floor level cultural change was more gradual and the process of constructing closer management–union relations was, according to one senior GMB steward in Bristol, only hindered by 'a few stewards who are still in the 1960s, they are still in the old "them and us" structure. They won't change; they are diminishing gradually.' But to suggest that a radical change in leadership style, from adversarial to co-operative, had taken place would be wide of the mark, since there is a history of co-operation and peaceful relations in the industry rather than relations marked by strong adversarialism (Ferner and Colling 1993).

However, there were cultural differences between plants, and Bristol workers were viewed by their Somerset counterparts as more entrenched in their ways. Whether these rural-based workers were more malleable than their urban counterparts is open to question. The reasons that the AEEU stewards in Somerset supported the partnership concept are more tangible. Stewards gave particular weight to the benefits associated with the introduction of the single-spine wage structure and greater access to and improved relations with top management. However, although they felt that progress had been made towards the partnership goal they commented that 'we're a long way from achieving it'. The main concern the stewards identified was their exclusion from being involved in the decision-making process. The union was forced to react to company proposals rather than their desired option to participate with management in drawing up policies affecting their members.

> Instead of the company working behind the scenes in coming out with proposals and we having always to challenge and address those issues, we want the management to work with us, so it wasn't a proposal, it was a joint thing.

Following privatisation single-table bargaining was introduced in the water companies which contributed to the improvement of management–union relations. This was more evident at Bristol Water where, along with the harmonisation of conditions, joint union–management working parties were established to examine and advocate solutions to specific problems. Whilst these co-operative management frameworks could appear to be a strategy designed to maximise the chances of successfully achieving change, the GMB senior steward believed that the union could also benefit:

> If it's something that you don't think is right, or you put something to the Company and they say, 'yes, I see what you are getting at, we'll put a working party together to look at it, it's not an issue'... it's a win-win thing again; it does work.

However, there is some evidence to suggest that management utilised these working parties as mechanisms to divert grievances. For instance, due to the increasing expressions of injustice at the way in which the performance-related pay system operated, management set up a working party to look at it rather than abandon the system.

While there were signs of partnership emerging at Bristol Water, at British Gas GMB forged a formal partnership agreement with management to replace the old adversarial relationship. This initiative was driven by a crisis in British Gas. The company was in severe economic difficulties in 1995, resulting in extensive redundancies. GMB, in line with its national policy, felt that protecting its members' interests at this time was best served through 'partnership'. Mechanisms such as regular open forums with shop stewards and quarterly LJC meetings between senior managers and senior shop stewards were introduced along with future job security assurances, in the form of no compulsory redundancies, to underpin the partnership agreement. However, the senior steward reported that to a certain extent the membership felt the union had let them down because of the prior acceptance of huge job losses, work intensification and the fragmentation of the workforce brought about by changes in working practices, such as home-based working. This has led to a feeling of isolation characteristic of the 'new' workplace.

In summary, there has been a significant shift in management–union relations in the privatised utilities, with more information and consultation, and with the opportunity for negotiating over change. This is particularly striking given the employers' need for rapid organisational and cultural transformation since privatisation and exposure to the market and competition. Respective management teams in privatised utility companies have chosen a strategy of negotiated change, using union representatives to establish agreement to change and to legitimise change as an alternative to confrontation. The streamlining of negotiating machinery, along with the harmonisation of conditions, single-table bargaining and in some cases outsourcing, has facilitated such developments. Paradoxically, the blurring of job demarcation has also contributed to both the GMB and AEEU co-operating more closely with management at the expense of souring relations with other unions. The language of partnership, however, was evident more at a notional rather than a tangible level. The exception to this was at British Gas, where a formal partnership agreement was enacted following the surfacing of economic difficulties in the company in 1995.

Employee discontents

The context for employee discontent has been a period of continuing job insecurity as the logic of privatisation and commercial competition induced the recasting of the organisation of work and employment relations in public and private utilities. To this must be added the effects of the regulators' input and trade-offs between wages and salaries, shareholder dividends and company profits, investment in the industries themselves, and prices charged to the customer. The GMB union, for instance, felt particularly aggrieved towards the regulator OFWAT (Office of Water Services) as it failed to take into account the impact of its decisions on the workforce in respect to pay and jobs, points that were raised to no avail by the GMB with Ian Byatt, the Director General of OFWAT. The 1994 OFWAT pricing review had heavily influenced Bristol Water management's decision to reduce the workforce by 200. Although this was not repeated following the December 1999 review the upward trend in employment levels recorded between March 1997 and March 1999 was not sustained.

Public-sector Magnox power stations

Fears over job security or more precisely closure of Magnox power stations was something that both BNFL senior management, trade unions and employees held in common, a fact that was instrumental in bringing about cultural and work organisational change. The union accepted a voluntary selective severance scheme even though reductions in the numbers employed resulted in the intensification of work for the remaining staff. For instance, at Hinckley 'A' the number of maintenance fitters had fallen from thirty in the early 1990s to ten in 1999. It was against this backdrop that a partnership arrangement emerged at Hinckley 'A' but one where the principles of this arrangement had yet to penetrate the thoughts and actions of middle managers. As the senior AEEU shop steward remarked:

> I believe most of the senior management are on board, it's when you get to the next layer . . . if you talk to some team leaders, this is where they don't know the meaning of partnership. They've got a job to do and that's it, it's got to be done at any end. This is the problem.

In particular, there was a concern that shift chargers, who are effectively responsible for running the site after 4.30pm, would not accept a weakening of their authority in respect to safety. Under the partnership arrangement, the right of workers to refuse to carry out work they considered as unsafe was re-enforced. But the fear of shop stewards was that their members would be cajoled into carrying out unsafe working practices because shift chargers had not been co-opted into the partnership way of working. In response to protests from shop stewards that this could well happen the company sent a letter to all staff saying that 'if the job is not safe it must stop'. That the company had to take this measure is indicative that partnership culture had yet to permeate management ranks, let alone the organisation as a whole.[7] However, this point should not be exaggerated given the pressure placed on shift chargers by senior managers to meet tight work schedules. These tensions gave rise to health and safety problems developing into key union grievances.

Another area of discontent at Hinckley was the use of agency staff, some of whom were formerly permanent members of staff. According to the senior AEEU steward:

> People have taken voluntary severance, their lump sum golden handshake and because the company needs them, then they bring them back as agency staff. It's a nonsense and it's annoying to the other engineers here.

The use of agency staff catalysed additional tensions in staff relations. At Hinckley 'A' agency staff made up around 7 per cent of the workforce and few were trade union members. The AEEU senior steward maintained that the agency notified its staff that they should not join a union. He commented, 'I know it's illegal, but you try and prove it.'

Outsourcing of services such as cleaning and maintenance was particularly prevalent at Oldbury, as a result of staff leaving through the voluntary severance scheme. In peak periods Oldbury was more heavily dependent on contractors than it had been before BNFL took control of Magnox power stations. The GMB shop steward observed:

> At one time, when the turbine needed to be stripped apart, that was CEGB [Central Electricity Generating Board] company people, now it's all Siemens, we don't get a look in at all on any of it. Ten years ago, that would have been nearly all our people with them doing the odd specialist jobs. It's completely the other way now.

One of the complaints of Oldbury permanent staff was that contract workers had had a negative effect on staff bonus payments because their productivity levels were below that of core workers. After protests from the unions BNFL agreed to change the criteria on which the bonus system was based to exclude the input of contract workers from the calculations.

To summarise, the company-union campaign to keep Magnox power stations operational and maintain employment security was uppermost in the minds of union representatives whose objective was to ensure that reductions in the workforce were achieved only through voluntary means. This impacted on the way in which unions approached labour-management relations and how they dealt with the discontents of their members. The result was a strengthening of the authority of the MJC in arbitrating over industrial relations' problems, which was favoured over the development of more participatory means, such as the mobilisation of union members around common discontents. Moreover, the partnership arrangement at Hinckley was beginning to impose co-operation on local labour-management relations enabling management to more readily increase the flexibility of the workforce and improve productivity through greater effort. But while the unions have felt it necessary to accept voluntary redundancies, and heavier workloads, in order to maintain unity with management in the fight to secure a future for Magnox power stations, they would not compromise over safety. On this important issue they successfully forced the company to accept the union's position.

The private-utilities sector

Health and safety was also an area of concern for workers employed by WPD. In contrast to the unifying qualities normally associated with health and safety matters, this issue actually served to antagonise relations between the trade unions and WPD's management. According to the AEEU stewards, trust had broken down between management, unions and staff following a number of fatal accidents.[8] Joint co-operation over health and safety had diminished. As one AEEU steward explained:

> On paper it would look brilliant. The reality is that it's nothing like it used to be. We used to have local committees. We used to meet all the time. We used to do a joint approach.

Increasingly, the AEEU experienced difficulties in recruiting safety representatives. The major complaint was that the company did not allocate enough time to union safety representatives to carry out their role due to pressure of work. This factor contributed to a rapid turnover of safety representatives, four in four years. One shop steward attempted to take the dual role of steward and safety representative but was forced to give up the safety role because of the pressure of his job as an engineer.

Despite complying with health and safety legislation, that is recognising union appointed safety representatives and having in place the relevant bodies and procedures, WPD eschewed a collective approach to health and safety and took to policing safety matters unilaterally. According to one steward trust over health and safety matters had broken down to the extent that spot checks take place frequently without the involvement of safety representatives or union stewards. The shop stewards likened this policy to macho management. Employees breaking health and safety regulations were threatened with dismissal. Managers apparently adopted an aggressive approach in dealing with health and safety matters spreading a climate of fear.

This approach contradicts recent research, which argues that the involvement of all employees in health and safety matters is of paramount importance (Vassie 1998) and that committees with greater employee input are more effective (Eaton and Nocerino 2000). Moreover, this approach leaves management open to the charge that to place undue emphasis on the culpability of workers in health and safety failings masks its drive to keep production going (Nichols 1997: 40).

Some union representatives recognised that the recent fatalities, and consequent court cases, pushed management into taking forceful top-down action.

> I think they think they can manage it and that's the way to manage it more, with a harder approach. It's because we've had accidents, we've had fatalities, which we never had previously.

Yet the AEEU thought that this approach was counterproductive, as indicated by the words of one of its stewards:

> I think health and safety is in people's minds now, they don't think it's for their benefit, which they should be feeling. They're feeling it's a stick. They're being beaten with this safety stick.

It does seem as though the unions were caught in a pincer movement. Pressure brought about by the intensification of work served to weaken union representative's involvement in managing health and safety procedures. Management's 'policing' attitude to health and safety further compounded this. This practice did not provide a good foundation on which to build a partnership. But as one AEEU steward remarked:

> I think the company is happy thinking that the partnership they've got is fine ... They've got a damned good partnership. If I had a partnership that was 70/30, so would I think it was a damn good one.

At British Gas, a partnership agreement signed in 1995 was accompanied by agreed changes in the organisation of work as discussed in the previous section. One consequence of these changes, and a source of discontent, was widespread work intensification. Home-based working for example was directly linked to achieving work targets, which since the original agreement that covered the installation and servicing of central heating systems has been widened to include other appliances. This was achieved by management without supplementary negotiation and was identified by a senior GMB steward as a critical issue because workloads were escalating. In addition, the introduction of computerised testing to diagnose problems, rather than call on the services of a technician as happened in the past, had increased the pace of work as 'waiting time' had been eliminated and estimated completion times reduced. Work was also more closely monitored by supervisory staff, adding to feelings of discontent associated with work intensification. One steward commented:

> You're working harder and you don't know what you are going to hit when you go into a house. Sometimes we've got what they call UCAD [universal computer-aided design] operators, which are physically monitoring how much work you are doing. They can see exactly where you are, and how much work is being done.

Work intensification was also identified as a concern at Wessex Water but it was a new pay structure that was the source of most grievances here. In the past new staff were placed on the bottom rung of the pay band for their grade of work and after six months, subject to satisfactory performance, they would automatically progress up the pay scale. The anomaly of the new pay system was that progression through the grade bands was now no longer 'automatic'. Increases were explicitly tied to performance. This could result in as much £2,000 a year difference between operators doing exactly the same job.

Individual performance-related pay was a particularly contentious issue at Bristol Water. It had a negative impact on employee morale and served to undermine team spirit. In contrast to the situation at Wessex Water feelings of injustice at the system had arisen because new staff could end up with higher pay than established staff for the same job. Moreover, some departments seemed to do better than others, intimating favouritism. Personnel was cited as one example of this because, according to the senior steward, if 'you are nearer the nucleus, you can shine'. The union response to this injustice over pay was to try to renegotiate the pay system and abolish the individual performance element and replace it with standard pay plus profit-related pay. But the union's hands were tied somewhat because they wanted to maintain good relations with the personnel manager, as one GMB steward indicated:

> This performance-related pay is the idea of the personnel manager. We don't really want to upset him, because he can be a friend to us, because he's a buffer between that and the director. He isn't a bad bloke, he's always been pretty fair, so we haven't said it's a load of rubbish and it's all your fault. We've just said I think it's time for change and we'll go down the road of trying to change it.

From the union viewpoint it is not the amount of money, which is small, but the injustice, particularly in a manual environment. Rather than mobilise the union membership around the issue shop stewards preferred not to upset the relationship they had built up with the personnel manager and agreed to set up a working party to look at the problem. By attempting to resolve the problem in this way the union stewards missed an opportunity to mobilise their members around an issue on which strong feelings prevailed. The stewards' action only served to distance themselves from their members and weaken combativeness.

To sum up, overall the legacy of the privatisation and marketisation of the public utilities surveyed was one of work intensification; changing systems of pay determination; and health and safety concerns. Whilst these issues often aroused a sense of unfairness and injustice there is little evidence of union representatives channelling this dissatisfaction into mobilising collective resistance. Rather in most cases the unions have remained reactive in the face of these pressures and often co-operated via joint councils or working parties in the introduction of change.

Conclusion

The privatisation of public utilities is now well advanced. Privatisation has increased the capacity of management to reshape the working environment so as to intensify capital accumulation. This chapter has traced the impact that privatisation has had on work organisation and management–union relations – and explored the union response. Workers in utility companies had experienced ownership changes; job losses; work intensification; and outsourcing of previously core operational functions. While remaining staff were better trained, more skilled and more flexible, some aspects of their employment conditions had deteriorated. Discontents were still harboured but there were few signs that, in any significant way, the unions were willing to pursue their resolution through membership mobilisation. Given there is a long history of non-participatory unionism in the former public utilities, and that dependent and detached partnership between the unions and employers was pursued at the utility sites visited, it is not surprising to find little evidence of rank-and-file activity. A further factor impeding membership mobilisation against collective grievances was that management continued to encourage representative bargaining through established bargaining or consultative bodies; at this level in particular the message was that management–union relations had improved. Management showed a willingness to negotiate change and unions reciprocated on the basis that co-operation offered the best hope of avoiding compulsory redundancies. This made it easier for utility employers to achieve the introduction of new ways of working and greater utilisation of flexible working practices. This led to the opening of divisions between unions contesting possession of the 'rights' to perform an increasing range of workplace tasks, as craft control over the labour process weakened.

Inhibiting the development of collective struggle was the marginalisation of those workers whose jobs had been outsourced creating further divisions within the workforce. Decentralisation of collective bargaining was minimal and opportunities for advancing participatory unionism as an alternative to partnership were handicapped. This was further compounded by the fact that the intensification of work impacted on the time some union representatives had to carry out their union roles proficiently. In one case this contributed to problems in recruiting and retaining health and safety representatives against a backdrop of a deteriorating health and safety environment. The development of a partnership approach, associated with a servicing model of union representation, acted to consolidate pre-existing co-operative industrial relations in the public and private utilities.

Our conclusion contradicts Fairbrother's (2000b) view that workplace activity in the sector was on the up. However, we recognise that workplace grievances in utilities did not remain individualised but had become collectivised and, therefore, the conditions were in place for union renewal based on 'organising' rather than 'servicing'. Unions, however, eschewed mobilisation and deflected collective grievances through neo-centralised institutional means, including non-bargaining bodies, and placed greater reliance on employer goodwill.

8   What future?

This book has sought to examine union response to change in the new workplace. In reality many of the workplaces surveyed have been reconstructed 'old' workplaces highlighting the fact that most British workplaces have been in operation for many years (Cully *et al.* 1999). This was a necessary choice to reflect how workplace unions have adapted to changing environments in these typical work settings. In any case, the array of organisational and cultural change, new management techniques, and new ways of organising work found in the workplaces qualify them in terms of 'newness'. The unions and workplaces surveyed also present a valid cross-section of contemporary British workplaces, ranging across the private and public sectors and representing a variety of occupations, crafts and skills. Most of the research data have come from the South West of England, and whilst the implication of this socio-geographical choice has not been fully explored, wherever possible data have been compared to that produced in the nationally-based 1998 Workplace Employee Relations Survey (WERS).

Research data have been deliberately gathered from union workplace representatives. This has been done to reflect the dynamic of change within the heartbeat of the union movement, and to counterbalance other studies which may reflect responses from employer's representatives on the one hand, or national trade union head offices on the other. The researchers have adopted a critical approach to recent literature on trade unions in the UK, which has often (but not always) presented a pessimistic view of unions' future. In essence the research has posed three key questions. First, to what extent has the long period of declining union organisation in the 1980s and 1990s affected the ability of workplace unions to challenge managerial prerogative? Second, how are unions in the workplace managing, if at all, to respond to new management initiatives? Third, is there evidence of any re-collectivisation of workplace relations in the unionised sectors? The conclusions of this book emphasise that despite many problems there is continued resilience of union organisation, from which further renewal is possible.

The new workplace

Within the research field presented there are both similarities and differences of experience. The similarities can be concluded from the following sections.

An era of instability in enterprise and organisation governance

In all sectors, both public and private, there was a distinct instability of ownership and/or governance. This development is part of the continued process of internationalisation taking place in the world economy. In the trading sector it is most pronounced. For example, of the fifteen manufacturing establishments surveyed only one had not been subject to a change in ownership in recent years, while one half of the insurance companies had been subject to take-over or merger. Similar experiences are recorded in the public utilities, where changes of ownership and mergers have also been an associated product of privatisation. The implications of this activity are sometimes severe. Many of changes of ownership have been accompanied by job rationalisation as new corporate structures have emerged from the old and the duplication of production of services has been eliminated. Job cuts have also been part of a more general rationalisation process in response to over capacity or as part of a simple asset-stripping operation. The increased pace of job cutting has enhanced feelings of job insecurity. This in itself would have had a number of secondary implications. First, in terms of maximising opportunities for management to increase worker exploitation (Cappelli *et al.* 1997: 4; Rubery 1996). Second, in terms of reducing feelings of well being and creating psychological stress and ill health (Gallie *et al.* 1998; ILO 2000). Increasing job insecurity may also have a deleterious effect on management-employee trust within the workplace making the consolidation of worker commitment more rather than less difficult to obtain. Appelbaum *et al.* (2000), for example, press this point in their preference for the high-performance work system based on mutual gains and partnership. However, like many business writers they fail to address the awkward fact that downsizing and job insecurity are inherent features of high-performance work systems (Biewener 1997). One additional implication, especially found from the aerospace data, is the effect job cutting has had on union activists. In five of our case studies union activists suffered almost total 'wipe-out' through selected redundancy during the early and mid-1990s; union organisation had to be rebuilt as a consequence. These events occurred in well-organised workplaces, the fear factor in other, less well-organised workplaces would have been equally if not more intense.

Another product of corporate instability is that prevailing decision-making structures within organisations have been changed either towards more centralised control and personnel or towards a more diffuse and variegated pattern. This has posed different problems for workplace unions in terms of adjustment. On the one hand, where decision-making has become more centralised, the workplace union has in turn become remote from the key decision-makers. Negotiation at local level is consequently more restricted in scope and content. In extreme cases this has meant that no contact at all had been made, either because workplace representatives simply could not identify who they could meaningfully talk to within the new corporate hierarchy or because real authority and control was located in corporate headquarters based overseas. On the other hand, where decision-making had become more diffuse, a danger sometimes arose that management at lower level operates to different standards and procedures, reflecting different styles in the management of employee relations. The latter case was evident in some insurance and manufacturing examples, and the former in the case of public utilities subject to foreign ownership. Old consistencies of consultation and negotiation have been disrupted and workplace unions have been faced with the need to adapt their own structures in response.

The consolidation of new ways of organising work

The surveys report an overwhelming trend towards the adoption of an array of new working methods with teamworking and problem-solving groups among the most prominent. More than two-thirds of the enterprises visited in the private sector had adopted these practices. The public-sector organisations reported a lesser incidence, but nevertheless included a third of the total. The incidence of flexible working arrangements was more varied, with a generally greater prominence of functional flexibility in the private organisations and a more equal distribution of numerical and temporal flexibility across all sectors. The data would suggest that a definite implantation of new working practices had taken root within the workplace, reflecting both the emulation of Japanese and lean production methods, as well as a management drive to flexibilise many aspects of working time, function and contract. It is these aspects, together with the predominance of performance-related pay, that clearly characterise the new workplace.

A shift towards entrepreneurial culture

In all sectors the attempted introduction of new cultural programmes and procedures aimed at raising customer consciousness were apparent. This 'new entrepreneurialism' has varied implications. At one level it can mean, as in insurance and aerospace, that old cultural and organisational values associated with the industry have been turned upside down. Insurance once displayed a conservative rule-bound and hierarchical organisational culture where the mass shifting of paper mountains dominated the organisation of work. Now, with the introduction of new 'products' and product competition and with the aid of ITS the value added of individual workers can be finely tuned and encouraged to be increased by new systems of pay and reward. A multiplicity of pay systems has resulted, ranging from individual performance-related pay, through to competency and even local market-related pay. Similarly in aerospace the old militaristic rule-bound culture has gradually given way to a customer-centred culture with the associated fragmentation of the workplace into business divisions and cost centres. As in some of the manufacturing examples, this has often meant a fragmentation of bargaining arrangements within the enterprise, combined with a withdrawal by employers from collectively agreed grade-related pay to individually based systems of performance reward. Even in the public services these processes can be traced, gas service engineers, for example, are now encouraged to be customer friendly and talk to the customer about new products and available services rather than just fix the broken boiler. In the NHS Trusts and local authorities the process of fragmentation is also apparent, as internal market testing and devolved budgets become the norm.

A distinct rise in employee discontent

The evidence clearly indicates a rise in employee discontent within this new workplace environment. There is notable reporting of an increase in discontent over management attitudes, staffing levels, workloads, working hours and flexibility as well as pay, grading and health and safety. The experience was common across all sectors, unions and organisations and confirmed by increasing use of grievance procedures to fend off the worst excesses of managerial prerogative. Additionally and possibly surprisingly given the changed political environment after the 1997 election, a hardening of management attitudes towards unions can also be traced. Reports of hardening management attitudes were approximately double the number of those reporting softening. The combination of hardening management attitudes and increasing discontent found in the surveys has important implications. First, it suggests that the conditions are ripe for re-enforcement of 'them-and-us' attitudinal groupings within the new workplace. Second, and following from the first, it indicates fertile ground for union mobilisation against the employer, and conversely, less fertile ground for any intended re-shaping of employee attitudes towards employer goal commitment or mutual gains-based employee relations.

Union responses

Such features of the new workplace described above form the root causes of the 'crisis of representation' presented and reviewed in the introductory chapter. New unionism, or the organising model, is one potential solution to the crisis implying as it does a more participatory approach, aggressive and innovative recruitment, and an emphasis (in the US version at least) on anti-corporate campaigning. The partnership route to renewal adopts a different perspective, reflecting ideas of mutual gains and, in its most regressive form, a retrenchment into business unionism. Lastly there are additional debates which focus on the perceived need for unions to adopt a new identity in this era of globalisation, to perhaps move beyond traditional economism of the workplace and to take on wider social goals in an effort to rekindle interest representation. Hyman (1999: 104–11), for example, argues that the pressures of increased international competition have led unions onto the defensive, to engage in concession bargaining, to participate in enterprise egoism, and 'to favour the relatively advantaged at the expense of the most insecure'. In this pessimistic scenario, it is argued that only a reformation of unions' identities to 'articulate a new discourse of workers' rights' can guarantee a sound future for unions in an increasingly unsolidaristic world. However, each of these remedies comes with its own associated problems. The organising model in the UK appears as a restrained version of its US exemplar, tempered by the conservatism of union leaderships, weakly diffused down the union hierarchies, and subject to the ongoing need to service members as well as recruit them. Partnership runs the severe risk of inducing passivity among the rank-and-file and dependence of union activists on employers' goodwill. Partnership agreements tend to be driven by employers' agendas and the prospects for engaging in Stewart and Martinez Lucio's (1998) 'new politics of production' are diminished as a result. Finally, while Hyman's (1999) stated need for broader solidaristic principles and action from within unions would be a welcome step forward for union renewal it runs the risk of ignoring union activity at the workplace, where members are recruited and, most importantly, where conflict between capital and labour is at its most acute. What then, is the reality of workplace unionism presented in this book? Are there examples of good practice from which lessons for union revival can be learnt?

In the introductory chapter a scheme of widening union influence (Figure 1.1) was outlined together with a model of the conditions necessary for successful union renewal (Table 1.1). It was argued first, that unions need to develop strategies to widen and deepen workplace bargaining agendas and to expand beyond their core workplaces if union renewal is to be realised. This entails invoking the core practice of the 'organising model', together with the adoption of more community and cross-union solidarity actions as suggested by Hyman (1999). It was also confirmed, by the evidence in Chapter 2, that there is a positive relationship between the introduction of new management practices and the generation of employee discontent, and then between the ensuing grievances and the scope of union bargaining activity. In other words, where unions at the workplace have engaged with management in opposing or moderating the process of change, they have retained and recruited members and increased their organisational strength. This analysis borrows something from previous work by Kelly (1998), where he adapts earlier examples of mobilisation theory, but also from others such as Darlington (1994a, b) who seek to define the importance of local union leadership intentions. The car sector studies of Stewart and Wass (1998) provide similar insights. These authors show how a union strategy of critical engagement with new management techniques, what one car plant convenor referred to as 'a strategy of disagreement', can allow shop stewards to gain control over the implementation of the social changes associated with new management techniques and effectively secure control over the organisation of work. In other words, unlike previous management attempts to change the workplace, often by imposition, trade unions can become directly engaged with organisational power, including such processes as teamworking and labour flexibility initiatives (1998: 82, 90). The research evidence presented in this book can be grouped into categories where such a process of engagement has been undertaken or otherwise. In different sectors and across the three different unions this evidence has been varied.

The importance of engagement

Evidence of practices of engagement emerge from all of the sectors surveyed. In the fifteen manufacturing examples, while there is a general picture of passivity in the face of corporate change and restructuring, there are two clear instances where the workplace union had positively adapted its practices to confront team-working. In one of these cases, a US-owned photocopying company, the MSF and AEEU had managed to re-organise itself so that union representative elections took place within the newly organised functionally based teams. From here it was possible to negotiate and if necessary obstruct the terms of change in work organisation engendered by the employer's team-based strategy. In a much smaller paper-producing company the GMB, working from 95 per cent shop floor union density, had managed to subvert some of the worse features of a management shift to team-working by retaining existing job demarcation patterns. Multi-tasking and concomitant work intensification had been successfully resisted.

In aerospace attempts to block transfer of work abroad under the pressures of internationalisation have so far been unsuccessful. However, the AEEU, in particular, through threats of action has been generally successful in blocking attempts to use on-site non-permanent labour which employers have sought to introduce to cut costs. This has been achieved by direct negotiation and sometimes with the threat of industrial action. As in the manufacturing examples the AEEU have often altered their internal structures, this time by shifting the power balance from group- to site-based representatives in order to counter management attempts to fragment site-wide pay and conditions agreements. Industrial action had to be threatened or taken in these examples to successfully preserve these site-wide agreements. Joint regulation of employment conditions has been preserved as a result. For the MSF, however, outcomes have been less successful, as the inability of the representatives to mobilise their members led to the break-up of site-wide regulation and a consequent victory for management over a subsequently more marginalised union.

The difference in union response in both manufacturing and aerospace may be partly explained by different organisational traditions within the two occupations represented by the unions, or by the more 'professional' orientation of MSF members. It must also be explained by the greater degree of activity of the AEEU stewards, in meeting management (and engaging), in meeting among themselves (and planning the terms of engagement), or communicating with members. Shifts towards team-working have also been met by the AEEU with efforts both to bring team-leaders within the orbit of union democratic procedures and then by challenging the managerial decentralisation implicit in team-working by threats of industrial action. Often the action was unofficial and short of strike action, involving various successful attempts to use a ban on overtime to force concessions. Although MSF has had less success in mobilising against work restructuring the same cannot be said in aerospace on the issue of pay and more general conditions of employment. Examples exist where a systematic approach to workplace communicating with members has enhanced the process of collectivisation and enabled the workplace union to confront management over pay issues. Mass meetings, sectional meetings, newsletters and two-way communications have all been successfully used, enabling strategic recruitment initiatives and the development of a positive organisational dynamic.

The insurance industry presents a different scenario. Operating from a lower membership base and degree of unionateness there are nevertheless examples where a 'back to basics' approach to organising has paid some dividend. The industry has been more prone than others to the introduction of new forms of pay determination, which has often disorientated workplace unions. The mass of individual grievances produced by individual performance pay has not led to a collective response from MSF in the vast majority of cases. Where organisational revival has come it has been from the exploitation of critical incidents of potential conflict over such issues as health and safety or working time and monitoring. In such cases the union has indeed engaged both with its members and management over the issue and raised its degree of perceived effectiveness as a result. In these instances it is clearly necessary to develop a critical mass of membership from which management authority and power can be challenged. How activists communicate with members has also proved to be important, with the more successful recruitment initiatives adopting an inclusive and participatory approach. The personal bravery of individuals in developing and progressing union activity in a hostile environment is also significant, particularly in the case of one cold recruitment initiative where the union was built from scratch by one or two individuals.

The examples from the public sector provide the most interesting of contrasts. Employee relations in both the local authorities and NHS Trusts surveyed were driven by partnership agendas, coming mainly from the employer as a conduit of Government policy. A potential problem of membership passivity was apparent, whereby the discourse of partnership leads to consultation and negotiations between management and union representatives at a central level. However, while centralised negotiations took place, the devolution of management authority within public services meant that the need for devolved union response was ever more important. Hence the 'paradox of partnership' was created. In the local authorities a second problem arose where the union had not attempted to revise its internal structures to match the more devolved managerial structures now apparent in the public sector. A process of detachment had ensued whereby the unions became remote from their members and their immediate interests. This process was compounded in the local authorities and one of the NHS Trusts by a passive attitude towards union activism and a dependence on full-time officials to service members' needs. In contrast, in two of the NHS Trusts, the workplace union had both decentralised its decision-making and continued to act independently of management interests (expressed through partnership). The unions had continued to adopt a traditional type of adversarialism backed up by increasing efforts to involve more members as activists within the negotiating framework. The participatory nature of these latter examples, together with an emphasis on self-sufficiency and political independence from full-time officers, had acted as a spur to union revival both in terms of membership gains and ability to engage with the employer.

Problems of detachment of union representatives from the membership were also found in the public and private utilities. In these cases privatisation and work restructuring had been generally subject to a process of negotiated change whereby the local union representatives (GMB and AEEU) had again conducted centralised negotiations with the employer. In many cases this negotiated form of change had taken place within a partnership discourse. The result appears to be that ordinary union members had become divorced from their representatives, and less able to maintain control over the terms of change at the point of production. Once again the process of detachment was further reinforced by a continuing dependence on full-time officers of the union to service members' needs from the outside. A hollow shell of union organisation can then be discerned, with low levels of participation and engagement, and declining prospects for the improvement of the union's organisational strength. For these studies at least, Fairbrother's (2000b) optimistic assessment of union renewal based on devolved participation is contradicted.

Resilience, recollectivisation, renewal

The research presents many contradictions of practice and many contrasts in union workplace experience. However, some important lessons for trade union resilience and renewal emerge. First, in those areas where a strong union tradition has been established, and where the necessary critical mass of members is present, it has been possible to renew and revive union power and organisation. This is most apparent in aerospace and some of the manufacturing examples. These are, of course, traditional areas of union organisation – the heartlands of the labour movement where in many cases the new discourse of partnership and co-operation has little resonance. Despite this there is a danger that such areas run the risk of being ignored in academic research and writing. But it is in these sectors that we can find the most positive examples of union engagement with the employer and of member participation in everyday union life. This is not to say that all these workplace are examples of good union practice. In many of the weaker cases union organisation can be tenuous, subject in some instances to the continuing goodwill of the employer. But in the strong workplaces it would appear that independent and assertive unionism prevails, and the dogged pursuit of grievance and discontent pays dividends for union organisation and strength.

Second, by the process of engagement, union members can be retained and recruited and the workplace union can thrive. This is true not only of manufacturing industries but also in insurance, where there is evidence of good communication practice and high levels of recruitment. In the public sector we found evidence of engagement in the politics of production, as well as evidence of detachment. Where unions adopt an independent approach, then engagement takes place both with the employer, involving local challenge to workplace reform, and with the membership, involving participatory practices and inclusiveness. The alternative is the development of patterns of detachment, passivity and dependence. This is reflected in public-sector cases of union support for partnership. Here is found detachment of the union representative from the members, passivity of the members in terms of non-involvement in union affairs and confrontation with management, and dependence on the union as a servicing agent from the outside rather than from within. To avoid such dangers the better organised workplace unions have revisited their own internal organisational dynamic, if necessary by adapting their own patterns of decision-making to reflect those of management.

In confronting the debates on individualism and collectivism within the new workplace what is presented here is a potential model of practice whereby it is indeed possible to recollectivise the workplace. Such a process of recollectivisation is based on the continued development of internal workplace solidarity, spurred by an environment where workplace injustice is growing and employee discontent is rife. We are not saying that the more pessimistic accounts of union decline are completely misplaced, as we do not wish to paint an over-optimistic picture of vibrant union renewal. But at the same time, we have uncovered a surprising degree of union pro-activity, influence and in some cases a militancy of a nature that rarely gets reported. This is particularly so in sectors and unions often written off as being 'traditional' and subject to 'terminal decline'.

To look at this another way one might ask why it is, in the context of the legacy of widespread decollectivisation at work (Smith and Morton 1993), that Britain's unions remain resilient in the face of sustained attacks from the employer and the state? Why, in an area of Britain not noted for strong trade union consciousness or worker militancy, have many workplace unions in large workplaces been more pro-active as agents of change at work, and more adept at recollectivising the workplace, than the pessimistic national surveys and writers of a managerialist persuasion would suggest?

The answer lies not in new types of leadership style or union approaches such as partnership. Instead, we find a strong correlation between workplace restructuring and use of new management techniques, the subsequent employee discontent, and the consequent mobilisation and recollectivisation. Indeed, rather than human resource management automatically reducing the scope for trade unionism, it can create the conditions for it.

Appendix

Research design

Semi-structured interviews

Trade union activists were the prime units of analysis for the research although additional contextual data were collected by interview with full-time trade union officials and, in some sectors, managers. The interviews were carried out between 1998 and 2000. Each lasted on average an hour and a half and each was taped. The semi-structured interview schedules covered a range of organising issues: changing organisational context; work restructuring; management-union relations; patterns of member grievances and union responses; workplace bargaining agendas; and union organising and recruitment strategies. A total of 108 workplace representatives were interviewed: 42 AEEU representatives, 18 GMB representatives and 48 MSF representatives. In addition, interviews were carried out with 15 full-time union officers (two from the AEEU, four from the GMB and nine from MSF). The following is a list of interviews by sector.

Aerospace

Eighteen AEEU and 19 MSF representatives were interviewed at the following firms: Allied Signals, BAe Systems, BAe Sowerby Research Centre, GKN-Westland Aerospace, GKN-Westland Helicopters, Matra-BAe Dynamics, Matra-Marconi Space, Messier-Dowty, Rolls-Royce and Smiths Industries. Five personnel managers were interviewed at BAE Systems, GKN-Westland, Messier-Dowty, Rolls-Royce and Smiths Industries.

Manufacturing

Seventeen AEEU, three GMB and four MSF representatives were interviewed at the following firms: AlloyCo, BrakeCo, CarCo, CerealCo, CheeseCo, ComponentCo, CopyCo, HydraulicCo, InjectorCo, OptoCo, PagerCo, PaperCo, PlasticCo, RubberCo, ValveCo.

Insurance

Ten MSF representatives were interviewed at the following firms: Das Legal, Friends Provident, London and Manchester, Northern Star, Norwich Union, Prudential and *CompanyA*.

Privatised utilities and nuclear power

Seven AEEU representatives and eight GMB representatives were interviewed at the following firms: Bristol Water, British Gas, Great Western Railways, Magnox Electric, Oldbury Power Station, SWEB, Wessex Water and Western Power Distribution.

NHS trusts

Thirteen MSF representatives were interviewed at the following NHS workplaces: CAMR Trust, Frenchay NHS Trust, Gloucester Royal NHS Trust, Honiton Community Trust, National Blood Transfusion Service, Southmead NHS Trust, Taunton and Somerset NHS Trust and United Bristol Hospital Trust.

Local government

Seven GMB representatives were interviewed at CityA and CityB local authorities. Three local authority policy officers were interviewed at CityA local authority.

Universities

Two MSF representatives were interviewed at the Universities of Bristol and Plymouth.

The questionnaire survey

Two questionnaire surveys were used for the research and both were distributed consecutively to lay representatives of the three unions between 1999 and 2000. The first was a survey of *all* workplace representatives at a sample of each of the unions' organised workplaces. This collected information on the use of different management practices in the representatives' work areas, views on management-union relations and union influence, patterns of member grievances and collective bargaining issues, and organising and recruitment activity.

The total number of responses received was 356. For MSF, 196 responses were received from representatives in a sample of 54 establishments, a response rate of 46 per cent. For the AEEU, 122 responses were received from representatives in a sample of 17 establishments, a response rate of 51 per cent. For the GMB, access was restricted to one urban area within the South West region: 38 responses were received from representatives in 10 establishments, a response rate of 66 per cent. The second survey was of senior workplace representatives (or convenors) at the same sample of workplaces. It collected information on union membership, recruitment patterns and organising facilities. The total response for the survey was 70, a response rate of 76 per cent for MSF and 100 per cent for the AEEU and GMB.

Notes

1 Unions facing up to crisis

1 The Certification Office returns on membership of trade unions affiliated to the TUC in 1999 and 2000 indicates a rise in membership for the first time since 1985, although density has fractionally fallen.
2 Whilst the number of days lost through work stoppages has declined a TUC Survey (2000) reports a doubling in the number of strike ballots in the year up to May 2000 compared with the previous year.
3 *Social Trends* 29, 1999 chart 5.16 .
4 The survey, of 5,300 employees in the public, private and voluntary sectors was funded by the British Occupational Health Research Foundation. (TUC Press Release, 14 February 2000).
5 The arguments put by Brenner go beyond an analysis of falling profit rates and raise contentious propositions about capital restructuring and the role of working-class organisations in contesting capital's logic. This latter concern has been the cause of much debate on the left inspiring a number of pro- and counter arguments. See, for example, Callinicos (2000) and Gindin (2000).
6 In the book, about the fight by an aluminium works union local against closure, the authors describe a range of tactics including research exposés, links with unions at home and abroad, street theatre, and lobbying of shareholders, all in addition to traditional picketing and solidarity.
7 The TUC annual survey on recognition in 2001 (*Focus on union recognition: TUC, 2001*) reports that unions won 159 new recognition deals in 2000, more than twice that achieved in 1999.
8 'New unionism: a message from John Monks' in *New Unionism: Organising for Growth*, TUC (undated).
9 *The GMB and Employers – Partnerships for Success*, London, GMB.

3 Job reform and recollectivisation in the aerospace industry

1 For example, a cursory analysis of the Chief Executive of BAe's recent book describing this cultural change will find a plethora of new management discourse terms: 'drivers and enablers', 'vision', 'values', 'leadership', 'business excellence review', 'customer value', 'partnership value', 'people value', to name but a few (Evans and Price 1999).

2 MSF Unity Left (formerly the TASS Broad Left) comprises groups of lay activists and full-time officers committed to left-wing, working-class politics. Its principal objectives are to secure the election of Unity Left supporters to key regional and national positions and the support of Unity Left motions at the MSF national conference.

3 Matra Marconi Space closed the Bristol site in 1999 to concentrate on its core activity of 'commercial communications' at other plants. Whether or not the growing strength of MSF at the Bristol site was a factor in this decision is a moot point.

4 Manufacturing change in an era of corporate instability

1 This is arguably an exaggerated assessment. The UK remains second to the US in the rate of overseas direct investment and as such is a major player as a world source of FDI.

2 Some caveats need to be expressed here. The returns on a membership of trade unions affiliated to the TUC in 1999 indicated a rise in membership for the first time since 1985, although density had fallen by 0.1 per cent over the year. Whilst the number of days lost through work stoppages has declined, a TUC Survey (2000) reported a doubling in the number of strike ballots in the year up to May 2000 compared with the previous year.

3 These figures are seasonally adjusted.

4 SIC 1980.

5 SIC 1992.

6 This shift in managerial attitudes, according to the 1998 WERS survey, was even more likely when workplace mergers or splits accompanied a change in ownership.

7 At InjectorCo *kaizen* was implemented under the *leitmotif*, Total Quality.

8 On 2 October 2001 it was revealed that the company was to shed 1,350 jobs at its UK plant in addition to the 330 people already facing redundancy. In effect manufacturing at the plant was to cease.

9 As at November 2000.

10 It must be stated that in the case of CopyCo the plant's location in a small town in a rural West of England area helped to create a feeling of community solidarity.

5 The insurance industry – back to basics

1 'Update' Newsletter (MSF Circular No. 98/13).

2 MSF headquarters *WWW* site, September 1998.

3 See 'How to: competency based pay' in *People Management*, 4, 19, 1 October 1998.

4 Source: interview notes with MSF regional officers; MSF recruitment data reports.

7 Negotiated privatisation in public utilities

1 At the time of writing this chapter it seemed unlikely that moves to partially privatise BNFL would take place before 2005. Preparations to clean up and

decommission nuclear plants were not far enough advanced to consider part privatisation until after the next election.

2 Magnox management introduced generic working in two stages. Shift workers were targeted first before any attempt was made to incorporate day workers. The reasons for this were unclear.

3 Although Bristol Water has always been a private company it tied itself to the agreements and followed the practices of public-sector water authorities before privatisation.

4 On the 26 April 1993, 120 print and bindery workers were locked out by the Bristol print firm J.W. Arrowsmith (about one kilometre from Bristol Water's main depot). Union recognition was withdrawn and only workers agreeing to sign new individual contracts were considered for re-employment. Only a few workers took up this 'offer'. The others were sacked and immediately established a daily picket calling for their re-instatement and union recognition. After twelve months the GPMU print union concluded the dispute but without securing the pickets main aims, re-instatement and union recognition.

5 Enron was the parent company of Wessex Water. At the end of November 2001, long after our site visit, Enron was put into the hands of an administrator and within a few days filed for bankruptcy to become the biggest corporate failure in the history of capitalism.

6 *FullCircle,* Issue 16, November 1999, BNFL Magnox Generation.

7 Notably, this practice, the right to say no to doing work employees deem to be unsafe, is now (November 2001) BNFL policy.

8 According to the stewards, three fatalities had occurred in the previous 30 months, all of which were followed by an enquiry conducted by the Health and Safety Executive.

References

Abbot, B. (1998) 'The emergence of a new industrial relations actor: the role of the Citizens' Advice Bureaux', *Industrial Relations Journal*, 29, 4: 257–69.

Ackers, P. and Payne, J. (1998) 'British trade unions and social partnership: rhetoric, reality and strategy', *The International Journal of Human Resource Management*, 9, 3: 529–550.

Albert, M. (1993) *Capitalism against Capitalism*, London: Whurr.

Allen, J. (1995) 'Crossing borders: footloose multinationals' in J. Allen and C. Hammet (eds) *A Shrinking World? Global Unevenness and Inequality*. Oxford: Oxford University Press, 233–54.

Appelbaum, E., Bailey, T., Berg, P. and Kalleberg, A.L. (2000) *Manufacturing Advantage: Why High Performance Work Systems Pay Off*, Ithaca, New York: Cornell University Press.

Atkinson, A. (2001) *Is Rising Income Inequality Inevitable? A Critique of the Transatlantic Consensus*, World Institute for Development Economics Research.

Auerbach, P. (1989) 'Multi-nationals and the British economy' in F. Green (ed.) *The Restructuring of the UK Economy*, Hemel Hempstead: Harvester Wheatsheaf.

Bacon, N. and Storey, J. (1996) 'Individualism and collectivism and the changing role of trade unions', in P. Ackers, C. Smith and P. Smith (eds) *The New Workplace and Trade Unionism*, London: Routledge.

Bacon, N. and Storey, J. (2000) 'New employee relations strategies in Britain: towards individualism or partnership?', *British Journal of Industrial Relations*, 38, 3: 407–27.

Bain, P. and Taylor, P. (2001) 'Two steps forward, one step back: interest definition, organisation and deflected mobilisation amongst call centre workers'. Paper presented to the *19th International Labour Process Conference*, Royal Holloway College, London, 26–28 March.

Batstone, E., Boraston, I. and Frenkel, S. (1977) *Shop Stewards in Action: The Organisation of Workplace Conflict and Accommodation*, Oxford: Basil Blackwell.

Beck, U. (1992) *Risk Society*, London: Sage.

Bell, D. (1973) *The Coming of Post-Industrial Society*, New York: Basic.

Beynon, H. (1973) *Working for Ford*, Harmondsworth: Penguin.

Beynon, H. (1984) *Working for Ford*, Harmondsworth: Penguin, 2nd edition.

Biewener, J. (1997) 'Downsizing and the New American Workplace: Rethinking the High Performance Paradigm', *Review of Radical Political Economics*, 29, 4: 1–22.

Bluestone, B., Jordan, P. and Sullivan, M. (1981) *Aircraft Industry Dynamics: An Analysis of Competition, Capital and Labor*, Boston Massachusetts: Aubern House.

Blundell, P. and Pirie, C. (1997) 'Response to the challenge', in *The Manufacturing Challenge in Aerospace*, IMechE Seminar Publication, Bury St Edmunds: The Institution of Mechanical Engineers.

Blyton, P. and Turnbull, P. (1998) *The Dynamics of Employee Relations*, London: Macmillan, 2nd edition.

Boddy, M. (1986) 'Bristol economy: key sectors: Insurance' *School of Advanced Urban Studies*, Bristol University.

Boddy, M., Lovering, J. and Bassett, K. (1986) *Sunbelt City? A Study of Economic Change in Britain's M4 Growth Corridor*, Oxford: Oxford University Press.

Bradley, R. and Pirie, C. (1997) 'Set the scene and outline the change' in *The Manufacturing Challenge in Aerospace*, IMechE Seminar Publication, Bury St Edmunds: The Institution of Mechanical Engineers.

Bradley, H., Erickson, M., Stephenson, C. and Williams, S. (2000) *Myths at Work*, Cambridge: Polity.

Braverman, H. (1974) *Labour and Monopoly Capital*, New York: Monthly Review Press.

Brecher, J. and Costello T. (1999) 'A new labor movement in the shell of the old?' in R. Tillman and M. S. Cummings (eds) *The Transformation of U.S. Unions*, London and Boulder: Rienner.

Brenner, R. (1998) 'The economics of global turbulence: a special report on the world economy, 1950–98.' *New Left Review*, 229.

Bronfenbrenner, K., Friedman, S., Hurd, R. W., Oswald, R. A. and Seeber, R. L. (1998) (eds) *Organising to Win: New Research on Union Strategies*, Ithaca and London: ILR Press.

Brown, C. (1999) 'No better under Labour for care workers', in S. Cohen (ed.) *What's Happening? The Truth about Work and the Myth of Partnership*, London: Trade Union Forum Pamphlet.

Brown, W. (1993) 'The contraction of collective bargaining in Britain', *British Journal of Industrial Relations*, 31, 2: 189–200.

Brown, W., Deakin, S., Hudson, M., Pratten, C. and Ryan, P. (1998) 'The Individualisation of Employment Contracts in Britain', Research Paper for the Department of Trade and Industry, Centre for Business Research, Department of Applied Economics, University of Cambridge, June 1998.

Bryan, D. (1995) 'The Internationalization of Capital and Marxian Value Theory', *Cambridge Journal of Economics*, 19: 65–89.

Bryson, A. (2000) 'Have British workers lost their voice, or have they gained a new one?', *PSI Research Discussion Paper 2*, London: Policy Studies Institute.

Burchell, B. Ladipo, D. and Wilkinson, F. (eds) (2002) *Job Insecurity and Work Intensification*, London: Routledge.

Cabinet Office (1999) *Modernising Government*, White Paper, Cm 4310.

Callinicos, A. (1989) *Against Postmodernism: A Marxist Critique*, Cambridge: Polity.

Callinicos, A. (2000) 'Capitalism, competition and profits: a critique of Brenner's theory of crisis', *Historical Materialism*, 4: 21.

Cappelli, P., Bassi, L., Katz, H., Knoke, D., Osterman, P. and Useem, M. (1997) *Change at Work*, New York: Oxford University Press.

Carling, W. and Soskice, D. (1997) 'Shocks to the system: the German political economy under stress', *National Institute Economic Review*, 159: 57–76.

Carr, F. (1999) 'Local bargaining in the National Health Service: new approaches to employee relations', *Industrial Relations Journal*, 30, 3: 197–211.

Carter, B. (1988) 'Trade unionism and the new middle class: the case of ASTMS', in P. Armstrong, B. Carter, C. Smith, and T. Nichols, (eds) *White Collar Workers Trade Unions and Class*, London: Croom Helm.

Carter, B. (1991) 'Politics and process in the making of manufacturing, science and finance', *Capital and Class*, 45: 35–72.

Carter, B. (1997) 'Adversity and opportunity: towards union renewal in MSF' *Capital and Class*, 61: 8–18.

Carter, B. (2000) 'Adoption of the organising model in British trade unions: some evidence from manufacturing, science and finance', *Work Employment and Society*, 14, 1: 117–36.

Carter, B. and Fairbrother, P. (1998) 'Coherence or contradiction? The TUC's "new unionism" project', paper presented to *Work, Employment and Society* Conference, Cambridge.

Carter, B. and Fairbrother, P. (1999) 'The transformation of British public-sector industrial relations: from "model employer" to marketized relations', *Historical Studies in Industrial Relations*, 7: 119–46.

Carter, B. and Poynter, G. (1999) 'Unions in a changing climate: MSF and UNISON experiences in the new public sector', *Industrial Relations Journal*, 30, 3: 499–513.

Carter, R. (1972) 'Conservative militants – the case of ASTMS', in Hyman, R. and Price, R. (eds) *The New Working Class? White-Collar Workers and their Organizations*, London: Macmillan.

Casey, B., Metcalf, H. and Millward, N. (1997) *Employers' Use of Flexible Labour*, London: Policy Studies Institute.

Castells, M. (2000) *The Rise of the Network Society*, Oxford: Blackwell, 2nd edition.

Caves, R. E. (1980) 'Productivity differences among industries', in R. E. Caves and L. B. Krause (eds) *Britain's Economic Performance*, Washington, D.C.: Brookings Institution.

Child, J., Faulkner, D. and Pitkethly, R. (2000) 'Foreign direct investment in the UK 1985–1994: the impact on domestic management practice', *Journal of Management Studies* 37, 1: 141–66.

Clark, T. N. and Hoffman-Martinot, V. (1998) *The New Political Culture*, Boulder, Colorado: Westview.

Claydon, T. (1998) 'Problematising partnership: the prospects for a co-operative bargaining agenda', in P. Sparrow and M. Marchington (eds) *Human Resource Management; The New Agenda*, London: Financial Times/Pitman.

Clegg, H. A. (1970) *The System of Industrial Relations in Great Britain*, Oxford: Basil Blackwell.

Coates, D. (1984) *The Context of British Politics*, London: Hutchinson.

Coates, D. (2000) *Models of Capitalism: Growth and Stagnation in the Modern Era*, Cambridge: Polity.

Cockburn, C. (1995) *Strategies for Gender Democracy*, Brussels: European Commission.

Corby, S. and Blundell, B. (1997) 'Trade unions and local bargaining in the NHS', *Health Manpower Management*, 23, 2: 49–54.

Cosh, A., Hughes, A., Singh, A., Carty, J. and Pender, J. (1990) *Take-overs and Short-termism in the UK*, London: Institute of Public Policy Research.

Coyle, D. (1997) *Weightless World: Strategies for Managing the Digital Economy*, Oxford: Capstone Publishing.

Cressey, P. and Scott, P. (1992) 'Employment, technology and industrial relations in clearing banks – is the honeymoon over?' *New Technology, Work and Employment*, 7, 2: 83–94.

Cully, M., Woodland, S., O'Reilly, A. and Dix, G. (1999) *Britain at Work*, London: Routledge.

Danford, A. (1999) *Japanese Management Techniques and British Workers*, London: Mansell.

Darlington R. (1994a) 'Shop stewards organisation in Ford Halewood: from Beynon to today', *Industrial Relations Journal*, 25, 2: 136–49.

Darlington, R. (1994b) *The Dynamics of Workplace Unionism*, London: Mansell.

Darlington, R. (1998) 'Workplace union resilience in the Merseyside Fire Brigade', *Industrial Relations Journal*, 29, 1: 58–73.

Dearlove, J. (2000) 'Globalisation and the study of British politics', *Politics* 20, 2: 111–18.

Delbridge, R., Lowe, J. and Oliver, N. (2000) 'Worker autonomy in lean teams: evidence from the world automotive components industry', in S. Procter, and F. Mueller, (eds) *Teamworking*, Basingstoke: Macmillan.

Delbridge, R., Turnbull, P. and Wilkinson, B. (1992), 'Pushing back the frontiers: management control and work intensification under JIT/TQM factory regimes', *New Technology, Work and Employment*, 17, 2: 97–106.

Denzin, N. K. (1999) 'Dennis Hopper, McDonald's and Nike', in B. Smart (ed.) *Resisting Macdonaldization*, London: Sage.

Department of Trade and Industry (1998) *Fairness at Work*, White Paper, Cm 3968, London: DTI.

Department of Trade and Industry (1999) *Our competitive future: UK competitiveness indicators 1999*, London: DTI.

Dicken, P. (1998) *Global Shift: Transforming the World Economy*, London: Paul Chapman.

Driffield, N. (1999) 'Indirect employment effects of foreign direct investment into the UK', *Bulletin of Economic Research* 51, 3: 207–21.

Du Gay, P. and Salaman, G. (1992) 'The Cult(ure) of the Customer', *Journal of Management Studies*, 29, 5, 61: 5–33.

Durand, J. P. (1999) 'The diversity of employee relationships', in J. P. Durand, P. Stewart, and J. J. Castillo (eds) *Teamwork in the Automobile Industry*, Basingstoke: Macmillan.

Eaton, A. and Nocerino, T. (2000) 'The effectiveness of health and safety committees: results of a survey of public-sector workplaces', *Industrial Relations*, 39, 2: 265–90.

Edwards, P., Hall, M., Hyman, R., Marginson, P., Sisson, K., Waddington, J. and Winchester, D. (1992) 'Great Britain: still muddling through?', in A. Ferner and R. Hyman (eds) *Industrial Relations in the New Europe*, Oxford: Blackwell.

Edwards, R. C. (1979) *Contested Terrain: The Transformation of the Workforce in the Twentieth Century*, New York: Basic Books.

Egan, A. (1982) 'Women in banking', *Industrial Relations Journal*, 13, 3: 20–31.

Eisenscher, M. (1999) 'Labor: turning the corner will take more than mobilization', in R. M. Tillman, and M. S. Cummings (eds) *The Transformation of U.S. Unions*, London and Boulder: Rienner.

Evans, R. and Price, C. (1999) *Vertical Take-off: The Inside Story of British Aersopace's Comeback from Crisis to World Class*, London: Brealey.

Fairbrother, P. (1994a) 'Privatisation and local trade unionism', *Work, Employment and Society*, 8, 3: 339–56.

Fairbrother, P. (1994b) *Politics and the State as Employer*, London: Mansell.

Fairbrother, P. (1996) 'Workplace trade unionism in the state sector', in P. Ackers, C. Smith and P. Smith (eds), *The New Workplace and Trade Unionism*, London: Routledge.

Fairbrother, P. (2000a) 'British trade unions facing the future', *Capital & Class*, 71: 47–78.

Fairbrother, P. (2000b) *Trade Unions at the Crossroads*, London: Mansell.

Fantasia, R. (1988) *Cultures of Solidarity; Consciousness, Action, and Contemporary American Workers*, Berkeley: University of California Press.

Ferner, A. (1989) *Ten years of Thatcherism Changing Industrial Relations in British Public Enterprises*, Warwick: School of Industrial and Business Studies, University of Warwick.

Ferner, A. and Colling, T. (1993) 'Electricity supply', in A. Pendleton and J. Winterton (eds), *Public Enterprise in Transition: Industrial Relations in State and Privatised Corporations*, London: Routledge.

Fisher, L. (1999) 'Strong workplace union fights health "Reforms"', in S. Cohen (ed.), *What's*

Happening? The Truth about Work and the Myth of Partnership, London: Trade Union Forum Pamphlet.

Flanders, A. (1975) *Management and Unions: The Theory and Reform of Industrial Relations*, London: Faber and Faber, 2nd edition.

Flecker, J. and Hofbauer, J. (1998) 'Capitalising on subjectivity: the "new model worker" and the importance of being useful', in P. Thompson and C. Warhurst (eds) *Workplaces of the Future*, London: Macmillan.

Fosh, P. (1993) 'Membership participation in workplace unionism: the possibilities of union renewal' *British Journal of Industrial Relations*, 31, 4: 577–92.

Foster, D. and Scott, P. (1998) 'Conceptualising union responses to contracting out municipal services, 1979–97', *Industrial Relations Journal*, 29, 2: 137–50.

Freeman, R. and Medoff, J. (1984) *What Do Unions Do?* New York: Basic Books.

Friedman, A. (1977) *Industry and Labour: Class Struggle at Work and Monopoly Capitalism*, London: Macmillan.

Gall, G. (1993) 'Industrial relations in banks: a comment on Cressey and Scott', *New Technology, Work and Employment*, 8, 1: 67–71.

Gall, G. (1998a) 'The changing relations of production: union derecognition in the UK magazine industry', *Industrial Relations Journal*, 29, 2: 151–61.

Gall, G. (1998b) 'The prospects for workplace trade unionism: evaluating Fairbrother's union renewal thesis', *Capital & Class*, 66: 149–57.

Gall, G. (1999) 'Union resilience in a cold climate: the case of the UK banking industry', in M. Upchurch (ed.) *The State and Globalization: Comparative Studies of Labour and Capital in National Economies*, London: Mansell.

Gall, G. and McKay, S. (2001), 'Facing "fairness at work": union perception of employer opposition and response to union recognition', *Industrial Relations Journal*, 32, 94–113.

Gallie, D. (1991) 'Patterns of skill change: upskilling, de-skilling or the polarisation of skills? *Work, Employment and Society*, 5, 3: 319–51.

Gallie, D., Rose, M. and Penn, R. (1996) 'The British debate on trade unionism: crisis and continuity', in D. Gallie, R. Penn, M. Rose (eds) *Trade Unionism in Recession*, Oxford: Oxford University Press.

Gallie, D., White, M., Cheng, Y. and Tomlinson, M. (1998) *Restructuring the Employment Relationship*, Oxford: Oxford University Press.

Gaster, L. (1999) 'Quality management in local government – issues and experiences', *Public Policy and Administration*, 14, 3: 35–54.

Gerlich, P. (1992) 'A farewell to corporatism?', *West European Politics*, 15: 132–46.

Giddens, A. (2000) *The Third Way and its Critics*, Oxford: Polity Press.

Gindin, S. (2000) 'Turning points and starting points: Brenner, left turbulence and class politics', in L. Panitch and C. Leys (eds) *Working Classes Global Realities: Socialist Register 2001*, London: Merlin Press.

Glynn S. and Booth A. (1996) *Modern Britain*, London: Routledge.

GMB (1998) *The GMB and Employers – Partnerships for Success*, London: GMB.

Gray, R. (1981) *The Aristocracy of Labour in Nineteenth-century Britain, c.1850–1900*, London, Macmillan.

Great Britain Office of National Statistics (2001a), Dataset lmsl, Employee jobs by industry 1978–2000 (*www.statistics.gov.uk/statbase*)

Great Britain Office of National Statistics (2001b), Dataset amistat, Acquisitions and mergers 1969–2000 (*www.statistics.gov.uk/statbase*)

Green, F. (2001) 'It's been a hard day's night: the concentration and intensification of work in late twentieth-century Britain', *British Journal of Industrial Relations*, 39, 1: 53–80.

Greenaway, D., Hine, R. C. and Wright, P. (1999) 'An empirical assessment of the impact of trade on employment in the United Kingdom', *European Journal of Political Economy*, 15: 485–500.

Greene, A. M., Black, J. and Ackers, P. (2000) 'The union makes us strong? a study of the dynamics of workplace union leadership at two UK manufacturing plants', *British Journal of Industrial Relations*, 38, 1: 75–93.

Greene, A., Hogan, J. and Grieco, M. (2001) 'E-collectivism and distributed discourse: new opportunities for trade union democracy', Paper presented to the *TUC/LSE Conference on Unions and the Internet*, May 12th.

Gripaios, P. (2000) *The South West Economy Trends and Prospects*, University of Plymouth, 12th edition.

Guest, D. (1990) 'Human resource management and the American dream', *Journal of Management Studies*, 27, 4: 378–97.

Guest, D. (1992) 'Employee commitment and control' in F. J. Hartley and G. M. Stephenson (eds) *Employee Relations*, Oxford: Blackwell.

Guest, D. and Peccei, R. (2001) 'Partnership at work: mutuality and the balance of advantage', *British Journal of Industrial Relations*, 39, 2: 207–36.

Hales, C. (2000) 'Management and empowerment programmes', *Work, Employment and Society*, 14, 3: 501–19.

Harman, C. (1995) *The Economics of the Madhouse*, London: Bookmarks.

Harrison, B. (1994) *Lean and Mean: The Changing Landscape of Corporate Power in the Age of Flexibility*, New York: Basic Books.

Hasluck, C. (1999) *Employment Prospects and Skill Needs in the Banking, Finance and Insurance Sector*. DfEE Skills Task Force, Research Group, Paper 9.

Hassel, A. (1999) 'The erosion of the German system of industrial relations', *British Journal of Industrial Relations*, 37, 3: 483–505.

Hayes, P. and Allen, M. (2001) 'Partnership as a union strategy: a preliminary evaluation', *Employee Relations*, 23, 2: 164–87.

Healy, G. and Kirton, G. (2000) 'Women, power and trade union government in the UK', *British Journal of Industrial Relations*, 38, 3: 343–60.

Heery, E. (1996) 'The new new unionism', in I. Beardwell (ed.) *Contemporary Industrial Relations: A Critical Analysis*, Oxford: Oxford University Press.

Heery, E. (1997) 'Performance-related pay and trade union membership', *Employee Relations* 19, 5: 430.

Heery, E. (1998) 'The relaunch of the Trades Union Congress', *British Journal of Industrial Relations*, 36, 3: 339–60.

Heery, E. and Abbott, B. (2000) 'Trade unions and the insecure workforce' in E. Heery and J. Salmon (eds) *The Insecure Workforce*, London: Routledge.

Heery, E. and Simms, M. (2001) *Research Bulletin No. 9*, New Unionism Project, Cardiff University.

Heery, E., Simms, M., Delbridge, R., Salmon, J. and Simpson, D. (2000), 'The TUC's organising academy: an assessment', *Industrial Relations Journal*, 31: 400–15.

Heery, E., Simms, M., Simpson, D., Delbridge, R., Salmon, J. and Stewart, P (1999) 'Organising Unionism Comes to Britain', Mimeo, Cardiff Business School.

Herriot, P. and Pemberton, C. (1996) 'Contracting careers', *Human Relations*, 49, 6: 759–90.

Hill, S. (1991) 'Why quality circles failed but total quality management might succeed', *British Journal of Industrial Relations*, 29, 4: 541–68.

Hirst, P. and Thompson, G. (1996) *Globalization in Question*, Cambridge: Polity Press.

Hirst. P. and Thompson, G. (2000) 'Globalization in one country? The peculiarities of the

British', *Economy and Society*, 29, 3: 335–56.

Hochschild, A. R. (1983) *The Managed Heart: Commercialization of Human Feeling*, Berkeley: University of California Press.

Horsman, M. and Marshall, A. (1994) *After the Nation State*, London: Harper Collins.

Howell, C. (1999) 'British trade unionism in crisis', in A. Martin and G. Ross (eds) *The Brave New World of European Labor*, New York and Oxford: Berghahn.

Hutton, W. (1995) *The State We're In*, London: Jonathan Cape.

Huws, U. (1999) 'Material world: the myth of the weightless economy', in L. Panitch and C. Leys (eds) *Global Capitalism versus Democracy; Socialist Register 1999*, Woodbridge: Merlin Press, 29–55.

Hyman, R. (1989) *The Political Economy of Industrial Relations*, Basingstoke: Macmillan.

Hyman, R. (1997) 'The future of employee representation', *British Journal of Industrial Relations*, 35, 3: 309–36.

Hyman, R. (1999) 'Imagined solidarities: can trade unions resist globalization?', in P. Leisink (ed.) *Globalization and Labour Relations*, Cheltenham: Edward Elgar.

IDS (2001) London: Income Data Services July report.

Industrial Management and Data Systems, (1997), 97: 37.

International Labour Organisation (2000) *Mental Health in the Workplace: Introduction*, Geneva: ILO.

Jeffreys, S. (2000) 'Western European trade unionism at 2000' in L. Panitch and C. Leys (eds) *Working Class Global Realities; Socialist Register 2001*, London: Merlin.

Juravich, T. and Bronfenbrenner, K. (1999) *Ravenswood: The Steelworkers' Victory and the Revival of American Labor*, Ithaca: Cornell University Press.

Kapstein, E. (1999) *Sharing the Wealth: Workers and the World Economy*, New York: W. W. Norton.

Kelly, J. (1996) 'Union militancy and social partnership', in P. Ackers, C. Smith and P. Smith (eds) *The New Workplace and Trade Unionism: Critical Perspectives on Work and Organisation*, London: Routledge.

Kelly, J. (1998) *Rethinking Industrial Relations*, London: Routledge.

Kelly, J. and Heery, E. (1989) 'Full time officers and trade union recruitment', *British Journal of Industrial Relations*, 27, 2: 196–213.

Kenney, M. and Florida, R. (1993), *Beyond Mass Production: The Japanese System and its Transfer to the U.S.*, Oxford: Oxford University Press.

Kessler, I. (1991) 'Workplace industrial relations in local government', *Employee Relations*, 13, 2: 2–29.

Kitson, M. and Mitchie, J. (1998), 'Deindustrialisation is bad for your wealth', in R. Delbridge and J. Lowe (1998), *Manufacturing in Transition*, London: Routledge.

Klandermans, B. (1997) *The Social Psychology of Protest*, Oxford: Blackwell.

Knell, J. (1999) 'Partnership at work', *Employment Relations Research Series* 7, DTI/Industrial Society.

Knights, D. (1990) 'Subjectivity, power and the labour process', in D. Knights and H. Willmott, *Labour Process Theory*, Basingstoke: Macmillan.

Kochan, T. (1999), 'Rebuilding the social contract at work: lessons from leading cases', Institute for Work and Employment Research, Sloan School of Management.

Kochan, T. and Osterman, P. (1994) *The Mutual Gains Enterprise*, Boston, Massachusetts: Harvard Business School Press.

Labour Research (1998) *Hard Work Ahead for Unions*, London: Labour Research Department.

Laffin, M. (1989) *Managing under Pressure: Industrial Relations in Local Government*, Basingstoke: Macmillan.

Lane, T. and Roberts, K. (1971) *Strike at Pilkingtons*, London: Fontana.

Legge, K. (1995) *Human Resource Management: Rhetorics and Realities*, Basingstoke: Macmillan.

Linstead, S. (1995) 'Averting the gaze: gender and power on the perfumed picket line', *Gender, Work and Organisation*, 2, 4: 190–206.

Lloyd, C. (1997) 'Decentralisation in the NHS: prospects for workplace unionism', *British Journal of Industrial Relations*, 35, 3: 427–46.

Lloyd, C. (1999) 'Regulating employment: implications for skill development in the aerospace industry', *European Journal of Industrial Relations*, 5, 2: 163–85.

Lovering, J. (1986) 'The restructuring of the defence industries and the role of the state', University of Bristol, School for Advanced Urban Studies Working Paper 59, Bristol.

Lovering, J. (1990) 'Military expenditure and the restructuring of capitalism: the military industry in Britain', *Cambridge Journal of Economics*, 14: 453–67.

Lovering, J. (1998) 'Opening Pandora's box: *de facto* industrial policy and the British defence industry', in R. Delbridge and J. Lowe, (eds) *Manufacturing Transition*, London: Routledge.

LRD (Labour Research Department) (1997) *Stress, Bullying and Violence – A Trade Union Guide*, London: LRD Publications.

Mahnkopf, B. (1992) 'The skill-oriented strategies of German trade unions: their impact on efficiency and equality objectives', *British Journal of Industrial Relations*, 30, 1: 61–81.

Maksymiw, W. (1990) *The British Trade Union Directory*, London: Longman.

Marginson, P. (1994) 'Multinational Britain: employment and work in an internationalised economy', *Human Resource Management Journal*, 4, 4: 63–80.

Marquand, D. (2000) 'Revisiting the Blair paradox', *New Left Review*, May–June 2000.

Martinez Lucio, M. and Stewart, P. (1997) 'The paradox of contemporary labour process theory: the rediscovery of labour and the disappearance of collectivism', *Capital and Class*, 62: 49–78.

Martinez Lucio, M., Jenkins, J. and Noon, M. (2000) 'Management strategy, union identity and oppositionalism: teamwork in the Royal Mail', in S. Procter and F. Mueller (eds) *Teamworking*, Basingstoke: Macmillan.

McAdam, D. (1988) 'Micromobilization contexts and recruitment to activism', *International Social Movement Research*, 1: 125–54.

McGovern P. (1998) *HRM, Technical Workers and the Multinational Corporation*, London: Routledge.

McIlroy, J. (1998) 'The enduring alliance? Trade unions and the making of new Labour 1994–97', *British Journal of Industrial Relations*, 36, 4: 537–64.

McIlroy, J. (2000) 'New Labour, new unions, new left', *Capital and Class*, 71: 11–45.

McNally, D. (1998) 'Globalisation on trial: crisis and class struggle in East Asia', *Monthly Review*, 50, 4: 1–15.

Millward, N., Bryson, A. and Forth, J. (2000) *All Change at Work? British Employment Relations 1980–98, as portrayed by the Workplace Industrial Relations Survey series*, London and New York: Routledge.

Moody, K. (1997) *Workers in a Lean World*, New York: Verso.

Moran, M. (1991) *The Politics of the Financial Services Revolution*, London: Macmillan.

Morris, T., Storey, J., Wilkinson, A. and Cressey, P. (2001) 'Industry change and union mergers in British retail finance', *British Journal of Industrial Relations*, 39, 2: 237–56.

Müller, F. and Purcell, J. (1992) 'The Europeanisation of manufacturing and the decentralisation of bargaining: multinational management strategies in the European automobile industry', *International Journal of Human Resource Management*, 3, 1: 15–44.

Müller-Jentsch, W. (1988) 'Trade unions as intermediary organisations', *Economic and Industrial Democracy*, 6: 3–33.

Nevin, E. and Davis, E. (1979) *The London Clearing Banks*, London: Elek Books.

Nichols, T. (1991) 'The labour process before and after the labour process debate' paper presented to the 9th Labour Process Conference, University of Aston, Birmingham.

Nichols, T. (1997) *The Sociology of Industrial Injury*, London: Mansell.

Nichols, T. (2001) 'The condition of labour – a retrospect', *Capital and Class*, 75: 185–98.

Nichols, T. and Armstrong, P. (1976) *Workers Divided*, London: Fontana.

Nichols, T. and Beynon H. (1977) *Living with Capitalism: Class Relations and the Modern Factory*, London: Routledge and Kegan Paul.

Nickson, D., Warhurst, C., Witz, A. and Cullen, A. (2001) 'The importance of being aesthetic: work, employment and service organisation', in A. Sturdy, I. Grugulis and H. Willmott (eds) *Customer Service: Empowerment and Entrapment*, Basingstoke: Palgrave.

Noon, M. and Blyton, P. (1997) *The Realities of Work*, Basingstoke: Macmillan.

O'Connell Davidson, J. (1993) *Privatisation Employment Relations: The Case of the Water Industry*, London: Mansell.

O'Doherty, D. and Willmott, H. (2001) 'Debating labour process theory: the issue of subjectivity and the relevance of poststructuralism', *Sociology*, 35, 2: 457–76.

Ogden, S. (1993) 'Water', in A. Pendleton and J. Winterton (eds) *Public Enterprise in Transition: Industrial Relations in State and Privatised Corporations*, London: Routledge.

Ohmae, K. (1990) *The Borderless World: Power and Strategy in the Interlinked Economy*, London: Collins.

Ohmae, K. (1996) *The End of the Nation State*, New York; Free Press.

Ollerenshaw, P. and Wardley, P. (1996) 'Economic growth and the business community in Bristol since 1840', in M. Dresser and P. Ollerenshaw (eds) *The Making of Modern Bristol*, Tiverton: Redcliffe Press, 124–156.

Olson, M. (1971) *The Logic of Collective Action*, Cambridge, Massachusetts: Harvard University Press.

O'Reilly, J. (1992) 'Banking on flexibility: a comparison of the use of flexible employment strategies in the retail banking sector in Britain and France', *International Journal of Human Resource Management*, 3, 1: 35–58.

Oxenbridge, S. (1997) 'Organising strategies and organising reform in New Zealand service sector unions', *Labor Studies Journal*, 22: 3–27.

Panitch, L. (1994) 'Globalization and the state' in R. Miliband and L. Panitch (eds) *The Socialist Register 1994*, London: Merlin Press.

Pendleton, A. and Winterton, J. (1993) 'Introduction: public enterprise industrial relations in context', in A. Pendleton and J. Winterton (eds) *Public Enterprise in Transition: Industrial Relations in State and Privatised Corporations*, London: Routledge.

Peters, T. and Austin, N. (1985) *A Passion for Excellence*, New York: Harper and Row.

Peters, T. J. and Waterman, R. H. (1982) *In Search of Excellence*, New York: Harper and Row.

Phelps-Brown, H. (1990) 'The counter-revolution of our time', *Industrial Relations*, 29, 1: 1–14.

Pickard, J. (1990) 'Engineering tools up for local bargaining', *Personnel Management*, March 1990.

Pollert, A. (1981) *Girls, Wives, Factory Lives*, London: Macmillan.

Pratten, C. (1976) *Labour Productivity Differentials within International Companies*, Cambridge: Cambridge University Press.

Proctor, S. and Mueller, F. (2000) 'Teamworking: strategy, structure, systems and culture' in S. Proctor and F. Mueller (eds), *Teamworking*, Basingstoke: Macmillan.

Ramsay, H., Scolarios, D. and Harley, B. (2000) 'Employees and high-performance work systems: testing inside the black box', *British Journal of Industrial Relations*, 38, 4: 501–31.

Regional Trends (1992–2000) Great Britain Central Statistical Office.

Rinehart, J., Huxley, C. and Robertson, D. (1997) *Just Another Car Factory? Lean Production and its Discontents*, Ithaca and London: ILR Press.

Ross, A. M. and Hartman, P. T. (1960), *Changing Patterns of Industrial Conflict*, New York: John Wiley & Sons.

Rubery, J. (1996) 'The labour market outlook and the outlook for labour market analysis' in R. Crompton, D. Gallie and K. Purcell (eds) *Changing Forms of Employment: Organisations, Skills, Gender*, London: Routledge.

Salama, A. and Easterby-Smith, M. (1994) 'Cultural change and managerial careers', *Personnel Review*, 23, 3: 21–33.

SBAC (2000) *UK Aerospace Statistics 1999*, London: Society of British Aerospace Companies.

Schonberger, R. J. (1996) *World Class Manufacturing: The Next Decade*, New York: Free Press.

Scott, J. (1997) *Corporate Business and Capitalist Classes*, Oxford: Oxford University Press.

Seidl, M. and Kleiner, B. (1999) 'Downsizing in the aerospace industry', *Aircraft Engineering and Aerospace Technology: An International Journal*, 71, 6: 546–9.

Smith, C. (1987) *Technical Workers: Class, Labour and Trade Unionism*, Basingstoke: Macmillan.

Smith, P. and Morton, G. (1993) 'Union exclusion and the decollectivisation of industrial relations in Britain', *British Journal of Industrial Relations*, 31, 1: 97–114.

Smith, P. and Morton, G. (2001) 'New Labour's reform of Britain's Employment Law: the devil is not only in the detail but in the values and policy Too', *British Journal of Industrial Relations*, 39, 1: 119–38.

Smith C. and Whalley P. (1996) 'Engineers in Britain: a study in persistence', in P. Meiskins and C. Smith (eds) *Engineering Labour*, London: Verso.

Snape, E. (1994) 'Union organising in Britain: the views of local full time officials', *Employee Relations*, 16, 8: 48–62.

Snape, E. (1995) 'The development of "managerial unionism" in Britain: the view from below', *Work, Employment and Society*, 9, 2: 559–68.

Standing, G. (1997) 'Globalization, labour flexibility and insecurity: the era of market regulation', *European Journal of Industrial Relations*, 3, 1: 7–37.

Stewart, P. and Martinez Lucio, M. (1998) 'Renewal and tradition in the new politics of production' in P. Thompson and C. Warhurst (eds) *Workplace of the Future*, London: Macmillan.

Stewart, P. and Wass, V. (1998) 'From "embrace and change" to "engage and change": trade union renewal and the new management strategies in the UK automotive industry', *New Technology, Work and Employment*, 13, 2: 77–93.

Stirling, J. (2001) 'Britain at work: letting the facts speak for themselves' *Capital & Class*, 73: 173–83.

Storey, J., Cressey, P., Morris, T. and Wilkinson, A. (1997) 'Changing employment practices in UK banking: case studies', *Personnel Review*, 26, 1/2: 24–42.

Streeck, W. (1997) 'German capitalism: does it exist? Can it survive?', in C. Crouch and W. Streeck (eds) *The Political Economy of Modern Capitalism*, London: Sage.

Stuart, M. and Martinez Lucio, M. (2000) 'Changing employment relations and "partnership" in the health and private sectors', *Journal of Management in Medicine*, 14, 4: 310–56.

Tailby, S. (2001) 'The financial services sector: UK sector overview report'. Draft of work in progress for the New Understanding of European Work Organisation Project, Employment Studies Research Unit, University of the West of England (unpublished).

Tailby, S. and Winchester, D. (2000) 'Management and trade unions: towards social partnership', in S. Bach and K. Sisson (eds) *Personnel Management: A Comprehensive Guide to Theory & Practice*, Oxford: Blackwell, 3rd edition.

Thornley, C. (1994) 'Nursing pay policy: chaos in context'. Paper presented to Cardiff Business School Employment Research Unit 1994 Annual Conference, Cardiff.

Thornley, C. (1998) 'Contesting local pay: the decentralisation of collective bargaining in the NHS', *British Journal of Industrial Relations*, 36, 3: 413–34.

Tilly, C. (1978) *From Mobilization to Revolution*, New York: McGraw Hill.

Troy, L. (1990) 'Is the US unique in the decline of private sector unions?', *Journal of Labor Research*, 11: 111–43.

TUC (1997) *Partners for Progress: Next Steps for the New Unionism*, London: TUC.

TUC (1999) *Partners for Progress: New Unionism in the Workplace*, London: TUC.

TUC (2000) *Trade Union Trends*, September, London: TUC.

TUC (2001) *Trade Union Trends*, September, London: TUC.

TUC Partnership Institute (2001) *Winning at Work*, London: TUC.

Undy, R. (1999) 'New Labour's "industrial relations settlement": the third way?', *British Journal of Industrial Relations*, 37, 2: 315–36.

Undy, R., Ellis, V., McCarthy, W.E.J. and Halmos, A. (1981) *Change in Trade Unions*, London: Hutchinson.

Upchurch, M. (2000) 'The crisis of labour relations in Germany', *Capital & Class*, 70: 65–94.

Upchurch, M., and Donnelly, E. (1992) 'Membership patterns in USDAW 1980–1990: survival as success?', *Industrial Relations Journal*, 23, 1: 60–8.

Valkenburg, B. (1996) 'Individualisation and solidarity: the challenge of modernisation', in P. Leisink, J. Van Leemput and J. Vilrokx (eds) *The Challenges to Trade Unions in Europe: Innovation or Adaptation*, Cheltenham: Edward Elgar.

Vassie, L. (1998) 'A proactive team-based approach to continuous improvement in health and safety management', *Employee Relations*, 20, 6: 577–93.

Voss, K. and Sherman, R. (2000) 'Breaking the iron law of oligarchy: union revitalization in the American labor movement', *American Journal of Sociology*, 106: 303–49.

Waddington, J. (2001) 'United Kingdom: restructuring services within a de-regulated regime', in D. E. Dolvik (ed.), *At Your Service? Comparative Perspectives on Employment and Labour Relations in the European Private Sector Services*. SALTSA, Work & Society, 27.

Waddington, J. and Kerr, A. (1999) 'Trying to stem the flow: union membership turnover in the public sector', *Industrial Relations Journal*, 30, 3: 184–96.

Waddington, J. and Whitston, C. (1996) 'Empowerment versus intensification: union perspectives of change at the workplace', in P. Ackers, C. Smith and P. Smith (eds), 1996, *The New Workplace and Trade Unionism*, London: Routledge.

Warhurst, C. and Thompson, P. (1998) 'Hands, hearts and minds: changing work and workers at the end of the century', in P. Thompson and C. Warhurst (eds), *Workplaces of the Future*, Basingstoke: Macmillan.

Webb, J. (1999) 'Work and the new public service class?', *Sociology*, 33, 4: 747–66.

Webb, T. (1998) *The Armour-Plated Ostrich: The Hidden Costs of Britain's Addiction to the Arms Business*, London: Comerford & Miller.

Western Development Partnership (1994) 'Securing our future – the aerospace industry in and around Avon', Bristol: Western Development Partnership.

Wilkinson, A., Marchington, M., Ackers, P. and Goodman, J. (1992), 'Total quality management and employee involvement', *Human Resource Management Journal*, 2, 4: 1–20.

Willman, P., Morris, T. and Aston, B. (1993) *Union Business: Trade Union Organisation and Financial Reform in the Thatcher Years*, Cambridge: Cambridge University Press.

Willmott, H. (1990) 'Subjectivity and the dialectics of praxis: opening up the core of labour process analysis', in D. Knights and H. Willmott (eds) *Labour Process Theory*, Basingstoke: Macmillan.

Winchester, D. and Bach, S. (1995) 'The state: the public sector', in P. Edwards (ed.), *Industrial Relations: Theory and Practice in Britain*, Oxford: Blackwell.

Womack, J. P., Jones, D. T. and Roos, D. (1990), *The Machine that Changed the World: The Triumph of Lean Production*, New York: Rawson Macmillan.

Wood, S. (1999) 'Getting the measure of the transformed high-performance organisation', *British Journal of Industrial Relations*, 37, 3: 391–417.

Woodward, S., Hendry, C., Alport, E., Harvey Cook, J., Vielba, C., Dobson, P. and Hockaday, N. (2000) *Employers Skill Survey: Case Study Banking, Finance and Insurance Sector*, DfEE, September.

Yates, M. D. (2001) 'The "new" economy and the labor movement', *Monthly Review*, 52, 11: 28–43.

Index

For Product Safety Concerns and Information please contact our EU
representative GPSR@taylorandfrancis.com
Taylor & Francis Verlag GmbH, Kaufingerstraße 24, 80331 München, Germany

www.ingramcontent.com/pod-product-compliance
Ingram Content Group UK Ltd.
Pitfield, Milton Keynes, MK11 3LW, UK
UKHW021121180425
457613UK00005B/175